Preventing Money Laundering and Terrorist Financing

Preventing Money Laundering and Terrorist Financing

A PRACTICAL GUIDE FOR BANK SUPERVISORS

SECOND EDITION

Pierre-Laurent Chatain,
Emile van der Does de Willebois, and
Maud Bökkerink

WORLD BANK GROUP

Contents

BOXES

FIGURES

TABLES

Foreword

The COVID-19 (coronavirus) crisis was a reminder, if any were needed, that criminal creativity thrives in times of chaos, exploiting people's fears. Unsafe face masks, counterfeit drugs, and suspect medical equipment flooded the market, touted as miracle cures against the coronavirus by unscrupulous actors wanting to turn a quick profit. Companies with no record in health won big government contracts and, as people's situation deteriorated, organized crime stepped in to lend a "helping hand" to those suffering financial distress. Where most people saw a global public health and economic crisis, criminals saw an opportunity.

What this criminal behavior, indeed almost all financial economic crime, has in common is that the funds involved move through the formal financial system. The service providers that execute those transactions are in a good position to gather firsthand intelligence on what is happening. For this reason, banks and other financial institutions have anti-money-laundering and countering the financing of terrorism (AML/CFT) obligations to find out who is paying whom and why and, if necessary, to alert the authorities. Financial institutions are the first line of defense against this criminal behavior; they are the gatekeepers to the international financial system.

But they cannot manage this task on their own; they require support from authorities to understand what threats they are exposed to, what criminal groups and typologies are prevalent in their system, and how exactly they are to undertake their obligations. They need a guiding, sometimes firm, hand.

Financial sector supervisors play a crucial role in this regard. Through off-site supervision and on-site visits, they ensure that the financial sector understands and effectively implements its AML/CFT obligations, providing guidance and, where necessary, enforcing with sanctions commensurate to the breach.

As a development institution, the World Bank cares deeply about protecting societies against the harm inflicted by money laundering and the profit-generating crime that is at its core. Organized crime, corruption, and terrorism are all "global public bads" that have a disproportionate effect on developing societies, particularly on persons living in fragile and conflict-afflicted states. Where organized crime takes root, small businesses pay protection money; where corruption thrives, patients pay bribes for medical treatment; where terrorist groups and warlords rule, it takes courage just to attend school. While we need to fight those ills directly, through our work on governance and our assistance to sector-specific operations, we also need to attack them on the back end by following the money. But protecting the integrity of the financial sector is also an objective in its own right: the criminal capture of financial institutions can damage the financial sector as a whole, weaken financial stability, and erode public trust in the financial sector. Examples abound of the harm done by financial institutions in the hands of criminal enterprise. Supervisors are the guardians of their finan-cial sector's integrity, ensuring that only persons deemed to be "fit and proper"—that is, sufficiently expert and of integrity—can take up a controlling position within that sector.

We have reissued this handbook to assist supervisors on the basics of supervision of financial institutions' AML/CFT obligations. Since its original publication 12 years ago, this handbook has proved to be an often consulted, frequently downloaded publication, commended for its highly prac-tical and directly applicable content. However, given technological progress and the development of fintech and crypto assets, developments in supervisory practice, unprecedented changes wrought by the COVID-19 pandemic, and overall changes in criminal behavior, we have updated the text to include new good practices and to ensure alignment with the 2012 Financial Action Task Force global AML/CFT standard. Surely the most important of changes in the standards are the fundamen-tal orientation on risk and the need to adapts one's AML/CFT system to target the risks to which a country is exposed. These changes are especially important for the wide variety of countries served by the World Bank, which are constrained by resources and have vastly different risk profiles. Risk and how it should inform supervisory practice are now integral parts of this handbook.

We hope that a new generation of AML/CFT supervisors will find this handbook useful. Surely now it is imperative to make sure that criminals and corrupt officials do not siphon off much-needed resources to their own unproductive and nefarious ends. The United Nations Sustainable Development Goals recognize the importance of the fight against illicit financial flows. We want to help you, our client countries, be effective in that fight.

Indermit S. Gill
Vice President, Equitable Growth, Finance, and Institutions
The World Bank

Acknowledgments

The original version of this handbook, published in 2009, was written by Pierre-Laurent Chatain (team leader), John McDowell, Cédric Mousset, Paul Allan Schott, and Emile van der Does de Willebois, all of the World Bank, with the participation of Kamil Borowik. The handbook was revised and updated in 2020–21 by Maud Bökkerink (consultant, Bökkerink Compliance International), under the supervision of Pierre-Laurent Chatain and Emile van der Does de Willebois (lead financial sector specialists, Finance, Competitiveness, and Innovation, World Bank). The team is also grateful to Yasmin De Magalhaes Pinto Almeida (young professional, World Bank) for her assistance.

The authors would like to thank the peer reviewers of the updated version: Kristel Grace Poh (senior financial sector expert, International Monetary Fund); Andy Watson (senior associate, Financial Crime Advisory Department, United Kingdom Financial Conduct Authority); Florabelle Santos (director, Financial System Integrity Department, Bangko Sentral ng Filipinas); and Juan Ortiz (senior financial sector specialist, World Bank).

The authors would also like to thank Jean Pesme (global director, Finance, Competitiveness, and Innovation, World Bank) and Ayhan Kose (chief economist and director, Prospects Group, Equitable Growth, Finance, and Institutions, World Bank) for their support and guidance throughout the process.

Abbreviations

ACIP	AML/CFT Industry Partnership (Singapore)
ACPR	Autorité de Contrôle Prudentiel et de Resolution (France)
AMCM	Autoridade Monetaria de Macau
AML	anti-money-laundering
AUSTRAC	Australian Transaction Reports and Analysis Centre (Australia)
BCBS	Basel Committee on Banking Supervision
BCP	Basel Core Principles for Effective Banking Supervision
BMA	Bermuda Monetary Authority
BNM	Bank Negara Malaysia
BSA	Bank Secrecy Act (United States)
CFATF	Caribbean Financial Action Task Force
CFT	combating the financing of terrorism
CNBV	Comisión Nacional Bancaria y de Valores (Mexico)
CSSF	Commission de Surveillance du Secteur Financier (Luxembourg)
DNB	De Nederlandsche Bank (The Netherlands)
EBA	European Banking Authority
ECCB	Eastern Caribbean Central Bank
EDD	enhanced due diligence
EU	European Union
FATF	Financial Action Task Force
FCA	Financial Conduct Authority (United Kingdom)
FEC	Financial Expertise Center (The Netherlands)
FIAU	Financial Intelligence Analysis Unit (Malta)
FinCEN	Financial Crimes Enforcement Network (United States)
FIN-NET	Financial Crime Network (United Kingdom)
FINTRAC	Financial Transaction and Reports Analysis Centre (Canada)
FIOD	Fiscal Information and Investigation Service (The Netherlands)
FIU	Financial Intelligence Unit
FRFI	federally regulated financial institution

FSI	Financial Stability Institute
FSRB	FATF-style regional body
IO	Immediate Outcome
MAS	Monetary Authority of Singapore
ML	money laundering
NRA	national risk assessment
OCC	Office of the Comptroller of the Currency (United States)
OECD	Organisation for Economic Co-operation and Development
OFAC	Office of Foreign Assets Control (United States)
OSFI	Office of the Supervisor of Financial Institutions (Canada)
RBS	risk-based supervision
SARLAFT	Risk Management System for ML/TF (Colombia)
SFC	Superintendencia Financiera de Colombia
STR	suspicious transaction report
SuRF	supervisory risk-based framework (Malaysia)
TF	terrorism financing

CHAPTER 1

Designing an Effective AML/CFT Supervisory Framework

OVERVIEW

A jurisdiction's anti-money-laundering (AML) and combating the financing of terrorism (CFT) framework has three primary objectives. The first is to deter money launderers and financiers of terrorism and the proliferation of weapons of mass destruction from using a jurisdiction's financial system. The second is to detect and report such activities, when and where they occur. The third is to prosecute and punish those involved in such illicit activities.

Although each government agency has its own priority, a jurisdiction as a whole has common objectives, such as the need to advance the domestic security agenda, safeguard the integrity of the financial sector, and avoid or minimize negative international ramifications from money laundering (ML) and terrorism financing (TF). Political will is the most important prerequisite for achieving these national objectives. A national government demonstrates its clear political commitment to establishing a robust AML/CFT framework by passing appropriate laws and regulations; by granting suitable powers to authorities and agencies in the jurisdiction; by dedicating necessary resources to relevant ministries, authorities, and agencies; and by prosecuting cases and obtaining convictions. A supervisor demonstrates its political will by conducting a rigorous supervisory on-site/off-site program that focuses on the highest risks and asks the difficult questions, including to entities that are politically connected or otherwise close to vested interests.

Establishing an effective AML/CFT framework requires significant collaboration and cooperation from all of the jurisdiction's stakeholders, including the private sector. As gatekeepers, the private sector—the financial institutions and designated nonfinancial businesses and professions—plays a critical role in preventing and detecting ML/TF through its risk mitigation and compliance systems.

AML/CFT supervisors generally have the following primary responsibilities:

- Ensuring that only fit and proper persons own, control, and manage banks and other financial institutions and that licensing requirements are sound;

- Understanding the ML/TF risks facing the jurisdiction, the financial and other sectors, and individual institutions;

- Supervising covered entities to ensure their effective assessment and management of ML/TF risk and compliance with AML/CFT preventive measures and, where necessary, applying effective, proportionate, and dissuasive sanctions for violations of AML/CFT laws and regulations; and

- Fostering an environment of collaboration with financial and other sectors with respect to ML/TF risks, AML/CFT compliance, and supervision.

A robust, risk-based AML/CFT supervision framework promotes the overall safety and soundness of the financial system and helps to prevent criminals from abusing the system for ML/TF purposes. This framework includes a program for off-site AML/CFT activities as well as on-site inspections informed by the risk profile of the jurisdiction, sector, and individual institutions. While the AML/CFT supervisor is not charged primarily with identifying and investigating individual cases of ML/TF, it may identify such cases, especially during on-site inspections, and be required to make referrals to the appropriate authorities, such as the financial intelligence unit (FIU). This unit may require AML/CFT supervisors to determine whether a transaction is suspicious or whether an institution or an institution's employee may be involved in or facilitating illicit activities. AML/CFT inspections will typically examine an institution's policies, procedures, and controls; review customers' files and records; and test transactions for compliance with the domestic AML/CFT requirements.

There are essentially three organizational approaches to AML/CFT supervision: (a) supervision by a banking supervisor or specialized AML/CFT supervisor, (b) supervision by the FIU, and (c) supervision shared between the FIU and a banking or AML/CFT supervisor. Whichever model is selected, a clear rationale for the decision is needed. In addition, policy makers need to consider some guiding principles when developing and implementing an effective, risk-based system for AML/CFT supervision:

- Have adequate resources to carry out their responsibilities, including human, financial, and technological resources;

- Enjoy a reasonable degree of operational independence and autonomy;

- Have access to all information from banks and other financial institutions without undue restrictions, including information on the ML/TF risks in their business activities and processes;

- Be authorized to carry out both off-site and on-site supervision, including under outsourcing arrangements;

- Have the power to make rules or issue guidance and enforce compliance, including the power to impose proportionate and dissuasive sanctions; and

- Be held accountable for their actions and be as transparent as possible.

This chapter addresses the key building blocks for designing and implementing an effective risk-based AML/CFT framework. It examines the importance of an AML/CFT supervisory framework in general, collaboration and coordination with stakeholders, principles and models for risk-based AML/CFT supervision, and organizational approaches to risk-based AML/CFT supervision.

THE IMPORTANCE OF AN AML/CFT SUPERVISORY FRAMEWORK

While the context and risks vary from jurisdiction to jurisdiction, some common issues are universally applicable for supervisors and policy makers when establishing an effective, risk-based AML/CFT supervisory framework. Other important factors underpinning the effectiveness of a jurisdiction's AML/CFT framework include the size, maturity, and sophistication of the regulatory and supervisory framework and the degree of financial inclusion. All of these factors can affect the level of ML/TF risks of a jurisdiction and influence the effectiveness of the AML/CFT measures in place.

Combating Crime

An effective AML/CFT framework is an important part of combating domestic and transnational crimes that generate illicit financial flows domestically and internationally. An effective AML/CFT framework requires a solid understanding of the risks to which the country is exposed. To this end, many countries have conducted a national risk assessment, which provides an important source of information for identifying the ML/TF threats facing a jurisdiction, such as corruption, drug trafficking, human trafficking, fraud, environmental crimes, tax evasion, and terrorism. A national risk assessment constitutes a key input for the development of national strategies and action plans based on

ML/TF risks and other AML/CFT priorities. Part of such strategies can involve the development of risk-based AML/CFT mechanisms by all stakeholders, including for supervisory purposes.

Devising a National Strategy

To establish an AML/CFT framework that meets international standards or to strengthen an existing framework, jurisdictions should collaborate on the development of a national strategy that is informed by a national risk assessment and other sources of risk information. Such a strategy should include well-identified policies and clear objectives and be subject to periodic reviews to ensure that it keeps pace with changes in the risk profile of a jurisdiction as well as national and international requirements. Once a strategy has been established and areas of responsibility have been clearly assigned, an action plan is needed for achieving the strategic goals.

To formulate an AML/CFT strategy, it is necessary to designate an authority or to have a coordination mechanism (for example, a national AML/CFT coordination committee). The coordination mechanism should include representatives of the various stakeholders that play a role in a jurisdiction's AML/CFT system. A key output of this coordination mechanism would be agency- and sector-specific action plans, with realistic implementation time frames, that address the key threats and vulnerabilities contributing to national ML/TF risks. This coordinating mechanism should also monitor progress in achieving national AML/CFT policy goals.

Many jurisdictions form working groups to guide and monitor implementation of the action plan, usually consisting of technical officials from the public sector and relevant agencies and high-level support to ensure that the action plan is implemented. Since much of the implementation concerns action by obliged entities, it is important to include representatives from the private sector. These working groups will guide and coordinate the specific actions needed. Of course, in many cases, individual ministries or agencies are solely responsible for implementing rules and regulations, and they can independently finalize and implement them. Nonetheless, a collaborative approach to implementation will result in a more robust and effective AML/CFT framework.

Supervising Gatekeepers of the Financial System

As gatekeepers, banks play a critical role in mitigating the risks that criminals will misuse the financial system. To do so, these entities must comply with several AML/CFT requirements, including requirements for risk assessments of their business; customer due diligence, including enhanced due diligence for politically exposed persons and other higher-risk situations and simplified due diligence where warranted; monitoring of transactions; reporting of suspicious transactions; and record-keeping requirements. Failure to comply with these and other obligations (for example, targeted financial sanctions) can attract enforcement measures, both administrative and criminal.

In addition to these obligations, banks need to make sure that neither their directors nor their employees become engaged in criminal acts, whether unwittingly or deliberately. Supervision contributes to the objective of ensuring, as far as possible, that an institution or its employees do not engage in ML/TF activities.

AML/CFT supervisors contribute to the effectiveness of the prevention and detection mechanisms in identifying cases and issuing suspicious transaction reports (STRs) that the FIUs and law enforcement authorities use to investigate and prosecute ML/TF activities and underlying predicating offenses.

In most jurisdictions, banking and other financial services are a very important part of the financial system. Banking is the conduit for most domestic and international payments; it intermediates deposit-taking and lending activities and other financial products and services. Given their role in domestic and international payment systems, banks and other payment service providers hold a central and strategic position in a jurisdiction's AML/CFT framework. This gatekeeper role also exposes them to domestic and international ML/TF activities. In most, if not all, national risk assessments, the banking and payment service sectors have been assessed as having a high level of exposure to ML/TF risk. Therefore, the sectors dealing with payments should have in place adequately robust AML/CFT compliance systems to protect the integrity of the financial system and the wider economy.

All jurisdictions must balance the need to protect the banking and financial sectors from ML/TF abuse by implementing AML/CFT requirements, on the one hand, and the need to minimize the risk of unnecessarily restricting access to financial services by the poorer segments of society (financial inclusion), on the other hand. These citizens, as well as others, may have difficulty, for example, satisfying the customer due diligence requirements imposed on financial institutions. The Financial Action Task Force (FATF) recommendations and, in particular, the risk-based approach to AML/CFT compliance provide sufficient flexibility to mitigate the risk to financial inclusion by, for instance, applying simplified measures for lower-risk cases and expanding access through technological innovations in case of non-face-to-face situations. A risk-based approach may also foster financial inclusion for low-income segments of society; for example, jurisdictions may allow exemptions in or deviations from the application of the FATF recommendations based on an institution's proven low risks or allow financial institutions to be more flexible in their application of customer due diligence measures. The risk-based approach to compliance can contribute to greater inclusion, transparency, and traceability of financial flows in these ways.

Promoting Safe and Sound Banking Practices

In addition to an overall effective AML/CFT framework based on the FATF standards, policy makers also have a responsibility to promote safe and sound banking practices. A comprehensive and robust AML/CFT regime for banks can mitigate ML/TF risks in the banking sector. In this regard, the Basel Committee on Banking Supervision (BCBS) has issued a set of principles on bank supervision: the Core Principles for Effective Banking Supervision (BCPs). These principles contain several AML/CFT requirements (BCBS 2012). In particular, according to BCP 29, "The supervisor determines that banks have adequate policies and processes, including strict customer due diligence rules to promote high ethical and professional standards in the financial sector and prevent the bank from being used, intentionally or unintentionally, for criminal activities." The assessment methodology further requires that, among other requirements, AML/CFT policies and processes are integrated into the banks' overall risk management framework to enable supervisors to identify, assess, monitor, manage, and mitigate ML/TF risks at both the bank and the group-wide levels.

The BCBS has also issued guidelines on sound management of risks related to money laundering and financing of terrorism that, while intended primarily as guidelines for banks, also include guidelines for supervisors (BCBS 2020). With respect to banks, the guidelines cover (a) essential elements of sound ML/TF risk management; (b) customer acceptance policy; (c) identification, verification, and risk profiling of customers and beneficial owners; (d) ongoing monitoring; (e) management of information (including record keeping); (f) reporting of suspicious transactions; and (g) group-wide and cross-border risk management. These guidelines also require supervisors to implement a risk-based approach to AML/CFT supervision.

International Implications

All jurisdictions that are members of the FATF or a similar regional body have subscribed to the international AML/CFT standards, which impose specific obligations on banks and other financial institutions and their supervisors. Most of these standards are implemented through domestic laws and regulations that are enforced at the domestic level.

Jurisdictions generally want to safeguard the integrity of their financial system and not condone its misuse by criminals. Failure to implement AML/CFT standards, mitigate ML/TF risks, or enforce domestic requirements can have adverse consequences for a jurisdiction. It can also affect a jurisdiction's international reputation. In the end, it could lead to the FATF listing the jurisdiction as having strategic deficiencies and placing it under increased monitoring or even, in extreme cases, on the list of high-risk jurisdictions that have significant strategic deficiencies in their AML/CFT regime, which calls for further countermeasures against the jurisdiction. Such a listing increases the risk profile of a jurisdiction and subjects it and its institutions to enhanced scrutiny and due diligence, particularly when conducting cross-border financial transactions.

In addition, it can result in a loss of business for banks and can restrict their access to the international payment system if correspondent accounts are closed or restricted. All of these actions increase the costs of doing business in or with the jurisdiction, which adversely affects the financial sector and the broader economy, particularly those parts of the economy that rely on international transactions. Thus, failure to have in place an effective risk-based AML/CFT regime that meets international standards could raise costs for both domestic institutions and international trade.

IMPORTANCE OF COORDINATION

The importance of effective cooperation and coordination cannot be overemphasized. FATF Recommendation 2 and Immediate Outcome (IO) 1 require jurisdictions to have proper mechanisms for national AML/CFT cooperation and coordination. Such mechanisms should ensure that policy makers, supervisors, the FIU, law enforcement, and other competent authorities cooperate and coordinate domestically in the development and implementation of AML/CFT measures, which should include measures to combat the financing of weapons proliferation. These measures include conducting national risk assessments and developing national AML/CFT strategies, policies, and action plans.

Interagency Coordination

The specific agencies involved vary from jurisdiction to jurisdiction, but the following are generally involved in cooperation and coordination efforts to develop and implement an effective AML/CFT regime:

- Legislature;
- Executive branch or ministries;
- Judiciary
- Law enforcement, including prosecution, police, and customs;

- Financial intelligence unit; and

- Supervisors of financial institutions and designated nonfinancial businesses and professions.

Cooperation is important to ensure that there is one cohesive national strategy and policy. National agencies may have different objectives and priorities that can potentially create conflicts of interest. However, agreement on collective goals and effective cooperation can minimize the incidence of conflict and enhance the effectiveness of the overall regime. It can also minimize potential conflicts in cases of overlapping duties and responsibilities by assigning clear lines of responsibility under the jurisdiction's AML/CFT regime. Avoiding duplication and wasted resources is an added benefit.

It is critical to involve banks in (further) developing the AML/CFT regime, for instance, when developing the national risk assessments. Effective consultation and cooperation with private sector stakeholders are essential to obtain their support for the national AML/CFT measures and to ensure that the measures are tailored appropriately. Most ML/TF takes place in the private sector; given its first-hand experience of the country's ML and TF risks, the sector should be an integral part of this process. Consequently, the private sector is critical in efforts to mitigate national ML/TF risks and provide valuable input for the FIU and law enforcement through its role in reporting suspicious transactions.

Mutual Respect and Trust

A successful AML/CFT regime is one in which the private and public sectors have developed mutual trust. While the two may have different objectives and priorities, they also share common goals and, therefore, recognize the need to cooperate if they are to achieve an AML/CFT regime that benefits both. If the private sector trusts the public sector, it is more likely to participate fully and actively in achieving the objectives. The public sector should recognize that the private sector bears significant compliance costs for activities that largely, but not exclusively, assist the public sector in fighting crime. Trust is particularly important for reporting suspicious transactions, given the sensitive nature of the information that members of the private sector are required to submit to the public sector. FIUs require timely, accurate, and high-quality STRs to enhance their operations. Failure to establish a public-private working relationship based on mutual respect and trust will hinder the implementation of effective AML/CFT measures in the jurisdiction.

PRINCIPLES FOR AN EFFECTIVE AML/CFT SUPERVISORY FRAMEWORK

Any AML/CFT supervisory framework should adopt a risk-based approach consistent with the FATF recommendations and use both off-site and on-site supervision. Within that approach and guided by several principles, jurisdictions can devise their own framework. The following list, though not exhaustive, reflects the best practices observed in many jurisdictions.

To enable them to fulfill their role, supervisors should be given the following:

- Sufficient operational independence;

- Adequate legal and regulatory powers to carry out their functions, including access to information;

- Authority to issue regulations or guidance;

- Authority to impose appropriate sanctions, including the power to revoke licenses; and

- Adequate human, financial, and technological resources.

To ensure that they build the necessary trust, it is imperative that supervisors always be transparent and accountable in their actions so that all supervised entities can see that the law is being applied in a fair and objective manner.

Independence

While the organizational structure surrounding AML/CFT supervision may vary from jurisdiction to jurisdiction, the supervising authority, whether it is the financial supervisor or the FIU, must have sufficient operational independence.[1] Unless provisions are already in place to guarantee this independence, the supervisor should be covered by the jurisdiction's legal and regulatory mandate.

Independence, in general, means that the day-to-day activities of the supervisor are not subject to undue external influence, direction, or control by, for example, the government or the industry. The supervisors should be free to carry out their legally mandated responsibilities in all core functions, including licensing (where applicable), off-site and on-site examinations, and enforcement, including license restrictions and revocations. Independence is not absolute. Since the financial supervisor operates within the framework of the broader financial sector and economy, it is generally acceptable for the supervisor to adhere to national policies and direction as established by the legislature or by relevant government policy makers. For instance, the supervisor will be subject to national policy objectives such as good governance and anticorruption efforts. In other words, the supervisor is not free to act irresponsibly and should be held accountable for its actions.

Independence is critical for some of the supervisory functions and operations (for example, budgets, recruitment, resources, issuance of regulations or guidance, enforcement and sanctions, conduct of off-site and on-site examinations, and setting of supervisory policies and procedures). For this purpose, it is important for the supervisor to have a reliable source of funding that is not subject to manipulation by, for instance, ministers or government. In France, for example, the Supervisory College of the Autorité de Contrôle Prudentiel et de Resolution (ACPR, the Authority for Prudential Control and Resolution) is an independent administrative authority, and the board of the ACPR comprises three independent magistrates from the highest national jurisdictions (Court of Cassation, State Council, and the Court of Audit). In the United States, the heads of all five banking regulatory agencies and their respective board members serve for specific terms of five or seven years, rather than at the discretion of the president of the United States.

Accountability

In establishing the supervision body, policy makers should balance the need for operational independence with a framework of accountability to government and the public interest (for example, for the stability of the financial sector and protection of bank depositors).[2] Therefore, it is of paramount importance that the AML/CFT supervisor has in place a robust corporate governance framework and a system of transparent accountability for fulfilling its responsibility effectively and efficiently. Accountability can entail a system of reporting and review to an appropriate legislative or oversight body and periodic independent external audits. Accountability not only enhances the effectiveness of the supervision function but also fosters credibility and trust with the public and private sectors and promotes a culture of compliance by entities subject to the AML/CFT regime. High integrity of staff and good practices in governance strengthen the credibility of the AML/CFT supervisor.

In France, for example, the governor of the Banque de France (the French central bank), who is also the chair of the ACPR (the supervisory body for AML/CFT), annually reports the central bank's activities to the public through parliament. The central bank is also subject to independent oversight by the Court of Audit and the Inspection Générale des Finances, which are responsible for the oversight of public systems. In addition, the ACPR is required to disclose an overview of its operations to the public. The overview takes the form of an annual report, which includes, among other information, the number of on-site visits, sanctions imposed on noncompliant financial institutions, and follow-up letters sent about inspections.

In the United States, all bank regulatory agencies are required to file publicly available annual reports. These reports provide a detailed description of the agencies' initiatives, financial management results, enforcement actions, and outreach to industry, community, and consumer organizations.

In Canada, both the Office of the Supervisor of Financial Institutions (OSFI) and the Financial Transaction and Reports Analysis Centre of Canada (FINTRAC) are legally required to present parliament with annual reports on their activities as specified in their legislated mandates and on their plans and priorities for the coming fiscal year. Many other jurisdictions also require such disclosure.

Access to Information

Conventional practice and international AML/CFT standards provide that the supervisory body should have adequate powers to monitor and ensure compliance by banks and other financial institutions. These powers include the authority to compel the production of information, both documentary and oral, relevant to its supervisory mandate. Supervisors should have unfettered access to complete and accurate information in a timely manner. Bank secrecy or other confidentiality laws must not restrict their access to such information.

The AML/CFT supervisor should have access to information, including board minutes and resolutions, policies and procedures, books and records of the supervised institutions, customer files and accounts, transaction documents, business correspondence, risk management systems, risk assessment data and results, and monitoring and reporting systems. Supervisors should also have access to officials and staff (including compliance and audit staff) for verbal information, clarification, and explanations on any relevant matter.

With regard to access to STR information and copies of STRs filed with the FIU, the practice varies across jurisdictions. In some jurisdictions, legislation only allows the FIU, not the supervisor, to have access to STR information. In the absence of a clear, explicit, and specific legal prohibition to access STR information, supervisors have the legal power to access any information in possession of a financial institution. Supervisors should have access to STR data to be able to examine compliance with the requirement to report suspicious transactions, including assessing the quality, sufficiency, and timeliness of STRs filed. Supervisors need to examine the strength of the internal processes of monitoring for unusual and suspicious activities (both manual and automated)—that is, the internal reporting systems and processes for deciding whether or not to file an STR. This monitoring and reporting process should generally be tested for effectiveness by reviewing a sample of the STRs. Without access to STR data, it would not be feasible to conduct a proper review of compliance with the STR requirements or to sanction institutions for their failure to comply with their STR obligations.

The supervisor should also have the authority to consult with the FIU as part of its ongoing AML/CFT supervision. One objective of such consultation is to obtain feedback on the STR reporting of the institution, including the number and quality of STRs. This information assists the supervisor in determining the scope and focus of inspections. Information should be shared under strict confidentiality and should not breach any specific restrictions imposed by the AML/CFT legislation. In addition, the supervisor should have access to additional information such as reports on trends, typologies, and emerging threats to the financial sector and the wider economy.

Authority to Issue Regulations or Guidance

The AML/CFT supervisor, as the authority that evaluates and enforces AML/CFT compliance, is generally in the best position to issue AML/CFT regulations or guidance. However, in some jurisdictions, an appropriate industry body may be able to discharge this requirement. The supervisor should therefore have the authority to issue regulations or guidance when required (in case of changes in international standards, legislation, risks, or AML/CFT strategies). These instruments should be clear enough to minimize misinterpretation and facilitate a uniform understanding, without being too prescriptive or leaving too little room for financial institutions to undertake a risk-based approach. Insufficient clarity can undermine effective implementation and compliance and make enforcement more difficult. To encourage buy-in by the sectors, it is good practice for the supervisor to consult with the industry and any other relevant body prior to issuing such regulations or guidance. Some jurisdictions use consultative papers for this purpose.

Sanctioning Powers

FATF Recommendation 35 requires jurisdictions to ensure that a range of effective, proportionate, and dissuasive sanctions—whether criminal, civil, or administrative—is available to deal with institutions that fail to comply with AML/CFT requirements. The international standards specifically provide that the AML/CFT supervisor be lawfully vested with adequate powers both to supervise and enforce compliance as well as to impose sanctions for failure to comply with AML/CFT requirements. Under a risk-based AML/CFT regime, some jurisdictions apply enforcement measures proportionate to the type and severity of the infringement. Sanctions should have a deterrent effect on the institution as well as on the financial sector. Enforcement measures, moreover, may differ from and be in addition to those imposed by criminal courts.

A wide range of enforcement measures are available for breaches of legal requirements, ranging from warning letters to license revocations, so that supervisors can calibrate enforcement measures based on the severity and frequency of violations. These sanctions should entail both financial and nonfinancial penalties, including warning letters, directives, cease-and-desist orders, suspension or removal of directors and officers, license restrictions, suspensions and revocations, and monetary fines. The supervisor may also issue specific corrective instructions with implementation timelines and subject to penalty when these timelines are not met. Sanctions should apply to both the financial institution and to directors, officers, and employees so that the individuals involved are held accountable. Some jurisdictions have the power to impose a lifetime ban on employment at any financial institution.

Jurisdictions should also have administrative appeals procedures (for example, through appeals boards) to challenge supervisory actions. Administrative appeals are generally more expeditious than civil court proceedings, even though civil suits may be used to appeal the decisions of administrative tribunals. Depending on the infringement, the aim of an enforcement measure is to remedy the deficiencies or to penalize the institution. Some infringements, such as the failure to file or the late filing of STRs, are detected after the event and cannot be remedied retroactively. If remedial actions are not possible anymore, a monetary fine is an appropriate sanction. Supervisors often also have the authority or obligation to publish their enforcement actions.

In imposing sanctions, supervisors should adhere to the legal system of the jurisdiction, ensuring that due process is followed and that the legal or constitutional protection of rights and privileges is safeguarded.

Adequate Resources

International standards require a jurisdiction to provide AML/CFT supervisors with adequate financial, human, and technological resources. These resources should correspond to the size, sophistication, and complexity of the sector as well as the level of ML/TF risks in the jurisdiction and the sector. The level of compliance and quality of AML/CFT controls in the sector should also be considered.

Jurisdictions and supervisors often have limited resources, which restricts their ability to recruit and retain skilled supervisors, train staff, or acquire information technology systems. Training of supervisory staff, including on the use of a risk-based supervisory approach, is critical for the supervision of AML/CFT compliance. In addition, training programs need to be kept up to date in order to reflect developing ML/TF techniques and typologies affecting the sectors.

To mitigate the problem of limited resources, jurisdictions could take several measures to maximize the efficiency of resources. One such measure is to develop a risk-based approach to AML/CFT supervision that allows for more precise scoping and targeting of off-site and on-site activities to areas and institutions that present the highest level of ML/TF risk. Often, internal or external auditors also review AML/CFT systems and controls. Such audit reports are available to the supervisor. Where permitted, the use of external auditors is also an option to complement the supervisory function.

RISK-BASED AML/CFT SUPERVISION

Historically, AML/CFT supervisors took a rules-based approach that focused primarily on legal compliance without taking account of the risk profile of an institution, its customers, and its operations. Under such a general approach, supervisory practice would apply a fixed frequency of inspections, sometimes based on the size and complexity of an institution. Of course, changing from a rules-based to a risk-based system cannot be done overnight—it requires adequate preparation and access to relevant data to enable the supervisor to form a judgment on the overall risk profile of the institution, the higher- and lower-risk lines of business within it, and its risk relative to other institutions, and to draw up a national supervisory plan. Supervisors will require training in the methods available to gather relevant data and how to piece them together to form a coherent strategy.

A risk-based approach to AML/CFT supervision rests on the supervisor's understanding of ML/TF risks at three levels: (a) jurisdiction risks (as described in the national risk assessment); (b) financial sector risks (based on sectoral risk assessments); and, where possible, (c) institutional risks (based on knowledge of the risk profiles of institutions). These preconditions are essential for an effective, risk-based AML/CFT supervision framework. Such a framework would entail obtaining and assessing information on an institution's inherent ML/TF risks and on the institution's level of AML/CFT compliance. Much of this supervision involves off-site supervision, which serves as a key element for developing the annual inspection plan, budgeting, and resourcing.

Conducting AML/CFT supervision in a risk-based manner has the advantage of enabling the supervisor to focus on those institutions or business lines and processes within an institution that pose the highest risk. Additionally, risk-based supervision allows the supervisor to allocate its resources efficiently and effectively. In a risk-based approach to supervision, the frequency and intensity of supervision will be determined by the ML/TF risk profile of an institution. Two elements are key to assessing an institution's risk profile: (a) the level of risks inherent in its business lines and processes, including customers, products, services, transactions, geographic exposure, and delivery channels; and (b) the adequacy of its AML/CFT policies, procedures, and controls.

On-Site and Off-Site Supervision

An effective AML/CFT supervisory system conducts both on-site and off-site supervision. Similarly, an effective banking supervisory system includes both on-site and off-site supervision as well as regular contacts with bank management. The time dedicated to either on-site or off-site supervision depends on several factors, including the quantity and quality of information available from financial institutions, the (technical) capacity and experience of supervisors, prior examination reports, and the sophistication of analytical models.

Higher-risk institutions can be subjected to more intense and frequent off-site monitoring and on-site inspections, while lower-risk institutions can be subjected to less monitoring and fewer inspections; indeed, for the lowest-risk institutions, only off-site monitoring may suffice. The risk profile would also help the supervisor to develop more informed supervisory strategies, including with regard to the type and scope of examinations to conduct. In addition, risk-based supervision requires appropriate emphasis on the off-site function with respect to risk assessments and profiling so that more targeted inspections can be conducted based on risk. As described in chapter 8, suptech—the use of innovative technologies by supervisory authorities to conduct supervisory work and oversight more effectively and efficiently—is of increasing importance in setting up and enhancing the off-site supervision function.

Developing Risk Profiles

To develop a risk-based approach to AML/CFT supervision, it is necessary to have an integrated quantitative and qualitative approach to understanding and assessing ML/TF risks and AML/CFT compliance. This approach is different from the approach taken with respect to other categories of prudential banking risk (for example, credit, liquidity, market, and operational risks, which rely significantly on quantitative analysis).

Ideally, a risk-based approach to AML/CFT supervision should be guided by a policy and process for both off-site and on-site supervision. While no specific methodology or model is prescribed for such a risk-based approach, FATF Recommendations 1 and 26 and IO 3 provide the underlying factors and principles that should be considered. The following are some of the main quantitative and qualitative elements of a methodology for assessing and understanding ML/TF risks and AML/CFT compliance.

The interpretive notes to Recommendations 1 and 26 provide guidance on a risk-based approach to AML/CFT supervision. In practice, supervisors may have their own supervisory risk models for developing institutional risk profiles to inform their supervisory strategies and activities. This process may involve obtaining data from the financial institutions on inherent ML/TF risks and AML/CFT compliance and developing an assessment model based on the overall level of ML/TF risks and the quality of AML/CFT risk mitigation processes. Some supervisors have adopted prudential risk assessment frameworks to conduct this assessment, which may include an assessment of the quality of risk management systems. However, a tailored approach to assessing the inherent ML/TF risks and the quality of AML/CFT risk-mitigating measures is an essential tool for allocating resources to AML/CFT supervision and determining the intensity and frequency of AML/CFT supervisory activities.

Quantitative Factors

AML/CFT supervisors should assess the inherent ML/TF risks of the institutions they supervise. This assessment includes assessing each institution's inherent risks related to the type and number of customers, products, services, transactions, geographic areas, and delivery channels. Risk assessments should also consider the size, complexity, and nature of an institution. Several AML/CFT supervisory authorities have implemented various models for assessing risk, including rating and scoring models.

Qualitative Factors

The supervisor also needs to assess the adequacy and effectiveness of a financial institution's policies, procedures, and controls for mitigating ML/TF risks. The strength of controls should be proportional to a financial institution's assessed risks. Lower inherent risks allow for simpler measures of risk mitigation. Quite apart from the institution's own control measures, other external factors—such as the geographic areas where the bank operates, its clientele, and its exposure to United Nations–sanctioned entities or individuals—might not show up in hard data but nevertheless reflect real risk factors.

Chapters 3 and 4 address this risk-based AML/CFT supervisory framework and off-site AML/CFT supervision in more detail.

ORGANIZATIONAL APPROACHES FOR EFFECTIVE AML/CFT SUPERVISION

Neither the BCPs nor the FATF standards prescribe or give specific guidance on which type of model or supervisory arrangements a jurisdiction should use to supervise banks and other institutions subject to the AML/CFT regime. Obviously, different jurisdictions will take different approaches, and a universal model would never do those differences justice. However, the FATF standards and the BCPs more generally do require jurisdictions to implement a risk-based approach to AML/CFT supervision (FATF 2014).

The choice of supervisory model depends on several factors, including the legal framework that designates the AML/CFT supervisor; the history, culture, and practice of supervision; the experience of the supervisor; and, very important, the human, financial, and technical resources available. The choice of supervisory model may also be influenced by national priorities in the fight against ML/TF; for instance, the FIU may participate in on-site inspections along with the sectoral supervisors. Regardless of the choice of designated AML/CFT supervisor, any model will have both pros and cons.

Supervision by the Banking or Sectoral Supervisor

A common organizational model is to have the banking or sectoral supervisor supervise the AML/CFT compliance of banks and other financial institutions. There are several benefits to having the banking or sectoral supervisor also be responsible for AML/CFT supervision:

1. The financial supervisory authorities are usually highly skilled and knowledgeable about their sectors and individual institutions' (other) risks. They also have experience in reviewing the adequacy of policies, procedures, and controls to manage risks in general. This institutional repository of knowledge and sectoral data can be used easily for a risk-based framework for AML/CFT supervision.

2. The financial supervisors' knowledge about an institution's type of customers, products, and services, markets, geographic reach, and business processes places them in a good position to assess the ML/TF risk profile of institutions and supervise the adequacy of AML/CFT controls.

3. ML/TF risk is just one of the risks to which banks and other financial institutions are exposed, allowing existing supervisory processes and tools to be used for AML/CFT supervision and a holistic approach to be used for prudential and AML/CFT supervision.

4. The FATF recommendations and the BCPs require banks and other financial institutions to be subject to group supervision because many of the AML/CFT requirements also apply to financial groups. Financial groups therefore often adopt an enterprise-wide approach to risk mitigation and compliance for both prudential and ML/TF risks. This approach requires supervisors to understand ML/TF risks across the group and to extend the supervisory capacity to consolidated supervision of the group.

5. Banking and other financial sector supervisors supervise international banks and other financial institutions as either host or home supervisors. This supervision facilitates consolidated cross-border AML/CFT supervision and provides an effective and tested forum for international cooperation, including through supervisory colleges. In addition, most supervisors are part of regional and international supervisory groups, which provide an effective network for cross-border cooperation, including through memoranda of understanding, on a range of issues, including AML/CFT.

6. Banking and other financial sector supervisors have good knowledge of the corporate governance and compliance culture and history of individual institutions. These elements are important pillars for the effective implementation of AML/CFT compliance systems.

7. Banking and financial sector supervisors have relatively more leverage and prestige in the financial sector and more operational autonomy and resources than some other supervisors. This autonomy is particularly important for enforcement purposes.

Despite the benefits of designating the sectoral supervisors as AML/CFT supervisors, this model also has some potential disadvantages:

1. Not all sectoral supervisors fully embrace the importance of AML/CFT supervision. Consequently, they may not give adequate attention and priority to AML/CFT issues, even when a sector has been identified as high risk. Such inattention may give rise to tensions between different government agencies.

2. AML/CFT supervision will often be assigned to a specialized unit or team within the supervisory authority. The absence of coordination across functional lines can create conflicting priorities and supervisory silos within the same supervisory authority, leading to fragmented supervision.

3. Where interagency cooperation is weak, especially between the sectoral supervisor and the FIU, the FIU may not give the supervisor critical information on risks and compliance, such as emerging ML/TF threats as well as the quantity and quality of STRs filed.

Box 1.1 presents an example of an organizational model for AML/CFT supervision in which the prudential supervisor is also responsible for AML/CFT supervision (FATF and GAFILAT 2018).

BOX 1.1 Mexico: CNBV

The Mexican financial system consists of more than 3,000 licensed or registered financial entities. Several competent authorities are in charge of its regulation and supervision, depending on the sector. The Comisión Nacional Bancaria y de Valores (CNBV) supervises banks and other designated financial sectors for anti-money-laundering and combating terrorism financing (AML/CFT) and prudential purposes and has implemented a comprehensive and sophisticated model that takes into account the number and diversity of institutions, products, services, and consumers, among others. Furthermore, its AML/CFT regulation and supervision are at the forefront of international standards and global trends in many aspects.

The CNBV employs both off-site surveillance and on-site inspections as part of its supervisory programs. The off-site component focuses on regular reports that institutions file on their activities, and supervisors prioritize their work based on the institution's risk profile. The results of the risk analysis feed directly into the updated risk assessments for each institution. The CNBV supervises the most important and highest-risk sectors using specialized AML/CFT risk matrixes that feed into the broader prudential risk model. While it schedules and targets AML/CFT inspections based mainly on AML/CFT factors, the AML/CFT inspectors work closely with the prudential supervisors in planning and executing on-site inspections in order to avoid unnecessary duplication for the supervised institutions, wherever possible. In planning its annual supervisory program, the CNBV also obtains input from the financial intelligence unit and law enforcement.

The CNBV conducts consolidated AML/CFT supervision of financial groups working with other domestic regulators through a supervisors' coordination group to exchange information, but it has no authority to conduct joint inspections with other supervisors. Where a bank has overseas operations, the CNBV works closely with the foreign supervisor to receive regular reports on its activities.

Sources: FATF and GAFILAT 2018. See also CNBV website (https://www.cnbv.gob.mx/).

Supervision by the FIU

Some jurisdictions have designated the FIU as the AML/CFT supervisor. In such cases, the supervisor focuses solely on AML/CFT supervision and does not engage in prudential or conduct supervision. This model has several benefits:

1. Because of its central role in a jurisdiction's AML/CFT regime, the FIU has specialized knowledge of the ML/TF risks facing the jurisdiction and its financial sector.

2. The FIU also plays an important role in drafting the jurisdiction's national risk assessments and national AML/CFT strategy.

3. The collection and analysis of STRs provide the FIU with essential information on the entities subject to the AML/CFT regime. Statistical information in the STRs can provide valuable input for supervisory purposes.

However, the model also has several drawbacks:

1. The organizational and institutional model of the FIU determines whether it has the appropriate skills and resources to discharge its AML/CFT supervision mandate. FIUs that are part of the organizational structure of a central bank or other supervisory authority may have supervisory experience since they are staffed and funded, at least initially, by the supervisory body. However, FIUs that are part of a government ministry or agency generally need to develop the necessary supervisory knowledge and skills. These FIUs often also have fewer resources to dedicate to their supervisory task.

2. An FIU supervisor does not have direct access to information from prudential supervision that is important for profiling ML/TF risk (for example, corporate governance, financial statistics, and audits).

3. Neither the FIU nor the sectoral supervisors can conduct consolidated supervision of a financial institution if such information is not shared among the supervisors (as should be the general practice). In practice, some FIU supervisors may be able to conduct joint or coordinated on-site inspections with sectoral supervisors.

4. Neither the FIU nor the sectoral supervisor can conduct consolidated cross-border AML/CFT supervision of international financial groups.

5. Having separate supervisors conduct prudential and AML/CFT supervision can lead to fragmented supervision. It also raises the possibility of interagency disagreements if different authorities arrive at different conclusions and recommendations on overlapping issues (for example, governance, audit, and compliance functions). A financial institution may also be subject to multiple inspections by two different supervisors, raising costs for the institution.

6. An FIU supervisor may not have powers, on its own, to apply certain sanctions for AML/CFT violations, such as removing directors or officers and restricting or revoking licenses.

Box 1.2 presents an example of an organizational model in which the FIU conducts AML/CFT supervision (FATF and APG 2015).

BOX 1.2 Australia: AUSTRAC

The Australian Transaction Reports and Analysis Centre (AUSTRAC) is Australia's financial intelligence unit and anti-money-laundering and combating the financing of terrorism (AML/CFT) regulator. It oversees the compliance of more than 14,000 Australian businesses with the AML/CFT laws, covering businesses in the financial services, gambling, bullion, and remittance sectors. These businesses range from major corporations to small businesses—from the big banks to a pub or club with poker machines or a small remittance service provider. AUSTRAC reviews whether these businesses have the systems and controls in place to minimize the risk that they will be exploited by criminals.

AUSTRAC has adopted a graduated approach to supervision that extends from low-intensity (media articles, guidance, forums, and presentations) through to moderate-intensity (behavioral reviews, letter campaigns, and desk reviews) and high-intensity (on-site inspections, enforcement consideration, remedial directions, enforceable undertakings, and civil penalties). This wide range of measures allows AUSTRAC to implement tailored responses, depending on the type of reporting entity and its inherent characteristics, such as its relative importance, its size, and the risks it faces. In addition, AUSTRAC's supervisory approach has been modified over time to take into account the stage of development of Australia's AML/CFT regime.

Sources: FATF and APG 2015. See also the AUSTRAC website (https://www.austrac.gov.au).

Supervision Shared between the FIU and the Banking or Sectoral Supervisor

The third model is to have the FIU and the banking or sectoral supervisors share responsibilities for AML/CFT supervision. This model has an important benefit, as facilitating the sharing of personnel, information, expertise, and other resources between the two agencies can potentially improve the overall quality of AML/CFT supervision due to the complementarity of resources and skills.

This model, however, requires the clear delineation of roles and responsibilities and coordination of supervisory activities, including a mechanism for resolving conflicts—for instance, concerning the assessment of findings or enforcement actions. Unless the lines of responsibility are clearly defined, there could be duplication of supervision and inefficient use of resources for both the supervised entities and the supervisors.

In developing jurisdictions with scarce supervisory resources, this option may not be practical. Weak interagency coordination can also lead to supervisory gaps in the scope of supervision as well as to differing interpretations of AML/CFT legislation that adversely affect the enforcement regime.

Box 1.3 presents an example of an organizational model of shared AML/CFT supervision between the FIU and other supervisors (FATF 2016).

BOX 1.3 Canada: FINTRAC and Other Supervisors

In Canada, market entry controls are applied at federal and provincial levels. The federal prudential regulator, Office of the Supervisor of Financial Institutions (OSFI), applies robust controls when licensing a federally regulated financial institution (FRFI). The regulatory regime involves both federal and provincial supervisors. The Financial Transactions and Reports Analysis Centre of Canada (FINTRAC), the financial intelligence unit, is responsible for supervising all financial institutions and designated nonfinancial businesses and professions for compliance with their obligations under the anti-money-laundering and combating terrorism financing (AML/CFT) legislation. Other (prudential) supervisors may incorporate AML/CFT aspects within their wider supervisory responsibilities and generally refer AML/CFT issues to FINTRAC.

OSFI is the prudential regulator for FRFIs and conducts risk assessments specific to money laundering (ML) and terrorism financing (TF) that apply an inherent risk rating to entities on a group-wide basis rather than an individual basis. It leverages its prudential supervisors to understand the vulnerabilities of individual FRFIs. It also collaborates with FINTRAC and other supervisors on their understanding of ML/TF risks.

FINTRAC has developed a risk assessment model that assigns risk ratings to sectors and individual reporting entities. The model is a comprehensive ML/TF analytical tool that considers various factors to predict the likelihood and consequence of noncompliance by a reporting entity. On the basis of its analysis, it rates reporting sectors and entities, and the ratings are then used to inform its supervisory strategy.

Since 2013, FRFIs have been supervised by OSFI and FINTRAC concurrently. This process has involved examinations of high- and medium-risk FRFIs by each agency concurrently, with OSFI taking a top-down (group-wide) approach and FINTRAC taking a bottom-up (individual entities or sector) approach. The two agencies coordinate their approaches during examinations but issue separate supervisory letters setting out their findings. Despite good supervisory coverage of FRFIs, the split of AML/CFT supervision generates some duplicative efforts. This approach may be desirable given the size and importance of FRFIs, but it suffers from insufficient coordination between the two agencies and duplication of supervisory resources.

Source: FATF 2016.

Coordination between Prudential and AML/CFT Supervision

Irrespective of the jurisdictional diversity of institutional arrangements in AML/CFT supervision, close coordination is needed between the sectoral supervisory authority and the AML/CFT supervisory authority. If the same authority conducts both prudential and AML/CFT supervision, coordination should be easier, at least in principle. As part of its "Guidelines on Sound Management of Risks Related to Money Laundering and Financing of Terrorism," the BCBS issued guidance in July 2020 on the interaction and cooperation between prudential and AML/CFT supervisors (BCBS 2020). This guidance sets out specific principles, recommendations, and descriptive examples to facilitate effective and efficient cooperation regarding authorization-related procedures for banks, ongoing supervision, and enforcement actions. It also describes possible methods of implementation, including mechanisms to facilitate cooperation at the jurisdictional and international levels. To ensure effectiveness and efficiency, the cooperation must not have a negative effect on the independence of either supervisory function in fulfilling its mandate. Moreover, the cooperation must not result in different supervisory functions unduly duplicating efforts. Information exchange should be created and maintained to ensure that supervisors have access to timely and appropriate information.

Furthermore, in December 2019, the European Supervisory Authorities (consisting of the European Banking Authority, the European Insurance and Occupational Pensions Authority, and the European Securities and Markets Authority) issued joint guidelines, known as the AML/CFT colleges' guidelines, on cooperation and information exchange for the purpose of AML/CFT between competent authorities supervising credit and financial institutions (Joint Committee of the European Supervisory Authorities 2019). These guidelines aim to foster cooperation between AML/CFT and prudential supervisors and to ensure that they exchange relevant information in a timely manner. The European Banking Authority has also published a report on the functioning of the AML/CFT colleges highlighting some good practices but also challenges (EBA 2020).

NOTES

1. See Basel Core Principle 2, https://www.bis.org/publ/bcbs230.pdf.
2. See Basel Core Principle 2, https://www.bis.org/publ/bcbs230.pdf.

REFERENCES

BCBS (Basel Committee on Banking Supervision). 2012. "Core Principles for Effective Banking Supervision." BCBS, Basel, September. https://www.bis.org/publ/bcbs230.htm.

BCBS (Basel Committee on Banking Supervision). 2020. "Guidelines on Sound Management of Risks Related to Money Laundering and Financing of Terrorism; Issued in January 2014 and Revised July 2020." BCBS, Basel. https://www.bis.org/bcbs/publ/d505.htm.

EBA (European Banking Authority). 2020. *Report on the Functioning of AML/CFT Colleges.* Paris: EBA, December 15. https://eba.europa.eu/eba-observes-improved-cooperation-between -authorities-through-newly-established-amlcft-colleges.

FATF (Financial Action Task Force). 2014. "Guidance for a Risk-Based Approach, the Banking Sector." FATF, Paris, October. http://www.fatf-gafi.org/media/fatf/documents/reports/Risk-Based -Approach-Banking-Sector.pdf.

FATF (Financial Action Task Force). 2016. "Anti-Money Laundering and Counter-Terrorist Financing Measures—Canada, Fourth Round Mutual Evaluation Report." FATF, Paris. https://www.fatf-gafi .org/media/fatf/documents/reports/mer4/MER-Canada-2016.pdf.

FATF (Financial Action Task Force) and APG (Asia-Pacific Group on Money Laundering). 2015. "Anti-Money Laundering and Counter-Terrorist Financing Measures—Australia, Fourth Round Mutual Evaluation Report." FATF, Paris; APG, Sydney. https://www.fatf-gafi.org/media/fatf /documents/reports/mer4/Mutual-Evaluation-Report-Australia-2015.pdf.

FATF (Financial Action Task Force) and GAFILAT (Latin America Anti-Money-Laundering Group). 2018. "Anti-Money Laundering and Counter-Terrorist Financing Measures—Mexico, Fourth Round Mutual Evaluation Report." FATF, Paris. https://www.fatf-gafi.org/media/fatf/documents/reports /mer4/MER-Mexico-2018.pdf.

Joint Committee of the European Supervisory Authorities. 2019. "Final Report on Joint Guidelines on Cooperation and Information Exchange for the Purpose of Directive (EU) 2015/849 between Competent Authorities Supervising Credit and Financial Institutions; the AML/CFT Colleges Guidelines." European Supervisory Authorities, Paris, December 16. https://esas-joint-committee .europa.eu/Publications/Guidelines/joint-guidelines-on-cooperation-and-information-exchange -on-AML-CFT.pdf.

CHAPTER 2

The Licensing Process and AML/CFT Due Diligence

OVERVIEW

A financial institution owned, controlled, or managed by criminals is at significantly greater risk of being used for money-laundering (ML) or terrorism financing (TF) purposes. International standards, therefore, provide that a jurisdiction should take the necessary legal or regulatory measures to prevent criminals or their associates from holding, being the beneficial owner of, having a significant or controlling interest in, or holding a management function in a financial institution.[1] Key to the success of such measures is having a properly designed and enforced licensing mechanism and fit and proper tests that are integral parts of a risk-based framework for prudential and anti-money-laundering and combating the financing of terrorism (AML/CFT) supervision.

The Basel Committee on Banking Supervision (BCBS) has established a set of minimum licensing criteria for supervisors to ensure that banks will be established and operated in a safe and sound manner and to mitigate the risk that they will be owned, controlled, or managed by persons who are not fit and proper.[2] The fit and proper criteria for board members and senior management include having (a) skills and experience in relevant financial operations commensurate with the intended activities of the bank and (b) no record of criminal activities or adverse regulatory judgments that make a person unfit to hold important positions in a bank. The licensing authority should determine whether the bank's (proposed) board understands the main risks associated with the bank, including ML/TF risks. The licensing authority should determine whether the proposed strategic and operating plans provide an appropriate system of corporate governance, risk management, and internal controls, including those related to the detection and prevention of criminal activities.

Fit and proper requirements for significant shareholders, beneficial owners, and managers should be implemented through domestic laws and regulations. Where appropriate, they should be complemented by additional requirements to consider ML/TF risks specific to the jurisdiction, the sector, and the institutions. The licensing process should be clearly structured, transparent, and based on independent and reliable information. The licensing authority should have the power to reassess periodically whether owners and managers are fit and proper as well as to reject any proposal for a change in significant ownership, including beneficial ownership or controlling interest, if the applications do not meet the licensing criteria. Further, the licensing authority should have adequate resources to discharge its duties. If the licensing authority and the sectoral or AML/CFT supervisor are not the same, the licensing authority should take into account the views of the sectoral or AML/CFT supervisor as part of the licensing process.

This chapter is arranged in two sections. The first section gives an overview of the licensing requirements for financial institutions, and the second section discusses considerations for an effective licensing process.

SUMMARY OF THE LICENSING REQUIREMENTS FOR FINANCIAL INSTITUTIONS

General Requirements

A bank robber once said that the best way to rob a bank is to own one. This situation also applies to ML/TF because if criminals own, control, or manage a financial institution, other criminals can use it more easily to launder illicit proceeds or to finance terrorism. The examples given in boxes 2.1 through 2.3

illustrate how banks that are managed or controlled by criminals or by persons who are not fit and proper can be abused for criminal and other illegal purposes, on a national scale.

BOX 2.1 The Bankers to the Narcotraffickers

Banco Continental S.A., part of a Honduran economic conglomerate owned and controlled by the politically connected Rosenthal family, was designated on October 7, 2015, by the US Department of the Treasury's Office of Foreign Assets Control (OFAC), together with its founder, Jaime Rolando Rosenthal Oliva, among other individuals and entities, as a specially designated narcotics trafficker, pursuant to the US Foreign Narcotics Kingpin Designation Act. Rosenthal and other individuals were designated as such for allegedly providing "money laundering and other services that support the international narcotics trafficking activities of multiple Central American drug traffickers and their criminal organizations" (US Department of the Treasury 2015).

Criminal indictments were also entered in the US Southern District of New York, with Yani Benjamin Rosenthal Hidalgo, Jaime Rosenthal's son, pleading guilty to a money-laundering charge in 2017. As part of his guilty plea, Yani Rosenthal admitted to using Banco Continental to process payments related to a trade-based money-laundering scheme and other activities of the Honduran drug-trafficking organization, Los Cachiros (itself designated as a narcotics trafficker by OFAC in September 2013). Banco Continental, in particular, provided loans to Los Cachiros, which were comingled with illicit funds derived from drug trafficking to finance other business ventures and were at times repaid with drug proceeds or drug-derived assets (US Department of Justice 2017).

According to OFAC, "Banco Continental S.A. served as an integral part of the Rosenthal money-laundering operations and facilitated the laundering of narcotics proceeds for multiple Central American drug-trafficking organizations" (OFAC 2015). This was the first time that OFAC designated a bank outside of the United States. As a result of the OFAC designation, the bank was forcibly liquidated by the Honduran banking regulator, the Comisión Nacional de Bancos y Seguros, shortly thereafter (OFAC 2015), with negative implications for the stability of the Honduran financial sector and for legitimate customers of the bank whose assets were temporarily frozen (CNBS 2015).

BOX 2.2 Fraudulent Connected-Party Lending Resulting in a Billion Dollar Loss

In November 2014, three of Moldova's largest banks—Banca Economii S.A., Banca Sociala S.A., and Unibank S.A.—collapsed after hundreds of millions of dollars were fraudulently dissipated abroad through a quick succession of transfers over the course of two days. An investigation conducted by investigative consulting firm Kroll at the behest of the National Bank of Moldova (the country's banking supervisor) found evidence of significant wrongdoing by the persons controlling these banks (National Bank of Moldova 2017).

(box continues on next page)

BOX 2.2 *(continued)*

Kroll found that, between 2012 and 2014, the three banks underwent significant changes in their shareholding. While seemingly unconnected, the individuals and entities amassing stakes in the three banks were all linked to Moldovan businessman and politician Ilan Shor, through a complex web of legal entities and arrangements (the Shor Group, including at least 77 companies). During this time period and accelerating in November 2014, the loan exposure of the three banks to the Shor Group companies increased from 25 percent to 80 percent, amounting to a total of US$2.9 billion in what were, in effect, related-party loans. While most of the proceeds of these loans were used to repay existing loans, US$600 million, or approximately US$1 billion factoring in interest (the equivalent of one-eighth of Moldova's gross domestic product), vanished and was presumably stolen by those orchestrating the fraud. The three banks had already seen significant deterioration in their balance sheets as a result of the connected-party lending and could not withstand the loss; their collapse triggered a banking crisis.

According to Kroll's investigation, the persons controlling the three banks exploited their position to misrepresent the liquidity ratios of the banks, secure loans against questionable collateral, bypass certain board members to approve the loans, and ignore the concerns of senior employees. These weaknesses in bank governance were foreshadowed by the findings of the International Monetary Fund and the World Bank Financial Sector Assessment Program in 2014. In particular, the assessment found, "Ownership changes have also resulted in nontransparent changes in board members and chief executive officers. Controlling shareholders—through the new management—are in some cases promoting imprudent activities, notably exceptional balance sheet growth funded by high-cost deposits, including interbank placements channeled via offshore banks. There are indications that a substantial portion of this funding has gone to finance owners' related-party transactions which—as the ultimate beneficial owners' identity is disguised—cannot be identified as such under National Bank of Moldova regulations. These transactions have introduced additional risk into some of the key banks in the system" (Ard and others 2014, 11).

BOX 2.3 The Digital Currency "Bank of Choice" for the Criminal Underworld

Liberty Reserve S.A. was incorporated in Costa Rica in 2006 and operated as a de facto digital currency, a deposit bank, and a payment services provider. Customers could acquire Liberty Reserve currencies, purportedly pegged to the dollar or the euro, through third-party exchangers; these funds were then deposited in Liberty Reserve accounts and available for transfer between Liberty Reserve accounts or for withdrawal through third-party exchangers. Liberty Reserve afforded customers a significant degree of anonymity, failing to conduct even minimal levels of customer due diligence and offering further anonymizing services for an additional fee. The only requirement for opening an account with Liberty Reserve was a working email address; the company did not validate or verify other information provided by the customer (such as name and address), and the requirements applied

(box continues on next page)

BOX 2.3 *(continued)*

to the third-party exchangers were similarly lax. In fact, numerous customers provided blatantly criminal names, such as "Hacker Account." In addition, for an additional transaction fee, customers could hide their account numbers when transacting in Liberty Reserves, significantly hampering traceability.

All of these characteristics, as well as its global reach as a digital currency that could be transferred easily across borders, made Liberty Reserve "the bank of choice for the criminal underworld," as characterized in a press release by the US Department of Justice (2013). Criminal charges were brought against the company and several of its principals and employees in May 2013. In its heyday, Liberty Reserve had an estimated 1 million customers operating 5 million accounts. Suspected sources of criminal funds laundered through Liberty Reserve included credit card fraud, identity theft, investment fraud, computer hacking, child pornography, and narcotics trafficking. In parallel to the criminal indictments, the US Department of the Treasury designated Liberty Reserve to be of primary money-laundering concern. Although inherently difficult to estimate (the indictment referred to US$6 billion in suspected laundered proceeds), Arthur Budovsky, founder of Liberty Reserve, admitted in his plea agreement to laundering more than US$250 million in illegal proceeds (US Department of Justice 2016).

Liberty Reserve was, in effect, operating a money-transmitting business with customers across the globe (including an estimated 200,000 customers in the United States), and doing so without any license. Budovsky had a prior conviction from in or around 2006 for operating another unlicensed money-transmitting business in the United States, GoldAge (a digital currency exchanger converting US dollars to e-gold). He appeared to have taken significant steps to distance himself on paper from Liberty Reserve to avoid negative repercussions of this conviction (among others, using the alias "Eric Paltz"). In 2009, prompted by Costa Rica's financial sector regulator, the Superintendencia General de Entidades Financieras, Liberty Reserve initiated the process of applying for a money-transmitting service license. Ultimately, due to the absence of even basic anti-money-laundering controls, it withdrew its application in November 2011 and took its operations underground. One of the charges brought against Liberty Reserve in the United States was operating an unlicensed money-transmitting business.

This case provides a clear reminder of the lengths to which criminals will go to avoid regulatory and supervisory oversight and the importance of enforcing adequate licensing requirements to prevent banks from being set up in part or in full to attract an illicit clientele.

Sources: US Department of Justice 2015; US Department of the Treasury 2013.

A robust licensing regime, which includes ensuring fit and proper ownership and management, is, therefore, a key building block of an effective risk-based AML/CFT supervisory regime. Market entry controls should be part of a comprehensive framework for prudential and AML/CFT supervision. The licensing process is typically undertaken by the sectoral supervisor but may be conducted by another licensing authority. In the latter case, adequate cooperation arrangements are needed between the sectoral (and AML/CFT) supervisor and the licensing authority. Such arrangements are needed to ensure that the supervisor's input is taken into account—for example, to ensure that the proposed risk management framework includes an appropriate AML/CFT compliance framework and independent compliance and audit functions.

The controls to guard against the involvement of criminals and their associates in the financial sector should apply to direct and indirect ownership and control of financial institutions. This application should include, at a minimum, identifying and verifying all significant shareholders, beneficial owners and others who may exert significant influence, and directors and senior management. Particular attention should be paid to politically exposed persons who might exercise control through corporate ownership, for example. A clear and explicit policy prohibiting or restricting the use of bearer shares or nominee shareholders should also be in place, including the obligation to declare all connected activities and relations between shareholders and managers.

International Standards

Both the BCBS and the FATF have established a set of minimum licensing requirements for supervisors, including fit and proper criteria. Taken together, these two international standards provide the foundation for establishing effective market entry and licensing or registration regimes that constitute an essential control against criminal abuse of the financial sector of any jurisdiction. When these entry-level controls are weak or nonexistent, the vulnerability to ML/TF risks increases significantly, adversely affecting the risk profile of individual institutions, the sector, and the whole jurisdiction. Giving criminals and their associates access to controlling and operating a bank compromises the integrity of the bank itself, and no amount of AML/CFT regulation can counter the risk of abuse.

Besides the market entry and licensing or registration regimes, the regulatory framework should provide for periodic review and reassessment of the fitness and propriety of the management, shareholders, and beneficial owners of licensed or registered institutions. Permissions to hold a qualifying holding or a managerial position in a bank or other financial institution should not be considered irrevocable and indefinite. The supervisors should have a framework for periodically reviewing compliance with the fit and proper requirements to ensure that management, shareholders, and beneficial owners comply with these requirements on a continuous basis and not only at the moment of receiving the license or registration.

Neither of the two international standards prescribes which agency should be the licensing authority, but it is implicit in the Basel Core Principles that the licensing authority should be autonomous, operationally independent, and free from undue political and industry influence.

Minimum Licensing Requirements

The Core Principles for Effective Banking Supervision (known as the Basel Core Principles, or BCPs) 5, 6, and 7 set out minimum criteria for the licensing of banks. To implement these principles, the BCBS has established a methodology that banking supervisors can use to conduct self-assessments or that bodies such as the International Monetary Fund and the World Bank under their Financial Sector Assessment Program can use to conduct independent assessments.

Principle 5: Licensing Criteria

BCP 5 states, "The licensing authority has the power to set criteria and reject applications for establishments that do not meet the criteria. At a minimum, the licensing process consists of an assessment of the ownership structure and governance (including the fitness and propriety of board members and senior management) of the bank and its wider group, and its strategic and operating plan, internal controls, risk management, and projected financial condition (including capital base). Where the proposed owner or parent organization is a foreign bank, the prior consent of its home supervisor is obtained."[3]

This principle has 11 essential criteria for assessing compliance with the licensing requirements process:[4]

1. The law identifies the authority responsible for granting and withdrawing a banking license. The licensing authority could be the banking supervisor or another competent authority. If the licensing authority and the supervisor are not the same, the supervisor has the right to have its views on each application considered and its concerns addressed. In addition, the licensing authority provides the supervisor with any information that may be material to the supervision of the licensed bank. The supervisor imposes prudential conditions or limitations on the newly licensed bank, where appropriate.

2. Laws or regulations give the licensing authority the power to set criteria for licensing banks. If the criteria are not fulfilled or if the information provided is inadequate, the licensing authority has the power to reject an application. If the licensing authority or supervisor determines that the license was based on false information, the license can be revoked.

3. The criteria for issuing licenses are consistent with those applied in ongoing supervision.

4. The licensing authority determines that the proposed legal, managerial, operational, and ownership structures of the bank and its wider group will not hinder effective supervision on both a solo and a consolidated basis. The licensing authority also determines, where appropriate, that these structures will not hinder the effective implementation of corrective measures in the future.

5. The licensing authority identifies and determines the suitability of the bank's major shareholders, including the ultimate beneficial owners, and others who may exert significant influence. It also assesses the transparency of the ownership structure, the sources of initial capital, and the ability of shareholders to provide additional financial support, where needed.

6. A minimum amount of initial capital is stipulated for all banks.

7. The licensing authority, at authorization, evaluates the bank's proposed board members and senior management as to their expertise and integrity (fit and proper test) and any potential conflicts of interest. The fit and proper criteria include (a) having skills and experience in relevant financial operations commensurate with the intended activities of the bank and (b) having no record of criminal activities or adverse regulatory judgments that make a person unfit to uphold important positions in a bank. The licensing authority determines whether the bank's board has sound knowledge of the material activities that the bank intends to pursue and the associated risks.

8. The licensing authority reviews the proposed strategic and operating plans of the bank. This authority includes determining that an appropriate system of corporate governance, risk management, and internal controls, including those related to the detection and prevention of criminal activities as well as the oversight of proposed outsourced functions, will be in place.

The operational structure is required to reflect the scope and degree of sophistication of the proposed activities of the bank.

9. The licensing authority reviews pro forma financial statements and projections of the proposed bank. This review includes an assessment of the adequacy of the financial strength to support the proposed strategic plan as well as financial information on the principal shareholders of the bank.

10. In the case of foreign banks establishing a branch or subsidiary, before issuing a license, the host supervisor establishes that no objection (or a statement of no objection) has been received from the home supervisor. For cross-border banking operations in its country, the host supervisor determines whether the home supervisor practices global consolidated supervision.

11. The licensing authority or supervisor has policies and processes to monitor the progress of new entrants in meeting their business and strategic goals and to determine that the supervisory requirements outlined in the license approval are being met.

Principle 6: Transfer of Significant Ownership

BCP 6 states, "The supervisor has the power to review, reject, and impose prudential conditions on any proposals to transfer significant ownership or controlling interests held directly or indirectly in existing banks to other parties."[5] This principle has six essential criteria:[6]

1. Laws or regulations contain clear definitions of "significant ownership" and "controlling interest."

2. There are requirements to obtain supervisory approval or provide immediate notification of proposed changes that would result in a change in ownership, including beneficial ownership or the exercise of voting rights over a particular threshold, or a change in controlling interest.

3. The supervisor has the power (a) to reject any proposal for a change in significant ownership, including beneficial ownership or controlling interest; (b) to prevent the exercise of voting rights in respect of such investments; and (c) to ensure that any change in significant ownership meets criteria comparable to those used for licensing banks. If the supervisor determines that the change in significant ownership is based on false information, the supervisor has the power to reject, modify, or reverse the change.

4. The supervisor obtains from banks, through periodic reporting or on-site examinations, the names and holdings of all significant shareholders or those exerting a controlling influence, including the identities of beneficial owners of shares being held by nominees, by custodians, and through vehicles that could be used to disguise ownership.

5. The supervisor has the power to take appropriate action to modify, reverse, or otherwise address a change of control that has taken place without the necessary notification to or approval of the supervisor.

6. Laws or regulations require banks to notify the supervisor as soon as they become aware of any material information that may negatively affect the suitability of a major shareholder or a party with a controlling interest.

Principle 7: Major Acquisitions

BCP 7 states, "The supervisor has the power to approve or reject (or recommend to the responsible authority the approval or rejection of), and impose prudential conditions on, major acquisitions or investments by a bank, against prescribed criteria, including the establishment of cross-border operations, and to determine that corporate affiliations or structures do not expose the bank to undue risks or hinder effective supervision."[7] It has five essential criteria:[8]

1. Laws or regulations clearly define (a) what types and amounts (absolute or in relation to a bank's capital) of acquisitions and investments need prior supervisory approval and (b) cases for which notification after the acquisition or investment is sufficient. Such cases are primarily activities closely related to banking and where the investment is small relative to the bank's capital.

2. Laws or regulations provide criteria by which to judge individual proposals.

3. Consistent with the licensing requirements, the supervisor determines that any new acquisitions and investments do not expose the bank to undue risks or hinder effective supervision and that, where appropriate, these new acquisitions and investments will not hinder the effective implementation of corrective measures in the future. The supervisor can prohibit banks from making major acquisitions or investments (including the establishment of cross-border banking operations) in countries with laws or regulations prohibiting information flows deemed necessary for adequate consolidated supervision. The supervisor considers the effectiveness of supervision in the host country and its own ability to exercise supervision on a consolidated basis.

4. The supervisor determines that the bank has, from the outset, adequate financial, managerial, and organizational resources to handle the acquisition or investment.

5. The supervisor is aware of the risks that nonbanking activities can pose to a banking group and has the means to take action to mitigate those risks. The supervisor considers the ability of the bank to manage these risks prior to permitting investment in nonbanking activities.

BCP 7 has one more criterion:[9]

1. The supervisor reviews major acquisitions or investments by other entities in the banking group to determine that they do not expose the bank to any undue risks or hinder effective supervision. The supervisor also determines, where appropriate, that these new acquisitions and investments will not hinder the effective implementation of corrective measures in the future. Where necessary, the supervisor is able to address the risks to the bank arising from such acquisitions or investments.

The FATF Requirements

In addition to the BCPs, the FATF has imposed more specific requirements for financial sector supervisors under Recommendation 26.[10] In particular, according to Assessment Criterion 26.3, "Competent authorities or financial supervisors should take the necessary legal or regulatory measures to prevent criminals or their associates from holding (or being the beneficial owner of) a significant or controlling interest, or holding a management function, in a financial institution" (FATF 2021, 75).

In addition, Core Issue 3.1 of Immediate Outcome (IO) 3 on effective AML/CFT supervision asks, "How well does licensing, registration, or other controls implemented by supervisors or other authorities prevent criminals and their associates from holding or being the beneficial owner of a significant or controlling interest or holding a management function in financial institutions, designated nonfinancial businesses and professions, or virtual asset service providers? How well are breaches of such licensing or registration requirements detected?" (FATF 2021, 103).

Box 2.4 provides some examples of market entry licensing controls from the 2015 FATF guidance on effective supervision and enforcement (FATF 2015).

BOX 2.4 Examples Illustrating Various Approaches to Market Entry

"Fit and proper tests": United States. All banking institution applicants are subjected to "fit and proper tests" that include background checks. Should applicants have a criminal history, they either are denied participation or undergo a thorough review to determine if their past criminal history would hinder their ability to operate a financial institution. In cases where applicants omit information that would expose their criminal record, federal laws or regulations allow for civil or criminal recourse. For example, the booklet on background investigations of the *Comptroller's Licensing Manual* incorporates policies and procedures used by the Office of the Comptroller of the Currency to review the background of persons and certain companies (filers) interested in entering the national banking system, acquiring control of a national bank, or influencing its operations (OCC 2009). The booklet on changes in directors and senior executive officers incorporates policies and procedures used by the OCC to review and evaluate changes in directors and senior executive officers (OCC 2009).

Prudential supervisor of federally regulated financial institutions: Canada. Under the Bank Act, the Office of the Superintendent of Financial Institutions (OSFI) arranges for criminal and other background checks on the planned owners and operators of financial institutions. In addition, OSFI has prudential guidance that requires banks and other financial institutions to conduct background checks on directors and senior managers of federally regulated entities when these persons change. OSFI refers to such persons as "responsible persons." When conducting an on-site assessment of anti-money-laundering/combating terrorism financing (AML/CFT), OSFI reviews the federally regulated financial institution's compliance with this guidance and tests the application by reviewing the conduct and results of background checks. These reviews are particularly useful for assessing the processes used to obtain background information for individuals who have not resided in Canada.

For new applicants for banking or other financial institution licenses, OSFI also reviews the planned risk assessment and compliance programs as part of the application process, with an emphasis on the applicant's business plan and model, prior to issuing letters patent by the minister of finance. If a potential financial institution does not seem to understand the risks or address the requirements satisfactorily, the application is delayed from proceeding to ministerial approval until the issues are resolved.

(box continues on next page)

BOX 2.4 *(continued)*

For applicants who already operate businesses that will be transferred to a financial institution status, the evaluation also includes an abbreviated on-site assessment as part of OSFI's exercise to determine operational readiness.

Visit to newly authorized institutions: Mexico. The supervisor visits newly authorized financial institutions prior to their start of operations. These visits are comprehensive reviews of all aspects of compliance with AML/CFT regulations, including a fit and proper test of the corporate structure (background of the legal person members), effective customer identification programs, know-your-customer policies, an AML manual (a document containing all relevant AML policies, procedures, and corporate governance schemes according to the applicable legal framework), an AML risk matrix, reporting obligations, and an automated system to detect and report suspicious transactions and currency transactions in a timely manner.

CONSIDERATIONS FOR AN EFFECTIVE LICENSING PROCESS

Defining a Licensing Policy

A licensing policy should at least address the following issues:

- Prohibition on the establishment and continuation of shell banks;

- Prohibition on the issuance of bearer shares by the financial institution, at any level of the ownership structure;

- Prohibition (or strict controls) on the use of nominee shares and nominee directors that can hide the identity of the ultimate beneficial owners of the financial institution;

- Prohibition on the use of nontransparent and opaque ownership and control structures for the financial institution;

- Prohibition on persons who are not fit and proper from holding, or being the beneficial owner of, a significant or controlling interest or holding a management function in a financial institution; and

- Application of enhanced licensing measures where persons holding, or being the beneficial owner of, a significant or controlling interest or holding a management function are from high-risk jurisdictions or are politically exposed persons.

The licensing policy and processes have to take into account the ML/TF risks and AML/CFT compliance measures presented in the licensing application. This licensing policy should take account of different licensing scenarios, such as *de novo* banks or financial institutions, financial institutions transforming into banks, international banks establishing branches or subsidiaries in the jurisdiction, private entities vs. publicly listed entities, and so forth. Shareholders may be subject to licensing requirements (fit and proper test) when they propose to control more than a certain percentage of an institution's shares or voting rights (qualifying holdings), as determined by the jurisdiction. The licensing authority may reject applications where a financial institution would be controlled by multiple holding companies or some other complex shareholding structure that would not allow for or would complicate identification of the beneficial owner or otherwise jeopardize the effectiveness of supervision. Some jurisdictions also require banks to be listed on a stock exchange and subject to the related disclosure requirements. As a matter of policy, a jurisdiction can prohibit offshore entities from holding directly or indirectly any ownership interests in a financial institution.[11]

Categories of ML/TF Risks to Consider at the Licensing Stage

In considering a license application, the supervisor or licensing authority should assess the following ML/TF–related risks: (a) ownership and control risk and (b) business-related risk.

Ownership and Control Risk

Ownership and control risk is the risk that criminals or their associates will own or control a financial institution and that directors, senior management, and key personnel will not be fit and proper. To mitigate this risk, the licensing authority should undertake the following when applying the licensing requirements:

- Identify the persons who will exercise effective influence and control over the bank, together or jointly as a group, including shareholders, beneficial owners, persons with a significant or controlling interest, directors, and senior management;

- Understand the primary reasons why these persons (such as their role and contributions) want to participate in the financial institution; and

- Establish the rationale for being involved with a financial institution in the jurisdiction if nonresidents are involved either directly or indirectly.

Business-Related Risks

Business-related ML/TF risks are risks associated with the bank's business lines—that is, the types of customers, products, services, geographic locations, and delivery channels. For instance, the licensing application should indicate what the target customer base will be (for example, retail, corporate, high-net-worth clients, or domestic or foreign customers). It should also indicate what products and services will be provided (for example, private banking, investment banking, fiduciary services, fund transfers, currency exchange, remittances, trade finance, or virtual assets). With respect to geography, the application should indicate if the financial institution will establish a network of branches and subsidiaries in the jurisdiction and abroad.

The licensing authority should ensure that the proposed AML/CFT program of the financial institution takes account of ML/TF risks and that the proposed framework is proportionate to these risks. Key to an AML/CFT program are adequate policies and procedures, independent compliance and audit functions, client due diligence, processes for monitoring transactions and reporting suspicious transactions, screening of staff, ongoing training (including for directors and senior management), and record keeping. A strong culture of compliance should underpin the AML/CFT framework. The proposed framework should be reviewed as part of the licensing process, taking into account the ML/TF risks of the jurisdiction and the sector as well as applicable legal and regulatory requirements.

Fit and Proper Procedures

In conducting fit and proper due diligence, the licensing or supervisory authority should obtain information about the shareholders, beneficial owners, persons with a significant or controlling interest, directors, and senior management (EBA 2016a, 2016b, 2017). The following information should be obtained and considered at a minimum:

- Evidence, such as police and judicial records, is needed to determine whether the persons or entities have a criminal and a civil record and, if so, the nature and seriousness of the offenses involved. In some jurisdictions, legal entities can be held criminally liable, while in others they can only be subject to civil action for the same types of offenses.

- Reliable information is needed on the business, professional, and work experience of the applicants that clearly demonstrates their competency and capacity to contribute to the success of the financial institution. This information can include a certificate of good conduct from past employers.

- For natural persons proposed as shareholders, reliable information is needed on their net worth (assets and liabilities) to ensure that they are solvent. Their financial standing should demonstrate their capacity to invest in the institution from own resources and to inject additional capital when needed. To ensure that no criminals or their associates are involved, it is especially relevant to determine that the sources of funds and the wealth of these persons are legitimate.

- For legal entities proposed as shareholders, due diligence should include (a) their business purpose, activities, and history; (b) their financial condition, preferably through independently audited accounts; (c) their corporate and ownership structure, including beneficial owners; and (d) their governance and reputation, including open-source information.

- For legal entities that will form the financial institution itself, the extent of due diligence will depend on whether the entity is a newly formed or an existing one. For a new entity, due diligence will be basic, including incorporation (if already formed) and proposed shareholding and directorships that will be part of the due diligence conducted on natural persons and legal persons as proposed shareholders of the bank.

- For legal entities already established and operational, further due diligence will be required to determine whether they are acceptable applicants (if there is no adverse news on these entities). In certain cases, enhanced due diligence will be required to investigate their business practices, regulatory and supervisory reputation, financial condition, and legal and judicial record.

- For nonresidents, whether natural or legal persons, further due diligence can involve consulting with parties in their jurisdiction of origin, including supervisors, law enforcement, and financial intelligence units.

- In general, use of open-source information is strongly recommended.

In conducting risk-based due diligence procedures, the licensing or supervisory authority should also consider risk factors with respect to the jurisdictions where the financial institution will operate as well as with respect to the jurisdictions where the shareholders, directors, and other related persons reside. For this purpose, supervisors should review the national risk assessments of the jurisdiction or jurisdictions involved as well as the AML/CFT framework of those jurisdictions. For jurisdictions with a weak AML/CFT framework or a high level of ML or TF and related offenses, due diligence on the applicant should be enhanced.

With regard to foreign banks wishing to open branches and subsidiaries in the jurisdiction, the due diligence process will be different from that for a *de novo* bank. In the first place, the host licensing or supervisory authority should obtain information from the home supervisor indicating that the institution is in good standing and has an adequate AML/CFT framework. In particular, the following minimum risk-based due diligence procedures should be considered, beyond the normal fit and proper procedures:

- Review the risk profile of the jurisdiction of origin and of any other jurisdictions in which the institution operates;

- Establish the regulatory and supervisory history of the institution, including compliance with AML/CFT requirements;

- Determine if the institution has been involved in ML/TF investigations;

- Review the adequacy of the institution's AML/CFT compliance framework and whether it is appropriate for the domestic requirements and risks;

- Review internal audit and compliance reports as well as external audit reports and management letters for AML/CFT issues; and

- Research open sources to obtain information on the reputation and background of the institution.

Transparency and Reliable Verifiable Information

The applicant is responsible for providing accurate and adequate information to the licensing authority so that the authority can make an informed decision on whether to grant a license. Providing false, misleading, or intentionally incomplete information may be grounds for refusal of a license, the imposition of administrative and civil sanctions, such as barring persons from participating in the proposed financial institution or the sector generally, or the application of fines. The licensing authority should at any time have the right to withdraw the license authorization if it identifies that the applicant willfully provided false or misleading information.

Supervisors can obtain information from multiple sources when they process license applications. In general, supervisors obtain information from the applicant and from other sources. To obtain information from the applicant, the supervisor can use questionnaires, (sworn) declarations, or similar mechanisms to obtain information on the natural and legal persons associated with the application. Such initial documentation should include the business proposal, projected financial statements, and information on the AML/CFT framework. The supervisor can interview shareholders, promotors, and other parties involved in the application process to collect information about the applicant. In addition, the supervisor can conduct its own due diligence, information gathering, and inquiries (with third parties such as other supervisors, domestically and abroad, law enforcement, financial intelligence units, intelligence service agencies, credit-rating and search agencies, the internet, and other reliable, publicly available information). In all cases, the supervisor should base its licensing decisions on reliable and verifiable information.

It is standard practice for supervisors to post their licensing requirements and procedures on their websites. These requirements and procedures should be reviewed periodically to ensure that they remain relevant and accurate, especially when changes are made to applicable laws, regulations, and policy.

With respect to the decision to grant or refuse a license, law and practice vary, with most jurisdictions requiring the supervisor to provide reasons for denying a license and others reserving the right not to provide any specific reason, usually on public interest grounds. For instance, if refusing a license may disclose sensitive information concerning an ongoing investigation into any person or entity involved in the application that would disqualify them from participating in the institution, then a specific explanation will not be required, or a general explanation may be given invoking public interest grounds. These cases, of course, can be challenged by the applicants.

Licenses can also be granted subject to terms and conditions, including regarding AML/CFT issues. One such condition could be to appoint a compliance officer at the management level or to require an independent AML/CFT audit within a specified period after the start of operations. Another condition may be to designate a board member or committee as responsible for dealing with AML/CFT issues.

Adequate Resources to Discharge Its Duties

The licensing authority should have adequate regulatory, human, technical, and financial resources to carry out its licensing responsibilities on an ongoing basis. These resources include the capacity to conduct a rigorous fit and proper assessment of all key persons. The regulatory framework for licensing should also provide the licensing authority with the necessary powers and authority to conduct all necessary due diligence on all matters relevant to making informed decisions on the applications. Staff involved in the licensing process should be professional and well trained to carry out their responsibilities.

Application of Licensing Requirements to Changes in Ownership, Control, and Senior Management Positions

After all due diligence processes have been completed and the application has been assessed thoroughly, a license can be issued subject to any terms and conditions that the licensing authority may impose. However, under a risk-based approach to supervision, the supervisor or licensing authority should conduct ongoing due diligence on the key players of the institution (significant shareholders, directors, and other key personnel) because their circumstances or characteristics can change, resulting in them no longer meeting the fit and proper requirements (for example, when a director is indicted or convicted of a crime after the license has been approved). The licensing policy should extend to due diligence requirements that arise after licensing. Likewise, if there are changes in ownership and control or if new owners and directors are brought on board, fit and proper due diligence on these persons should be conducted in accordance with licensing requirements.

NOTES

1. Financial Action Task Force (FATF) Recommendation 26.
2. Basel Core Principle (BCP) 5.
3. BCP 5, 25.
4. BCP 5, 26–27.

5. BCP 6, 27.
6. BCP 6, 27–28.
7. BCP 7, 28.
8. BCP 7, 28–29.
9. BCP 7, 29.
10. Each recommendation is assessed under different criteria according to *Methodology for Assessing Compliance with the FATF Recommendations and the Effectiveness of AML/CFT Systems* (FATF 2021, 12–14).
11. Offshore entities are located in offshore centers that are engaged primarily in business with nonresidents.

REFERENCES

Ard, Laura A., Carlos Enrique Caceres, Pierre-Laurent Chatain, Leif Michael Clark, Brett E. Coleman, Ghenadie Cotelnic, Jose Garrido, and others. 2014. "Moldova—Financial Sector Assessment." Financial Sector Assessment Program, World Bank, Washington, DC. https://documents.worldbank.org/curated/en/392881468288057798/Moldova-Financial-sector-assessment.

CNBS (Comisión Nacional de Bancos y Seguros). 2015. "Testimonio de clientes y cuenta habientes Banco Continental S.A." Press Release, CNBS, Tegucigalpa, October 14. https://www.cnbs.gob.hn/blog/2015/10/16/video-cnbs-16-10-2015-01/.

EBA (European Banking Authority). 2016a. "Implementing Technical Standards on Common Procedures, Forms, and Templates for the Consultation Process between the Relevant Competent Authorities for Proposed Acquisitions of Qualifying Holdings in Credit Institutions as Referred to in Article 24 of Directive 2013/36/EU of the European Parliament and of the Council." Final Report, EBA, Paris, September 22. https://eba.europa.eu/sites/default/documents/files/documents/10180/1586782/c772440c-89ab-4729-9cc1-04d73887f2ba/Final%20draft%20ITS%20on%20the%20procedures%20and%20forms%20(EBA-ITS-2016-05).pdf.

EBA (European Banking Authority). 2016b. "Joint Guidelines on the Prudential Assessment of Acquisitions and Increases of Qualifying Holdings in the Financial Sector." Final Report, EBA, Paris, December 20. https://esas-joint-committee.europa.eu/Publications/Guidelines/JC_QH_GLs_EN.pdf.

EBA (European Banking Authority). 2017. "Draft Regulatory Technical Standards under Article8(2) of Directive 2013/36/EU on the Information to Be Provided for the Authorisation of Credit Institutions, the Requirements Applicable to Shareholders and Members with Qualifying Holdings and Obstacles Which May Prevent the Effective Exercise of Supervisory Powers." Final Report, EBA, Paris, July 14. https://eba.europa.eu/sites/default/documents/files/documents/10180/1907331/de9abe89-7be5-4fea-aaf8-43bd4e67d71e/Draft%20RTS%20and%20ITS%20on%20Authorisation%20of%20Credit%20Institutions%20(EBA-RTS-2017-08%20EBA-ITS-2017-05).pdf.

FATF (Financial Action Task Force). 2015. "Guidance for a Risk-Based Approach: Effective Supervision and Enforcement by AML/CFT Supervisors of the Financial Sector and Law Enforcement." FATF, Paris, October. https://www.fatf-gafi.org/publications/fatfrecommendations/documents/rba-effective-supervision-and-enforcement.html.

FATF (Financial Action Task Force). 2021. *Methodology for Assessing Compliance with the FATF Recommendations and the Effectiveness of AML/CFT Systems; Adopted in February 2013, Amended October 2021.* Paris: FATF. https://www.fatf-gafi.org/publications/mutualevaluations /documents/fatf-methodology.html.

National Bank of Moldova. 2017. "NBM Published a Detailed Summary of the Second Investigation Report of the Kroll and Steptoe & Johnson Companies." Press Release, National Bank of Moldova, Kishinev, December 21. https://www.bnm.md/en/content /nbm-published-detailed-summary-second-investigation-report-kroll-and-steptoe-johnson.

OCC (Office of the Comptroller of the Currency). 2009. *Comptrollers Licensing Manual.* Washington, DC: OCC.

OFAC (Office of Foreign Assets). 2015. "Statement on Proposed Liquidation of Banco Continental." OFAC, US Department of the Treasury, Washington, DC, October 11. https://home.treasury.gov/ system/files/126/banco_continental_10112015.pdf.

US Department of Justice. 2013. "Manhattan U.S. Attorney Announces Charges against Liberty Reserve, One of World's Largest Digital Currency Companies, and Seven of Its Principals and Employees for Allegedly Running a $6 Billion Money Laundering Scheme." Press Release, US Department of Justice, Washington, DC, May 28. https://www.justice.gov/usao-sdny/pr /manhattan-us-attorney-announces-charges-against-liberty-reserve-one-world-s-largest.

US Department of Justice. 2015. "Southern District of New York Redacted Indictment *United States* v. *Liberty Reserve S.A., et al.*, Case No. 13-cr-368." Southern District of New York, US Department of Justice, Washington, DC. https://www.justice.gov/sites/default/files/usao -sdny/legacy/2015/03/25/Liberty%20Reserve%2C%20et%20al.%20Indictment%20-%20 Redacted_0.pdf.

US Department of Justice. 2016. "Founder of Liberty Reserve Pleads Guilty to Laundering More Than $250 Million through His Digital Currency Business." Press Release, US Department of Justice, Washington, DC, January 29. https://www.justice.gov/opa/pr /founder-liberty-reserve-pleads-guilty-laundering-more-250-million-through-his-digital.

US Department of Justice. 2017. "Former Honduran Congressman and Businessman Pleads Guilty in Manhattan Federal Court to Money Laundering Charge." Press Release, US Department of Justice, Washington, DC, July 26. https://www.justice.gov/usao-sdny/pr /former-honduran-congressman-and-businessman-pleads-guilty-manhattan-federal-court-money.

US Department of the Treasury. 2013. "Notice on Finding that Liberty Reserve S.A. Is a Financial Institution of Primary Money Laundering Concern." US Department of the Treasury, Washington, DC, May 28. https://www.fincen.gov/sites/default/files/special_measure/311--LR-NoticeofFinding-Final.pdf.

US Department of the Treasury. 2015. "Treasury Sanctions Rosenthal Money Laundering Organization." Press Release, US Department of the Treasury, Washington, DC, October 7. https://www.treasury.gov/press-center/press-releases/pages/jl0200.aspx.

CHAPTER 3

Introduction to a Risk-Based AML/CFT Supervisory Framework

INTERNATIONAL STANDARDS FOR RISK-BASED SUPERVISION

Financial Action Task Force (FATF) Recommendation 1 sets out the overarching risk-based require-ments for jurisdictions, including financial institutions and their supervisors. Paragraph 9 of the interpretive note to Recommendation 1 requires supervisors to review the money-laundering and terrorism financing (ML/TF) risk profiles and risk assessments prepared by financial institutions and to consider the results of this review in their supervision. With respect to financial institutions, part B of this interpretive note details the obligations and decisions in assessing ML/TF risks as well as the weapons proliferation financing risks. Immediate Outcome (IO) 3 establishes the requirements for supervisors to supervise, monitor, and regulate financial institutions appropriately for compli-ance with anti-money-laundering and combating the financing of terrorism (AML/CFT) require-ments commensurate with their risks, and IO 4 sets out the obligations for financial institutions to apply AML/CFT preventive measures commensurate with their risks and to report suspicious transactions.

In summary, these standards require financial institutions and supervisors to identify, assess, and understand the ML/TF risks and to apply proportionate risk mitigation and supervisory measures, respectively. Where risks are higher, mitigation and supervision should be enhanced, and where risks are lower, less rigorous measures may be applied. This principle also implies that where the risks are at a normal level (neither high nor low), the standard measures described in the recommen-dations apply.

Outcomes from FATF Evaluations with Respect to Supervision

The FATF recommendations set the standard for an effective risk-based AML/CFT supervisory approach. Recommendation 26 and IO 3 set out the main requirements for applying effective risk-based AML/CFT supervision to financial institutions.

As of November 2021, the FATF had published the mutual evaluation reports and follow-up reports of 119 jurisdictions.[1] Of these 119 jurisdictions, 30 are members of the FATF[2] and 89 are members of an FATF-style regional body (FSRB). Members of FSRBs are largely developing jurisdictions.

Jurisdictions have so far had mixed results from the assessment of compliance with Recommendation 26. As shown on figure 3.1, 87 percent of the assessed FATF members are largely compliant or compliant with this recommendation. In contrast, only 61 percent of the assessed FSRB members are largely compliant or compliant; 39 percent are partially compliant or noncompliant.

FIGURE 3.1 Compliance of FATF Members and FSRB Members with Recommendation 26, 2021

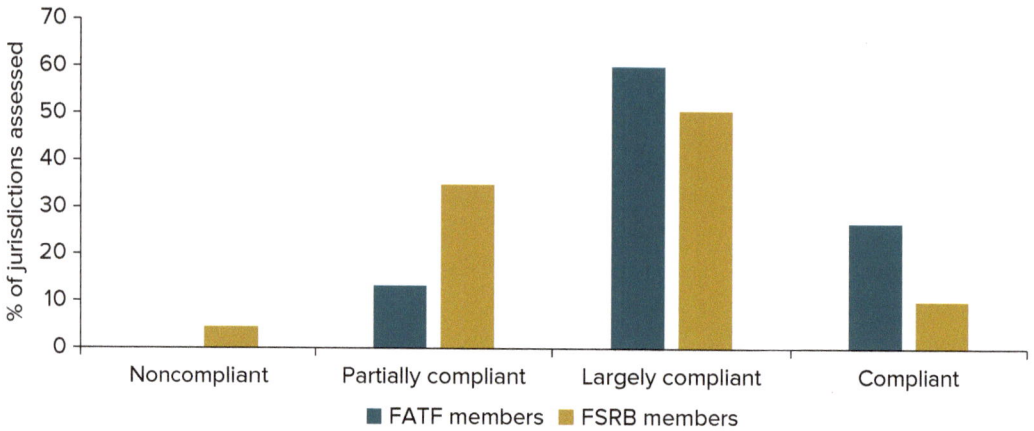

Source: FATF consolidated assessment ratings, updated November 8, 2021.
Note: FATF = Financial Action Task Force. FSRB = FATF-style regional body.

The assessments of effectiveness of supervision under IO 3 also show a divergence between FATF members and FSRB members. The differences are, however, smaller than with the technical compliance with Recommendation 26. Figure 3.2 shows that 17 percent of FATF members have substantial effectiveness, compared with only 7 percent of FSRB members. The percentage of jurisdictions rated as having moderate effectiveness is 73 percent among FATF members and 53 percent among FSRB members. Moreover, 10 percent of FATF members have a low effectiveness rating, versus 40 percent of the FSRB members.

FIGURE 3.2 Compliance of FATF Members and FSRB Members with IO 3, 2021

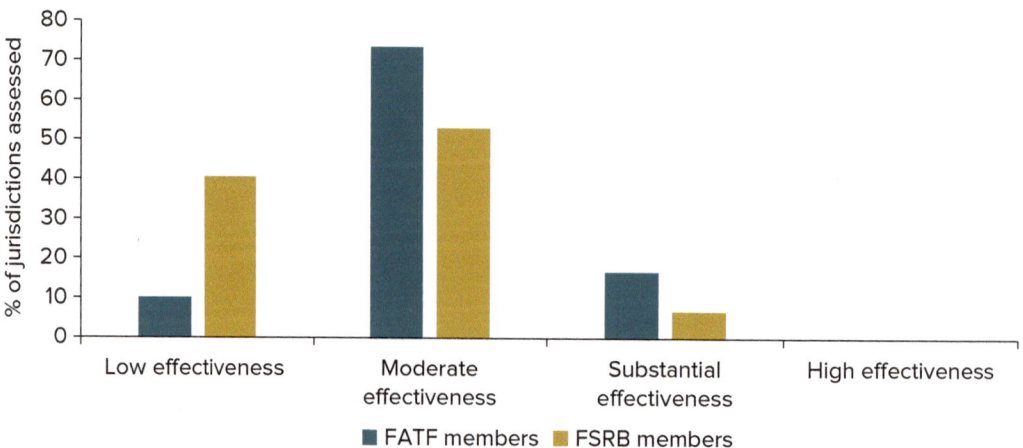

Source: FATF consolidated assessment ratings, updated November 8, 2021.
Note: FATF = Financial Action Task Force. FSRB = FATF-style regional body. IO = Immediate Outcome.

In all, of the 119 assessed jurisdictions, only 11 jurisdictions (5 FATF members and 6 FSRB members) have a substantial effectiveness rating. None of the jurisdictions has obtained a high effectiveness rating. In all, it is evident that jurisdictions have difficulty attaining an effective risk-based AML/CFT supervisory framework for all entities covered by the AML/CFT requirements.

FATF IO 3

IO 3 identifies six core issues for assessing the overall effectiveness of supervision in a risk-based framework. Core Issues 3.2 and 3.3, in particular, deal with the understanding of risk and risk-based supervision.[3] These six core issues are as follows:

- *Core Issue 3.1.* How well do licensing, registration, or other controls implemented by supervisors or other authorities prevent criminals and their associates from holding, or being the beneficial owner of, a significant or controlling interest or holding a management function in a financial institution, designated nonfinancial business or profession, or virtual asset service provider? How well are breaches of such licensing or registration requirements detected?

- *Core Issue 3.2.* How well do the supervisors identify and maintain an understanding of the ML/TF risks in the financial and other sectors as a whole, between different sectors and types of institutions, and in individual institutions?

- *Core Issue 3.3.* With a view to mitigating the risks, how well do supervisors, on a risk-sensitive basis, supervise or monitor the extent to which financial institutions, designated nonfinancial businesses and professions, and virtual asset service providers are complying with their AML/CFT requirements?

- *Core Issue 3.4.* To what extent are remedial actions or effective, proportionate, and dissuasive sanctions applied in practice?

- *Core Issue 3.5.* To what extent are supervisors able to demonstrate that their actions have an effect on compliance by financial institutions, designated nonfinancial businesses and professions, and virtual asset service providers?

- *Core Issue 3.6.* How well do supervisors promote a clear understanding by financial institutions, designated nonfinancial businesses and professions, and virtual asset service providers of their AML/CFT obligations and ML/TF risks?

FATF Guidance on the Risk-Based Approach

In March 2021, the FATF issued its "Guidance on Risk-Based Supervision" to encourage countries to move beyond a tick-box approach to monitoring the private sector's efforts to curb money-laundering and terrorism financing (FATF 2021b). The overarching goal is to make supervision more effective. To that end, the guidance is meant to help supervisors to address the full spectrum of risks and focus resources where the risks are highest. A risk-based approach is less burdensome on lower-risk sectors or activities, which is critical for maintaining or increasing financial inclusion.

Establishing a risk-based approach is not trivial, though. In fact, transitioning from rules-based supervision to risk-based supervision is a demanding process, which can be especially challenging in low-capacity countries. It requires a change in supervisory culture and staff mind-set. Supervisors need to work across government and with the private sector to develop an in-depth understanding of the risks facing their regulated entities.

As the FATF puts it, "This is important because every business operates differently and faces different risks. Supervisors need to have appropriate powers, skills, and resources as well as political and organizational support. They need to continuously update their understanding of risk and adjust and improve their supervisory approach" (FATF 2021b).

The FATF guidance is composed of three parts. Part 1 explains how supervisors should assess the risks facing their supervised sectors and prioritize their activities in line with the FATF standards' risk-based approach. Part 2 discusses strategies to address common challenges in risk-based supervision and provides jurisdictional examples, including examples of strategies for supervising designated nonfinancial businesses and professions and virtual asset service providers. Part 3 provides country examples from across the global network of supervision of the financial sector, virtual asset service providers, and other private sector entities.

The FATF guidance, while nonbinding, clarifies and explains how supervisors should apply a risk-based approach to their activities in line with the FATF standards. In addition to explaining common expectations, the guidance is also forward-looking and identifies innovative practices that can improve the effectiveness of AML/CFT supervision and thus the overall AML/CFT system.

In this document, the FATF defines what constitutes an effective risk-based supervisory framework. In such a framework, the supervisor identifies, assesses, and understands ML/TF risks within the sector(s) and entities under its purview and mitigates them effectively on an ongoing basis. This process involves implementing a sound risk assessment system that enables the identification, measurement, control, and monitoring of ML/TF risks as well as a risk-based supervisory approach that enables timely supervisory intervention to address any significant changes or elevation in risks (FATF 2021b, 12). More specifically, the supervisor undertakes the following:

- Develops and maintains a good understanding of ML/TF risks at the sector as well as the entity level based on a sound assessment of inherent risks and quality of mitigation measures and informed by national ML/TF risk assessment;

- Develops and implements a supervisory strategy that directs supervisory focus to higher or emerging ML/TF risks, while ensuring that appropriate, risk-based strategies are in place to address lower risks effectively and efficiently without unnecessarily affecting access to and use of financial services;

- Influences entities' behavior by ensuring that they have effective AML/CFT policies in place and, where issues are identified, provides targeted guidance and feedback, directing or overseeing remedial actions and exercising enforcement powers in a dissuasive and proportionate manner taking risk, context, and materiality into account;

- Monitors the evolving risk environment and stays agile to identify emerging risks and respond promptly;

- Is equipped with the expertise, powers, discretion, and tools needed and has adequate resources to perform its functions; and

- Coordinates with other competent authorities when relevant, including the financial intelligence unit (FIU), law enforcement agencies, and other supervisory agencies, as well as with foreign counterparts, sharing information, prioritizing risks, and carrying out joint supervisory activities as appropriate.

The Basel Core Principles

The Core Principles for Effective Banking Supervision (the Basel Core Principles, or BCPs) also require banking supervisors to apply a risk-based approach to supervision in general, including for AML/CFT. BCP 8 addresses a supervisory approach based on risks in general, stating, "An effective system of banking supervision requires the supervisor to develop and maintain a forward-looking assessment of the risk profile of individual banks and banking groups, proportionate to their systemic importance; identify, assess, and address risks emanating from banks and the banking system as a whole; have a framework in place for early intervention; and have plans in place, in partnership with other relevant authorities, to take action to resolve banks in an orderly manner if they become nonviable."[4]

BCP 8 has eight essential criteria:[5]

1. The supervisor uses a methodology for determining and assessing on an ongoing basis the nature, impact, and scope of the risks (a) that banks or banking groups are exposed to, including risks posed by entities in the wider group; and (b) that banks or banking groups present to the safety and soundness of the banking system.

2. The methodology addresses, among other things, the business focus, group structure, risk profile, internal control environment, and resolvability of banks and permits relevant comparisons between banks. The frequency and intensity of supervision of banks and banking groups reflect the outcome of this analysis.

3. The supervisor has processes to understand the risk profile of banks and banking groups and employs a well-defined methodology to establish a forward-looking view of the profile. The nature of the supervisory work for each bank is based on the results of this analysis.

4. The supervisor assesses banks' and banking groups' compliance with prudential regulations and other legal requirements.

5. The supervisor takes the macroeconomic environment into account in its risk assessment of banks and banking groups. The supervisor also takes into account cross-sectoral developments—for example, in nonbank financial institutions—through frequent contact with their regulators.

6. The supervisor, in conjunction with other relevant authorities, identifies, monitors, and assesses the buildup of risks, trends, and concentrations within and across the banking system as a whole. This assessment includes, among other things, banks' problem assets and sources of liquidity (such as the funding conditions and costs of domestic and foreign currency). The supervisor incorporates this analysis into its assessment of banks and banking groups and addresses proactively any serious threat to the stability of the banking system. The supervisor communicates any significant trends or emerging risks identified to banks and other relevant authorities with responsibilities for financial system stability.

7. Drawing on information provided by the bank and other national supervisors, the supervisor, in conjunction with the resolution authority, assesses the bank's resolvability, where appropriate, having regard for its risk profile and systemic importance. When bank-specific barriers to orderly resolution are identified, the supervisor requires, where necessary, banks to adopt appropriate measures, such as changes in business strategies; managerial, operational, and ownership

structures; and internal procedures. Any such measures take into account their effect on the soundness and stability of ongoing business.

8. The supervisor has a clear framework or process for handling banks in times of stress, such that any decisions to require or undertake recovery or resolution actions are made in a timely manner.

9. Where the supervisor becomes aware of bank-like activities being performed fully or partially outside the regulatory perimeter, the supervisor takes appropriate steps to call the matter to the attention of the responsible authority. Where the supervisor becomes aware that a bank is restructuring its activities to avoid the regulatory perimeter, the supervisor takes appropriate steps to address this situation.

RISK-BASED APPROACH TO SUPERVISION

A risk-based approach to AML/CFT supervision refers to (a) the process by which a supervisor, according to its understanding of ML/TF risks in the jurisdiction and of the supervised institutions, allocates its resources to AML/CFT supervision; and (b) the specific process of supervising institutions (that is, the frequency and intensity of off-site and on-site AML/CFT supervision).

The Joint Committee of the European Supervisory Authorities—a forum with the objective of strengthening cooperation between the European Banking Authority, the European Insurance and Occupational Pensions Authority, and the European Securities and Markets Authority—characterizes risk-based supervision as an ongoing, cyclical process that includes four steps (Joint Committee of the European Supervisory Authorities 2016, 3):

1. The identification of ML/TF risk factors, whereby competent authorities obtain information on both domestic and foreign ML/TF threats affecting the relevant markets;

2. The assessment of risk, whereby competent authorities use this information to obtain a holistic view of the ML/TF risk associated with each credit or financial institution ("firm") or group of firms, including the inherent risk to which the firm or group of firms is exposed and the risk-mitigating measures that a firm or group of firm has in place;

3. The allocation of AML/CFT supervisory resources based on this risk assessment, which includes decisions about the focus, depth, duration, and frequency of on-site and off-site activities and supervisory staffing needs, including technical expertise; and

4. The monitoring and review of the risk assessment and associated allocation of supervisory resources to ensure that they remain up to date and relevant.

Adopting a risk-based approach to AML/CFT supervision allows the supervisory authority to allocate its resources based on the risks assessed in the jurisdiction, in a sector, or in an institution. As a result, the supervisory authority can use its resources effectively and efficiently. To do so, the supervisor should have a clear understanding of the following (FATF 2021b, 75–76):

● The ML/TF risks and the policies, internal controls, and procedures associated with the institution or group, as identified by the supervisor's assessment of the institution or group's risk profile;

FIGURE 3.3 A General Framework for Risk-Based AML/CFT Supervision

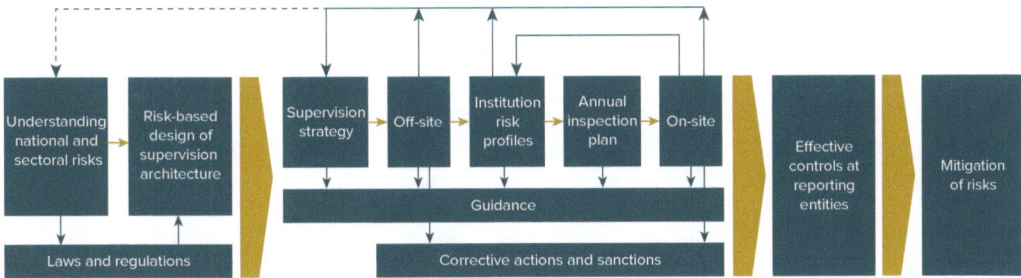

Source: World Bank risk-based approach toolkit.
Note: AML = anti-money-laundering. CFT = combating the financing of terrorism.

- The ML/TF risks present in the jurisdiction; and

- The characteristics of the financial institutions or groups, in particular, the diversity and number of financial institutions and the degree of discretion allowed under the risk-based approach.

The risk assessment of a sector or financial institution is not static. It will change depending on how risks evolve, at the national level and at the level of the sector or institution. The assessment of the ML/TF risk profile of a financial institution or group, including the risks of noncompliance, should therefore be reviewed both periodically and "when there are major events or developments in the management and operations of the financial institution or group" (FATF 2021b, Criterion 26.6, 76).

The supervisory activities will generally consist of off-site and on-site activities (figure 3.3). As a basic principle, off-site supervision should tackle everything that can be reviewed remotely, and on-site activities should focus on sample testing, interviews, and aspects that cannot be assessed remotely, such as the actual implementation of AML/CFT requirements.

Principles for a Risk-Based Approach to Supervision

Supervisors should formulate a risk-based regime for supervising compliance with AML/CFT requirements, including its effective implementation by financial institutions. A key objective of such a regime is to apply a proportional approach to AML/CFT supervision that establishes the intensity, frequency, and scope of oversight.

The supervisory regime should be comprehensive, transparent, and proportional to the ML/TF risks identified. In developing and implementing a risk-based AML/CFT supervisory regime, supervisors should adhere to some basic principles. The following are examples of some of these principles, but each supervisory body should adopt them in accordance with its jurisdiction's regulatory framework and practices, context, and experience:

- Supervisory authorities have appropriate discretion to apply the supervisory policies and procedures in a risk-sensitive manner and provide institutions with appropriate discretion to apply a risk-based approach. Rules-based stringencies and a zero-tolerance stance can easily undermine the risk-based approach.

- The supervisor employs a well-defined methodology to identify and assess ML/TF risks as well as the AML/CFT compliance measures of the supervised institutions and sector. Based on the

ML/TF risk profile of financial institutions and the understanding of risks in the sector, the supervisor develops its supervisory strategies and plans.

- The nature, intensity, and frequency of AML/CFT supervision is proportional to the ML/TF risk profile of the jurisdiction, sectors, and individual institutions. This approach allows the supervisor to formulate its operational plans, including for off-site and on-site supervision. It also allows for effective and efficient planning and deployment of available resources, including planning and budgeting for the annual calendar of supervisory activities.

- The supervisor uses a methodology, based on quantitative and qualitative information, to inform its AML/CFT supervision. The methodology includes prudential and AML/CFT data collection and analytical tools to form a comprehensive view of the risk of institutions and sectors. The supervisor uses the results of the national risk assessments to develop and update its ML/TF risk assessments.

- The supervisor informs and consults with the sectors and other relevant authorities in a clear and transparent manner on the application of its risk-based supervisory regime.

- The supervisor collaborates with foreign counterpart supervisors to ensure consolidated risk-based supervision of international groups, including through supervisory memoranda of understanding and colleges.

- Financial supervisors have adequate financial, human, and technical resources. They also have sufficient operational independence and autonomy to ensure freedom from undue influence or interference. The supervisory authorities ensure that staff maintain high professional standards, including standards concerning confidentiality, and are themselves of high integrity and appropriately skilled.

- The supervisor periodically reviews and updates the supervisory framework, taking into account changes in risks, but also changes in legislation and in the international AML/CFT standards, guidelines, and best practices.

Risk-Based Approach at the Bank Level

The FATF standards and BCPs for taking a risk-based approach to implementing national AML/CFT measures include obligations on *all* AML/CFT stakeholders—not just government agencies, the FIU, law enforcement, and supervisors, but also private sector entities, such as financial institutions and designated nonfinancial businesses and professions.[6]

From the perspective of individual financial institutions, the key requirement is to identify and assess the ML/TF threats inherent in their business activities, the ML/TF vulnerabilities in their processes, and the level of their AML/CFT controls. Financial institutions should assess the inherent risks of their (a) customer base, (b) products and services, (c) transactions, (d) geographic areas in which they operate or where their customers are located, and (e) delivery or distribution channels for their products, services, and transactions. These risk factors are not exhaustive, and financial institutions can assess additional risk factors depending on, among others, the risk and context of the jurisdiction and sector or the particular business models of individual institutions. In conducting a risk assessment, financial institutions should be free to determine how they do this, as long as the approach is coherent, consistent, and transparent to the supervisor.

The second key requirement of a risk-based approach is for financial institutions to mitigate the risks that have been identified and assessed. Financial institutions therefore need to have AML/CFT policies, procedures, and controls to mitigate those risks and comply with their legal and regulatory obligations. Such measures should be proportional to and consistent with the level of risks assessed, applying enhanced measures where risks are higher and simpler measures where risks are lower. Enhanced measures mean that the scope, intensity, and frequency of controls should be proportionately stronger to mitigate higher risks.

Unless circumstances call for specific prescriptions, supervisors should not prescribe the specific measures to be applied by institutions in their management of risks, except for cases where enhanced and simplified measures are already prescribed by law or regulation. Financial institutions should have flexibility in deciding the most effective way to assess and manage their risks, but decisions should be documented, and financial institutions should be able to demonstrate to a supervisor how they came to those risk management judgments. In deciding on the degree of discretion to grant a financial institution, the supervisor should take into account several factors, including the maturity and sophistication of the sector and institution as well as the institution's track record for AML/CFT compliance, but also for managing other risks. It is also important to take into account the supervisors' experience in conducting risk-based AML/CFT supervision. In jurisdictions where the financial sector and AML/CFT supervisory regime are not well developed, the capacity of financial institutions to assess and mitigate their ML/TF risks may not be fully developed. In such cases, the discretion and flexibility allowed under a risk-based approach should be limited and phased in until such time as the institution's or sector's understanding of risks and experience in mitigating risks improve.

While financial institutions have discretion to implement their own AML/CFT frameworks, supervisors should provide guidance on risk factors and the model or methodology that financial institutions could use to assess their inherent and residual ML/TF risks. Such guidance is intended to provide some consistency and allow comparisons across institutions. Notwithstanding the model used, the adequacy of the risk assessment will be influenced largely by the availability, accuracy, and up-to-date nature of information required for the conduct of risk assessments.[7]

The supervisor will review the effectiveness of the AML/CFT risk assessment relative to, among others, the degree and nature of inherent risks. The degree of complexity of a financial institution's risk assessment model should be commensurate with the nature, complexity, and size of its business. For less complex financial institutions, a simpler risk assessment will suffice, but a large complex institution will require a more elaborate risk assessment. The customer base, international presence, business products, and other factors contribute to the degree of complexity required. Appendix A discusses banks' business-wide risk assessment and risk mitigation processes in more detail.

AML/CFT SUPERVISORY CYCLE

Supervisors should apply an integrated, comprehensive approach to AML/CFT supervision. The risk assessments and risk profiles of financial institutions constitute an important component of the AML/CFT supervisory approach. Nevertheless, the risk-based supervisory regime needs to be harmonized with other supervisory activities, such as licensing, prudential supervision, and enforcement. In addition, collaboration and coordination with other supervisors and the FIU are also necessary in some cases. Figure 3.4 illustrates a basic AML/CFT supervisory cycle.

FIGURE 3.4 The AML/CFT Supervisory Cycle

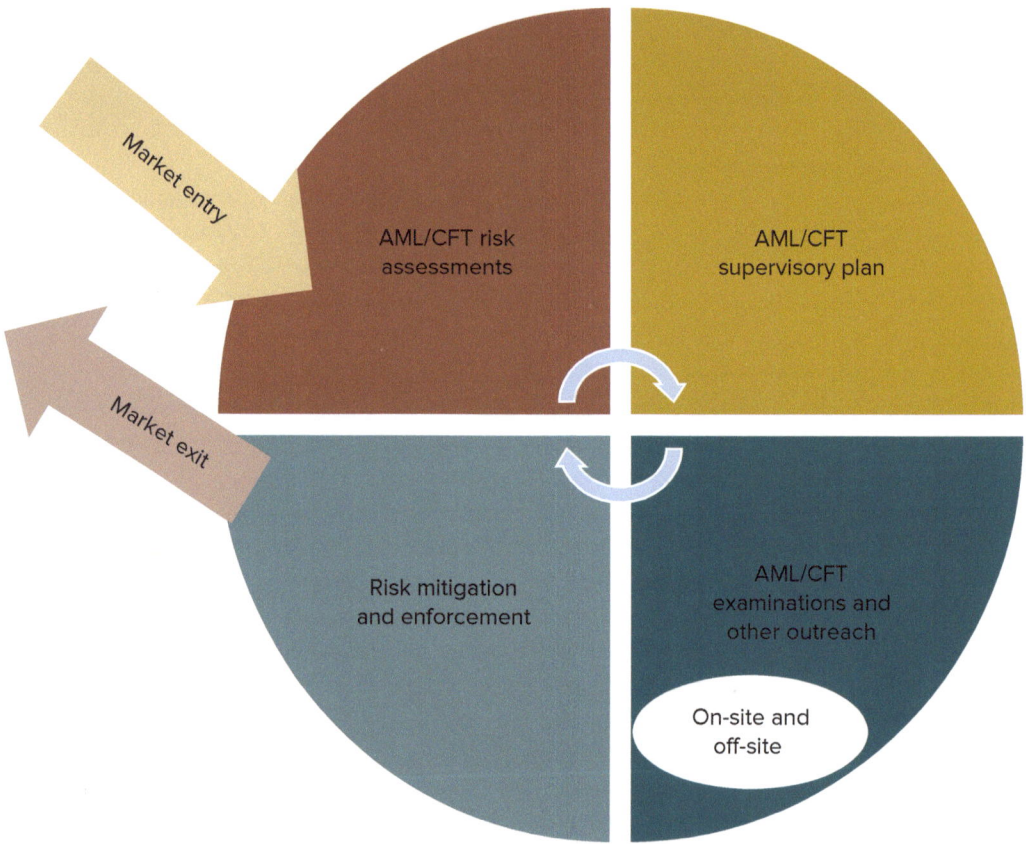

Source: World Bank.
Note AML = anti-money-laundering. CFT = combating the financing of terrorism.

Market entry and exit are critical controls for managing ML/TF risks in a sector. As part of the market entry process, fit and proper tests help to prevent criminals and their associates from participating in the financial sector.

For supervisors to implement an effective risk-based approach to supervision, they should take into account the ML/TF risks to which the jurisdictions, sectors, and institutions are exposed. As described in chapter 1, an important part of a risk-based approach to supervision lies in the development of risk profiles. This profiling is generally done by collecting data on inherent risks related to customers, products, services, transactions, geography, and delivery channels as well as information on the level of AML/CFT compliance of an institution.

Based on the risk profiles of institutions and the overall understanding of risks in a sector, the supervisor can plan its activities, including the planning, prioritization, and resourcing of on-site examinations and other outreach, such as compliance meetings and seminars. As part of the ongoing mitigation process, both on-site and off-site supervision are core elements of the supervisor's toolkit.

One of the key objectives of AML/CFT supervision is to identify noncompliance with the applicable laws and regulations and, where necessary, to apply proportionate and dissuasive enforcement measures and sanctions. Where financial institutions have been grossly negligent and in breach of their AML/CFT obligations or engaged in criminal ML/TF activities, supervisors can revoke their license.

Implementation of the AML/CFT supervision plan, in general, requires collaboration and consultation with other agencies, including other supervisors, law enforcement, and the FIU, domestically and, where possible, abroad, as the case requires.

Overview of the Risk-Based Off-Site AML/CFT Supervision Function

Under a risk-based approach to AML/CFT supervision, emphasis is placed on off-site supervision as a means of maximizing efficiencies and effectiveness in the use of supervisory resources, particularly for on-site examinations. A key focus of off-site AML/CFT supervision is understanding ML/TF risks at the institutional and sectoral levels. This understanding requires a supervision methodology and a process for identifying and assessing ML/TF risks and the adequacy of AML/CFT measures for each institution. This understanding is needed to establish the ML/TF risk profiles of each institution. The ML/TF risk profiles allow supervisors to plan, prioritize, and resource their supervisory activities in a more efficient and effective manner, including budgeting for the annual calendar of on-site inspections and other supervisory outreach, staffing levels, and training.

Where a financial institution is part of a financial group, the supervisor should consolidate and coordinate the institutional ML/TF risk profiles with those of other members of the group to ascertain a consolidated risk profile of the group. This effort requires collaboration and coordination with supervisory agencies that supervise different parts of the group.

The processes for off-site supervisory approaches are elaborated further in chapter 4.

Overview of the Risk-Based On-Site AML/CFT Examinations Function

The on-site inspection function should be closely aligned with the results of the off-site supervision function. The supervisor's approach to on-site inspections is based, to a large extent, on the risk profiles of financial institutions, with higher-risk entities requiring enhanced supervisory actions. Consequently, the type, objectives, frequency, scope, and duration of on-site inspections are determined mainly by the risk profile of the institution.

At the end of an examination, the risk profile of the institution should be updated, especially with respect to the adequacy of the internal risk mitigation systems in place. In addition, the draft and final reports should be shared with the prudential or other supervisors (provided that information-sharing arrangements are in place) to inform, coordinate, and agree on recommendations and follow-up actions, including with respect to enforcement and sanctions.

The processes for on-site examinations are elaborated further in chapter 5.

Supervision of Financial Institutions That Are Members of Financial Groups

Where a financial institution is a member of a financial group whose members are supervised by a single supervisor, the risk assessments, off-site supervision, and on-site inspections can all be coordinated internally among the relevant departments. Where a financial institution is a member of a financial group whose members are supervised by more than one supervisor, the supervisors should coordinate their activities. Procedures need to be established for the planning of inspections, including parallel or joint inspections, and for the sharing of supervisory information and examination results. A key objective of such coordination is to develop a harmonized framework for risk-based supervision as well as a methodology for consolidating and sharing risk assessments and profiles. It is also meant to avoid gaps in oversight that leave important entities within a financial group unchecked.

Where a financial institution is a branch, subsidiary, or affiliate of a foreign financial institution or group or is the parent company of branches, subsidiaries, or affiliates in other jurisdictions, the home and host supervisors should collaborate closely and coordinate their activities, including the exchange of AML/CFT–related information, to enable cross-border supervision of such groups. Cross-border supervision should be a condition of licenses and authorizations for such financial groups.

Example of a Risk-Based AML/CFT Supervisory Framework

Box 3.1 summarizes the risk-based AML/CFT supervisory framework of Bermuda, as assessed in September 2018 and reported by the Caribbean Financial Action Task Force in January 2020 (CFATF 2020).

BOX 3.1 Bermuda's BMA: Risk-Based Supervision of Compliance with AML/CFT Requirements

The Bermuda Monetary Authority (BMA) has implemented a risk-based framework for supervising anti-money-laundering and combating the financing of terrorism (AML/CFT) to assess compliance by banks and other entities subject to its supervision and to mitigate sectoral risks. This framework assesses the impact and probability of risks with respect to all aspects of the institution's operations and controls on an ongoing basis in order to facilitate a timely supervisory response to identified weaknesses. Sectors assessed as high risk (including banks) are prioritized for on-site examinations and off-site monitoring. These supervisory activities are conducted by the prudential and AML/CFT supervisory departments. On-site examinations are scheduled at the beginning of the year, but the calendar of inspections can be revised and is usually amended as the year progresses, largely, if not exclusively, based on changes in the risk profiles of institutions, including the results of updated risk assessments.

The BMA's risk-based framework for AML/CFT supervision is therefore underpinned by the risk profiles of each sector and their component institutions, which are significantly informed by recent national risk assessments. To understand the money-laundering/terrorism financing (ML/TF) risks facing sectors under its supervision, the BMA conducts an annual risk assessment at both the sector and entity levels, using data calls and questionnaires. The development of the BMA's supervision strategies, prioritization, and resourcing has been influenced by the outcomes of national

(box continues on next page)

BOX 3.1 *(continued)*

risk assessments and includes establishing the intensity and frequency of supervisory activities (on-site examinations), staffing, outsourcing, training, and related budgeting requirements. The BMA's annual supervisory inspection plan is subject to regular review; the plan takes into account any new information on ML/TF risks affecting the sectors or individual entities. The BMA's risk assessments are structured in three stages: understanding the inherent risk within a sector, assessing the effectiveness of the ML/TF controls in place, and estimating the level of residual risk in the sector. This risk assessment is used to inform the risk-based approach to AML/CFT supervision across all stages of the AML/CFT supervisory life cycle.

The BMA's off-site supervision also entails a review of the institution's AML/CFT policies and procedures. In addition, the prudential and AML/CFT units of the BMA hold regular outreach meetings with industry groups, external auditors, and other stakeholders to discuss supervisory issues, including ML/TF risk issues. As part of its supervisory function, the BMA reviews the working papers of external auditors to verify the scope of a financial institution's internal controls, corporate governance, and legal compliance framework. The independent audits are also a source of information on the effectiveness of the financial institution's AML/CFT program and compliance with the AML/CFT legislation.

The assessment of sectoral and institutional ML/TF risk profiles informs the supervisory strategy, objectives, scope, depth, and frequency of examinations, which include a mix of documentary reviews and interviews with key staff of financial institutions during inspections. The BMA uses on-site inspections to verify the adequacy of a financial institution's AML/CFT risk management and mitigation systems (policies, procedures, risk management, and internal controls) and to determine if they are commensurate with the institution's ML/TF risks, size, complexity, business model, and so forth. On-site inspections also verify compliance with national AML/CFT legal requirements, but do so taking a risk-based approach.

On completion of an on-site examination, a draft report containing the main findings and recommendations, including remedial actions and, where applicable, sanctions, is presented to the examined entity. The combined supervisory activity of the AML/CFT unit's on-site and off-site teams and the prudential unit teams complement each other and combine to ensure a highly effective, highly developed AML/CFT supervisory regime.

Source: CFATF 2020.

OUTLINE OF AN AML/CFT SUPERVISION MANUAL

Implementation of the supervisor's AML/CFT supervision regime should demonstrate that its supervisory approach is commensurate to these risks. An AML/CFT supervision manual that includes specific procedures for off-site and on-site supervision is useful. Box 3.2 provides a guide for structuring an AML/CFT supervision manual.

BOX 3.2 An Outline for Structuring an AML/CFT Supervision Manual

PART I: INTRODUCTION

- Scope and purpose of the manual
- International AML/CFT standards applicable to financial institutions
- The outcomes of the national risk assessment
- Legal and regulatory AML/CFT framework applicable to financial institutions and financial groups
- AML/CFT supervision strategy and action plan
- Structure of the AML/CFT supervisory department or unit and supervisory tools
- Types of AML/CFT supervision and outreach:
  - Off-site supervision
  - On-site supervision
  - Other outreach (compliance meetings, seminars, publications, and guidance).

PART II: OFF-SITE AML/CFT SUPERVISION METHODOLOGY AND PROCESSES

- Objectives of off-site supervision
- Methodology for collecting, analyzing, and assessing information on institutional and sectoral risks
- Risk-profiling and -planning processes
- Group and cross-border supervisory issues.

PART III: ON-SITE AML/CFT EXAMINATION PROCEDURES AND PROCESSES

- Objectives of on-site examinations
- Types and objectives of on-site examinations: full scope, targeted, thematic, and ad hoc
- Inspection planning:
  - Frequency, scope, intensity, and resourcing (based on risk profile, size, and complexity of the institution and compliance issues)
  - Information and meetings requirements
  - Administrative procedures (for example, team selection, letter to management, and other required processes)
- Core examination procedures:
  - Documentary review;
  - Staff interviews
  - Evaluation of internal controls and compliance procedures
  - Testing of customer files, transactions, and monitoring and screening systems.

PART IV: STRUCTURE AND CONTENT OF THE EXAMINATION REPORT

- Legal basis
- Business and ML/TF risk profile summary
- Objectives, scope, and types of the examination
- Inspection procedures applied
- Executive summary

(box continues on next page)

BOX 3.2 *(continued)*

- Examination findings
- Results of sample tests
- Recommendations, possible corrective measures, expected timelines.

PART V: FOLLOW-UP

- Recommendations for enforcement and sanctions
- Risk profile update: inherent risk, mitigation, and compliance
- Process and timelines for follow-up.

PART VI: STATISTICS

- Ongoing collection of statistics on supervisory activities (for example, number of risk assessments conducted or updated; number of off-site and on-site reviews; number of recommendations or enforcement actions and results of follow-ups; and other useful statistics to serve as metrics of the effectiveness of supervisory interventions)
- Analysis of statistics on supervisory activities and a feedback mechanism for findings to inform the supervisory process.

Source: World Bank.
Note: AML = anti-money-laundering. CFT = combating the financing of terrorism.

COOPERATION BETWEEN PRUDENTIAL AND AML/CFT SUPERVISION

From the perspective of operational risk, AML/CFT is considered within the overall risk profile of a financial institution. Consequently, prudential and AML/CFT supervisors should coordinate their supervision efforts, especially when AML/CFT oversight is separated from the rest of prudential supervision.[8] From the perspective of international standards, the Basel Core Principles include both prudential and AML/CFT elements, while the FATF standards also incorporate elements of these core principles.

Several supervisory issues overlap between prudential and AML/CFT supervision, specifically in the areas of corporate governance, internal audit, and compliance. In particular, special attention should be paid to coordinating the supervision of compliance with due diligence obligations on beneficial ownership and politically exposed persons, including in the context of licensing and fit and proper assessment of shareholders and senior management of banks. Consequently, the risk assessments, supervision planning, and conduct of inspections should be coordinated with the prudential supervision departments to enable a holistic approach to supervision, but also to avoid duplication or gaps.

Especially in jurisdictions where the prudential supervisor is not the same as the AML/CFT supervisor,[9] additional efforts are needed to coordinate and collaborate on AML/CFT supervision. The following issues need to be addressed when the prudential and AML/CFT supervisors are not the same:

- Do the AML/CFT supervisor and the prudential supervisor have the same or similar powers, including having access to all information required and the power to impose enforcement measures?

- Do the AML/CFT supervisor and the prudential supervisor have the same or similar legal protections?

- Do the AML/CFT supervisor and the prudential supervisor understand the overall context of their respective tasks?

- What is the standing of the supervisors within a sector?

- Do the supervisors have the mechanisms for cross-border cooperation with foreign supervisors, and do these exchange mechanisms cover a wide range of information, including data on beneficial ownership and politically exposed persons?

- Are there any restrictions for exchanging information between domestic prudential and AML/CFT supervisors, especially in relation to beneficial ownership and politically exposed persons?

- How are duplication of effort and the potential for conflicting supervisory actions minimized between the prudential and AML/CFT supervisors?

To address these issues, the Basel Committee on Banking Supervision (BCBS) updated its guidelines on cooperation between prudential and AML/CFT supervisors in 2020 (BCBS 2020). Annex 5 to the "Guidelines: Sound Management of Risks Related to Money Laundering and Financing of Terrorism" provides further guidelines to strengthen the interaction and cooperation between prudential and AML/CFT supervisors. In particular, the guidelines provide for prudential and AML/CFT cooperation and information sharing in the following areas (BCBS 2020, annex 5, 46, par. 8):

1. Authorization-related procedures of a bank, including license applications, assessments of qualifying holdings, and fit and proper tests both at the time of authorization and on a continuing basis thereafter;

2. Ongoing supervision, including assessment of governance, risk management, and internal control systems of a bank, business model and profitability drivers, operational risks, and compliance with AML requirements; and

3. Enforcement actions or revocation of a banking license.

The euro area provides an example of the need for cooperation between prudential and AML/CFT supervisors. An analysis from the European Parliament highlights the need for cooperation between prudential and AML/CFT supervisors in the euro area, where AML/CFT supervision mainly involves national competent authorities, and the European Central Bank is the prudential supervisor for significant institutions (European Parliament 2019). The analysis identifies areas for improving the integration of AML/CFT components into prudential supervision:

- AML/CFT supervisors should contribute their expertise to the authorization assessments of banks;

- Assessment criteria should be clearer when assessing whether the acquisition of a qualifying holding could increase the risk of ML/TF; and

- Prudential supervision should state specifically that institutions and their prudential supervisors need to assess the risk of financial crime.

The European Supervisory Authorities have also issued joint guidelines on cooperation and information exchange between competent authorities supervising credit and financial institutions, known as the AML/CFT colleges' guidelines (Joint Committee of the European Supervisory Authorities 2019). The AML/CFT colleges provide a permanent structure for cooperation and information exchange between supervisors from different European Union member states and third jurisdictions that are responsible for the AML/CFT supervision of the same institution. The guidelines set out the rules governing the establishment and operation of these colleges and structuring the exchange of information between AML/CFT and prudential supervisors, who are invited to participate in AML/CFT colleges as observers. The European Supervisory Authorities have since observed improved cooperation between authorities through these AML/CFT colleges (EBA 2020).

NOTES

1. The FATF publishes regularly on its website an overview of the consolidated ratings on both effectiveness and technical compliance for all jurisdictions assessed based on the 2012 FATF recommendations, which were updated in 2022, and the 2013 assessment methodology, which was updated in 2021 (FATF 2021a, 2022).
2. This number includes jurisdictions that are members of both the FATF and an FATF-style regional body.
3. Each core issue recommendation is assessed under different criteria according to *Methodology for Assessing Compliance with the FATF Recommendations and the Effectiveness of AML/CFT Systems* (FATF 2021a, 103).
4. BCP 8, 29.
5. BCP 8, 29–30.
6. Indeed, with respect to financial institutions—notably banks—the key AML/CFT requirements are contained in Recommendation 1 (risk assessment), IO 4 for effectiveness (understanding and mitigating risks), and in more specific risk-based obligations, such as Recommendation 10 on customer due diligence and Recommendation 18 on AML/CFT policies, procedures, and controls, including group-wide programs. The BCPs and the "Guidelines: Sound Management of Risk Related to Money Laundering and Financing of Terrorism" (BCBS 2020) include similar requirements for banks, which are required to have sound risk management programs in place to address all kinds of risks, including ML and TF risks. The supervisor needs to have a thorough understanding of those obligations to enable it to conduct effective supervision.
7. For examples of guidance on business-wide risk assessments, see DNB (n.d.); IFC (2019); and Wolfsberg Group (2015).
8. In certain countries, AML/CFT oversight is assigned to a dedicated department or unit within the overall supervisory body.
9. The FIU, for example.

REFERENCES

BCBS (Basel Committee on Banking Supervision). 2020. "Sound Management of Risks Related to Money Laundering and Terrorism Financing; January 2014, Revised July 2020." BCBS, Basel. https://www.bis.org/bcbs/publ/d505.pdf.

CFATF (Caribbean Financial Action Task Force). 2020. "Fourth Round Mutual Evaluation Report of Bermuda." CFATF, Port of Spain. https://www.cfatf-gafic.org/home /cfatf-news/616-fourth-round-mutual-evaluation-report-of-bermuda-2.

DNB (De Nederlandsche Bank, Dutch Central Bank). n.d. "Integrity Risk Analysis: More Where Necessary, Less Where Possible." DNB, Amsterdam. https://www.toezicht.dnb.nl/en /binaries/51-234068.PDF.

EBA (European Banking Authority). 2020. "EBA Observes Improved Cooperation between Authorities through Newly Established AML/CFT Colleges." EBA, Paris. December 15. https://eba.europa.eu/eba-observes-improved-cooperation-between-authorities-through-newly -established-amlcft-colleges.

European Parliament. 2019. "Anti-Money-Laundering: Reinforcing the Supervisory and Regulatory Framework." European Parliament, Brussels. https://www.europarl.europa.eu/RegData/etudes /IDAN/2018/614496/IPOL_IDA(2018)614496_EN.pdf.

FATF (Financial Action Task Force). 2021a. *Methodology for Assessing Compliance with the FATF Recommendations and the Effectiveness of AML/CFT Systems; Adopted in February 2013, Amended October 2021*. Paris: FATF. https://www.fatf-gafi.org/publications/mutualevaluations /documents/fatf-methodology.html.

FATF (Financial Action Task Force). 2021b. "Guidance on Risk-Based Supervision." FATF, Paris, March. https://www.fatf-gafi.org/media/fatf/documents/Guidance-Risk-Based-Supervision.pdf.

FATF (Financial Action Task Force). 2022. "The FATF Recommendations: International Standards on Combating Money Laundering and the Financing of Terrorism and Proliferation; Adopted in February 2012, Revised March 2022." FATF, Paris. https://www.fatf-gafi.org/media/fatf /documents/recommendations/pdfs/fatf%20recommendations%202012.pdf.

IFC (International Finance Corporation). 2019. "Anti-Money-Laundering (AML) & Countering Financing of Terrorism (CFT) Risk Management in Emerging Market Banks." Good Practice Note 2019. IFC, Washington, DC. https://www.ifc.org/wps/wcm/connect/e7e10e94-3cd8-4f4c-b6f8 -1e14ea9eff80/45464_IFC_AML_Report.pdf?MOD=AJPERES&CVID=mKKNshy.

Joint Committee of the European Supervisory Authorities. 2016. "Joint Guidelines on the Characteristics of a Risk-Based Approach to Anti-Money Laundering and Terrorist Financing Supervision, and the Steps to Be Taken When Conducting Supervision on a Risk-Sensitive Basis—The Risk-Based Supervision Guidelines." European Supervisory Authorities, Paris, November 16.

Wolfsberg Group. 2015. "Frequently Asked Questions on Risk Assessments for Money Laundering, Sanctions, and Bribery & Corruption." Wolfsberg Group, Ermatingen, Switzerland. https://www .wolfsberg-principles.com/sites/default/files/wb/pdfs/faqs/17.%20Wolfsberg-Risk-Assessment -FAQs-2015.pdf.

CHAPTER 4

Off-Site AML/CFT Supervision

OVERVIEW

In the past, supervision of anti-money-laundering and combating the financing of terrorism (AML/CFT) was conducted mainly through on-site examinations; it generally focused on legal and regulatory compliance and paid only basic attention to money-laundering/terrorism financing (ML/TF) risks. Off-site AML/CFT supervision was conducted in only a limited way. A key challenge for supervisors was the lack of systems and methodologies for transitioning from a rules-based approach to a risk-based approach to AML/CFT supervision.

A methodology and a process are needed for identifying and assessing ML/TF risks and for determining the adequacy of risk mitigation measures in order to understand the ML/TF risk profiles of banks. Off-site and on-site processes need to be set up and balanced, taking into account practical considerations, such as human, financial, and technological resources.

This chapter considers options for the AML/CFT off-site function. It provides examples of inherent and residual risk assessments and how to use off-site risk assessments for planning supervisory activities, such as on-site examinations and other types of supervisory outreach.

KEY OBJECTIVES OF A RISK-BASED APPROACH TO OFF-SITE AML/CFT SUPERVISION

As shown in the general framework for risk-based AML/CFT supervision illustrated in figure 3.3 in chapter 3, the off-site function is an integral part of the risk-based approach to AML/CFT supervision. It is an essential part of the process of identifying, assessing, and understanding ML/TF risk profiles and mitigating measures of financial institutions.

As indicated in the Financial Action Task Force (FATF) "Guidance on Risk-Based Supervision" (FATF 2021, sec. 66), off-site monitoring helps to keep supervisors up to date on the ML/TF risk landscape, inherent risk profiles of regulated entities, and potential weaknesses in these entities' control measures. The insights gained from performing off-site monitoring can thus guide the approach and the focus of supervisors' on-site reviews. For example, the results of preliminary evaluations can be used to tailor the nature, frequency, intensity, and focus of supervision as well as to guide the supervisory authority on how to pivot attention to higher-risk areas. Effective off-site monitoring entails collecting and analyzing data and information to enable ongoing monitoring of an entire sector; it is not intended to produce a snapshot of one or several entities.[1]

Core Responsibilities of Off-Site Supervision

A risk-based approach to AML/CFT supervision emphasizes use of the off-site function to determine the ML/TF profiles of financial institutions and develop the supervisory strategy and annual plan. Articulating the main objectives of the off-site function is useful for guiding the operational objectives and activities of this function. These objectives should be aligned with the supervisor's overall AML/CFT supervisory regime. Consequently, the following actions constitute core responsibilities of off-site supervision:

- Collect information from financial institutions on inherent risks related to the type and number of customers, products, services, transactions, geography, and delivery channels;

- Obtain information on the business-wide risk assessments of financial institutions and the AML/CFT compliance systems, audit and compliance reports, and open-source information, among others;

- Assess the ML/TF risks of financial institutions and develop their institutional risk profiles;

- Develop supervisory strategies and plans, including the annual calendar of inspections for individual financial institutions or groups;

- Monitor the ML/TF risks on an ongoing basis to identify new trends and red-flag indicators;

- Update the institutional risk profiles and trigger ad hoc inspections, as necessary;

- Hold meetings with the management and staff of institutions to support off-site supervision or in combination with on-site supervision;

- Develop sectoral risk assessments; and

- Liaise with other supervisors on other supervisory issues and with the financial intelligence unit (FIU) on the quality of suspicious transactions reports (STRs) and other ML/TF–related matters.

Other responsibilities of the off-site function include conducting periodic meetings with sector representatives to discuss ML/TF risks, general compliance issues, and other challenges facing the sector.

Resources and Information Requirements for Off-Site Supervision

To conduct effective off-site supervision, the supervisor needs to have adequate resources to carry out its responsibilities, including human, financial, and technological resources. In particular, supervisors need to have sufficient resources to conduct AML/CFT off-site supervision on a continuous basis. The amount and type of resources will depend on the following factors:

- Size, growth, and complexity of the financial sector;

- Level and trends of ML/TF risks;

- Experience and capacity of the supervisory authority;

- Availability of technological support for off-site processes, including suptech solutions (see chapter 8); and

- Economic and financial conditions in the jurisdiction.

Effective off-site supervision depends on the supervisor having timely access to all the information it needs to inform its activities and on the quality of information available. The supervisor should receive, on a periodic basis, information from financial institutions on their inherent ML/TF risks and AML/CFT compliance as well as ad hoc information when required. Over time, the supervisor can build statistical databases for analytical and monitoring purposes with respect to the level of ML/TF risk and adequacy of AML/CFT compliance. This effort will require developing internal data governance and information management systems to enable supervisors to analyze and use the available information efficiently. As described in chapter 8, supervisors can use suptech solutions to process these statistical databases and to improve their ability to identify the patterns and characteristics of potential ML/TF risks and vulnerabilities in the financial sector.

In addition, supervisors should collaborate with the FIU, which can provide useful information on ML/TF risks and emerging threats in the jurisdiction.

RISK PROFILING: A KEY PREREQUISITE FOR RISK-BASED SUPERVISION

Off-site supervision includes the identification and analysis of institutional and sectoral ML/TF risks. The results of this risk analysis are used to inform the type and intensity of other supervisory activities as well as the planning and resourcing of on-site inspections. This analysis requires supervisors to collect as much relevant information as possible about institutions' inherent ML/TF risks and the adequacy of their AML/CFT policies, procedures, and controls, including information on the business-wide risk assessment of financial institutions, the AML/CFT compliance systems, and audit and compliance reports (see appendix A for more detail on the business-wide risk assessment of financial institutions).

In the case of financial groups, group-wide information is required for a consolidated risk profile of the institution.

Information Requirements for Developing Risk Profiles

One of the biggest challenges for off-site supervision is to determine the extent of the information required to conduct risk profiling. The type and amount of information required will depend on various factors, including the availability of useful, up-to-date information within the supervisory body, availability of information within supervised entities,[2] stage of development of AML/CFT controls in the financial institutions, and resources of the supervisors.

The following subsections provide examples of the type of information required to conduct risk profiling for a financial institution.

General Institutional and Contextual Information

General information on the institution provides the broad contextual framework for the risk profile of the institution. It may also form the basis for establishing peer groups or clusters of institutions.[3]

- Corporate structure, including ownership and management structure, group structure, shareholding structure and beneficial owners, branch and subsidiary network, and years in operation;

- Financial information, including size, total deposits and assets, and business lines;

- Prudential and other supervisory information, including business model, governance, risk appetite, prior examination reports, compliance and enforcement history, external auditors' reports, and general reputation;

- Input from other competent authorities, including information from police, prosecutors, and intelligence agencies; tax, customs, and anticorruption authorities; and agencies dealing with targeted financial sanctions, for example;

- Results of national risk assessments as they relate to the financial sector and its customers, products, and services;

- Results of independent testing and audits that are provided to supervisory agencies;

- Information on risks obtained from public-private partnerships or other consultation mechanisms;

- Open-source information (media, adverse reporting) with respect to allegations or factual cases related to ML/TF or financial crime;[4] apart from news outlets, Transparency International and the Organized Crime and Corruption Reporting Project produce third-party reports;

- Findings from matters reported by whistleblowers and complaints; and

- Input from international counterparts, groups, and organizations (for example, reports of the FATF and FATF-style regional bodies and risk factor guidelines of the European Supervisory Authorities).

Inherent ML/TF Risks

Inherent risks are ML/TF risks intrinsic to a sector's or an entity's business activities before any AML/CFT controls are applied. Data are collected on inherent risks related to the type and number of customers, products, services, transactions, geography, and delivery channels. For these risk factors, information should be collected on the number and volume of the underlying topic. The following are some examples:

- Customers, including the number of clients that are natural persons, legal persons and arrangements, residents, nonresidents, politically exposed persons (domestic and foreign), nonprofit organizations, correspondent relations, and high-net-worth individuals;

- Products, services, and transactions, including the number and volume of cash deposits, wealth management and private banking services, trustee services, international funds transfers, currency exchanges, money remittances, trade finance, and virtual assets;

- Geography, including the number of customers (per type) who reside in or are active in high-risk jurisdictions, number and volume of fund transfers, and number and volume of remittances to or from high-risk jurisdictions;

- Delivery channels, including the number of business relationships that were established (in a period) through agents or intermediaries, and the number of business relationships established in a given period without reliable, independent digital identification systems; and

- Any other inherent risk factors the supervisors may consider appropriate given the context of the jurisdiction and sector.

    Annex 4A provides an example of a questionnaire that can be used to collect data on inherent ML/TF risk.

Risk Mitigation

Supervisors should obtain and assess information on a jurisdiction's AML/CFT policies, procedures, and controls. Based on the information obtained, the adequacy of the mitigation measures should be assessed. As a general guide, the off-site function should obtain sufficient information, including the following:

- Corporate governance and role of the board (especially in setting the bank's risk appetite and strategy), board governance, and board committees for AML/CFT compliance;

- Compliance information for management, compliance monitoring reports, reports on incidents, and internal and external audit reports;

- Compliance and audit functions, including independence, operational autonomy, qualifications and resources of (group) audit and compliance, role and responsibilities of the compliance function, scope of compliance work regarding monitoring, STRs, risk assessments, and training;

- Business-wide ML/TF risk assessment, AML/CFT policies, procedures, and controls, including on customer due diligence, transaction monitoring, targeted financial sanctions screening, and record keeping;

- Monitoring, analysis, and reporting of unusual and suspicious transactions, including security of information, decision-making arrangements, quality controls, and communications with the FIU; and

- AML/CFT resources, staffing, and training.

Annex 4B provides an example of a questionnaire that can be used to obtain information on AML/CFT controls.

Proliferation Financing

For the risk profile of financial institutions, the supervisor can decide to assess the risk of proliferation financing as a subset of the overall assessment of inherent risk. Since the same set of controls is generally used for proliferation financing as for targeted financial sanctions, no separate assessment of the adequacy of control measures specifically for proliferation financing is necessary for off-site supervision purposes. Proliferation financing assessment is a new requirement, and there is little literature addressing it. In its 2018 "Guidance on Counter Proliferation Financing," the FATF provides useful insights, in particular with respect to using a risk-based approach (FATF 2018; see also box 4.1).

BOX 4.1 Extract from FATF Guidance: Supervision of Proliferation Financing

Specifically, an effective supervisory model in the proliferation financing context often involves the following measures:

1. Competent authorities should communicate the consolidated list of persons and entities through their websites immediately after publication by the United Nations Security Council/Sanctions Committee, and preferably through one single website to prevent confusion to different supervised institutions.

2. Supervisors may encourage their supervised institutions to apply a risk-based approach in the context of proliferation financing, by making reference to the Financial Action Task Force (FATF) "Guidance for a Risk-Based Approach to Effective Supervision and Enforcement by AML/CFT Supervisors of the Financial Sector and Law Enforcement."

3. Supervisors should understand the proliferation financing contextual situation or exposure to potential sanctions evasion faced by supervised institutions and sectors in their country, for example, customers, products, geographical reach, and delivery channels. While not a binding requirement under FATF standards, supervisors may note that proliferation financing risks are distributed differently from money-laundering (ML) and terrorism financing (TF) risks between and within financial institutions. Adequately supervising the implementation of counterproliferation financing measures may require

(box continues on next page)

BOX 4.1 (*continued*)

supervisors to focus on different business units and different products from those which are relevant to AML/CFT supervision.

4. Supervisors should apply targeted financial sanctions screening as part of fit and proper tests to control market entry.

5. Supervisors should consider the capacity and counterproliferation financing experience of the supervised institutions and individual sectors and their understanding of targeted financial sanctions obligations.

6. Supervisors may determine risk-based methodology and procedures of supervisory activities, including frequency, comprehensiveness, and tools employed (for example, from issuing questionnaires to carrying out follow-up on remedial measures or from conducting interviews, sample testing, to reviewing records for on-site supervision).

7. Supervisors should adopt a risk-based approach for determining the frequency of off-site and on-site supervision.

8. Supervisors should determine, in the course of supervision, the extent of board and senior management oversight of proliferation financing matters and the adequacy of escalation of proliferation-financing-related issues to board and senior management.

9. Supervisors should focus on the effectiveness of sanctions screening, on processes and procedures to detect sanctioned entities, and on assets which are owned or controlled by them. They should also review whether supervised institutions are implementing customer due diligence measures sufficiently to identify and verify the beneficial owner of a customer or party to a transaction.

10. Supervisors should focus on supervised institutions' identification and management of false positives in the implementation of controls on persons and entities subject to targeted financial sanctions.

11. As far as the nonfinancial sector is concerned, supervisors may also note the vulnerabilities associated with company formation (which is also applicable to lawyers and trust or company service providers).

12. Countries should ensure that their legal frameworks allow supervisors' appropriate access to the books and records of each supervised institution to collect the widest range of information that a supervisor or a competent authority needs.

13. Supervisors should cooperate with foreign supervisory counterparts, where relevant, such as in instances where supervised institutions operate across borders, including through arrangements to share confidential information.

Source: Extracted, with minor edits, from FATF 2018.

STRUCTURED OFF-SITE ANALYSIS OF ML/TF RISKS

To be able to analyze risks in a comprehensive, consistent manner, supervisors need to standardize or harmonize risk-profiling methodologies. A risk-profiling methodology allows the supervisor to compare the risk profiles of institutions and to make sectoral and cross-sectoral risk assessments.

There are no internationally prescribed models or methodologies for assessing the ML/TF risks of financial institutions or for assessing the adequacy of AML/CFT risk controls, not in the least because the sources of information on inherent risks and compliance measures vary from jurisdiction to jurisdiction. The methodology should be tailored to the national context; the results of national risk assessments; factors such as the size, complexity, and maturity of a sector; availability of information; and experience and capacity of the supervisors.

This section discusses the assessment of inherent ML/TF risks and the adequacy of AML/CFT compliance measures. These two components can be used to assess the residual or net risks. The first option provides a simplified approach to the assessment of residual risk. The second option involves a more detailed analysis and is based on the risk assessment framework developed by the World Bank.

In both approaches, the supervisor should obtain the information through off-site reporting systems such as questionnaires because most of the required information will not be internally available or, if available, might not be up to date.

Rating systems and scales can vary from supervisor to supervisor and even by sector. Generally, though, a more basic system may be considered at the start of this process until the availability and reliability of information improves and supervisors gain experience with its use.

Simplified Approach

The following example illustrates a basic model for analyzing the inherent ML/TF risk factors. The application of weights is optional, and the specific weights used in table 4.1 are illustrative only; they are not prescriptive. Each supervisor will determine whether weights (or other analytical methods) are to be applied and, if so, what weights are appropriate to use for each inherent risk factor.

Supervisors should also be aware that a simplified approach will not be effective for a large financial institution that has several types of customers and multiple products, as it will be difficult to assign one or a few risk ratings to a complex and diverse customer base or to a diverse range of products.

Inherent Risk

Data on inherent risk factors can be obtained from financial institutions through questionnaires requesting statistical data on the risk factors and underlying topics of interest. In a simplified approach, the number of data points to be collected can be limited to a few—for instance, data on a few types of high-risk customers and products and geographic presence.

TABLE 4.1 Example of Risk Scores for Inherent Risk Factors

Risk score	From	To
Low (1)	0.01	1.00
Medium-low (2)	1.01	2.00
Medium-high (3)	2.01	3.00
High (4)	3.01	4.00

Source: World Bank.

For each data point, a rating will be given on the likelihood that ML/TF risks with respect to that specific risk (sub)factor will occur. With respect to risk scores, ranges of one to three, one to four, or one to five are generally used. Typically, a four-level scale (low, medium-low, medium-high, high) forces the supervisor to make an informed choice on the level of risk. A three- or five-level scale can also be used, but the supervisor should be careful not to assess all data points as "medium."

When scoring the risk (sub)factors, institutions with a large number of foreign, politically exposed persons (either absolute or relative) would get four points; institutions with a high number and amount of transactions in high-risk jurisdictions would get the most points; and institutions in the top 25 percentile of institutions with nonresident customers would get four points. After assessing every data point, an average rating is computed for each of the risk factors, as follows.

Subsequently, the average of the ratings of all risk factors will be the inherent risk rating for an institution. This inherent risk rating can also be calculated by giving weights to the risk factors. Using a weighted approach allows the supervisor to take into account the fact that some risk factors can be more relevant for a sector than others. The weights assigned in table 4.2 are indicative only; they can be adjusted depending on the circumstances of sectoral and jurisdiction risk. In this example, the total weighted inherent risk rating would be 2.25 (medium-high); if a simple average is used, the rating would be 2.0 (medium-low).

The supervisor can also use a more qualitative approach to assess risk factors (table 4.3).

While in theory this part of the risk assessment can also take into account the impact of risk on an institution's operations, doing so is not recommended for the simple fact that, unlike financial risks, the impact of an inherent ML/TF risk that materializes is difficult to quantify and measure with any degree of precision.

Mitigating Measures

In order to assess the mitigating measures of a financial institution, it is necessary to obtain the information mentioned under "risk mitigation." The off-site function will be needed to evaluate all documents and information obtained. This effort will require substantial resources and time. Instead of collecting different documents and information, (part of) the information for the assessment of mitigating measures can also be obtained from financial institutions through questionnaires or self-assessments.

During the off-site process, in general, only the existence and adequacy of mitigating measures can be assessed. Assessing the operational effectiveness of the measures is difficult and can only be done during on-site inspections.

TABLE 4.2 Example of Risk Ratings for Inherent Risk Factors

Inherent risk factor	Weight (%, optional)	Ratings	Weighted rating
1. Customer risk	40	3	1.2
2. Products, services, transactions risk	20	2	0.4
3 Geographic risk	25	2	0.5
4. Delivery channel risk	15	1	0.15
Total average and weighted inherent risk rating	100	2.0	2.25

Source: World Bank.

TABLE 4.3 Example of a Qualitative Assessment of Inherent Risk

Type of risk	1. Low	2. Low-medium	3. High-medium	4. High	Assigned score
Geography	The institution has only a domestic presence and activities.	The institution has mainly a domestic presence and very limited cross-border activities.	The institution has a domestic as well as an international presence. Some activities take place in high-risk jurisdictions.	The institution has a large number of subsidiaries, branches, or activities in high-risk jurisdictions.	
Products and services	The institution offers only low-risk products and services.	The institution offers mainly low-risk products and services.	The institution offers some high-risk products and services.	The institution offers a significant number of high-risk products and services.	
Type of customers	The institution has only low-risk types of customers.	The institution has mainly low-risk types of customers.	The institution has some high-risk types of customers.	The institution has a significant number of high-risk types of customers.	
Delivery channels	The institution only offers products and services through direct client contact.	The institution offers products and services mainly through direct client contact and limited non-face-to-face channels.	The institution offers products and services through direct client contact but also substantially through non-face-to-face channels.	The institution offers a significant percentage of products and services through high-risk delivery channels.	
Average (weighted) score for risk level					
Adjusted risk level based on a combination of factors or supervisory judgment					
Narrative on risk-level score					

Source: World Bank.

TABLE 4.4 Example of Risk Scores for Mitigating Measures

Rating	From	To
Strong (1)	0.01	1.00
Satisfactory (2)	1.01	2.00
Inadequate (3)	2.01	3.00
Weak (4)	3.01	4.00

Source: World Bank.

Similar to the inherent risk factors, all elements of the mitigating measures need to be rated. A scale of four qualitative ratings (strong, satisfactory, inadequate, and weak) is expedient, inviting the supervisor to make an informed assessment of the level of adequacy and not select the middle rating, as would be possible with a three- or five- point scale (table 4.4).

TABLE 4.5 Example of Ratings for Mitigating Measures

Mitigating measure	Weight (%, optional)	Rating	Weighted rating
1. Corporate governance and role of the board	20	2	0.4
2. Compliance and management information	10	2	0.2
3. Audit and compliance functions	25	1	0.25
4. AML/CFT policies, procedures, and controls	20	2	0.4
5. Suspicious transaction reporting	15	3	0.45
6. AML/CFT resources, staff, and training	10	2	0.2
Total average rating for mitigating measures	**100**	**2.14**	**1.9**

Source: World Bank.

Note: AML = anti-money-laundering. CFT = combating the financing of terrorism.

After assessing the elements of a mitigating measure, a (weighted) rating can be computed for that overall mitigating measure. Here, the application of weights is also optional, and the specific weights used in table 4.5 are illustrative only, not prescriptive. Each supervisor will determine if weights (or any other analytical method) are to be applied; and if so, what are the appropriate weights to use for each mitigation measure.

In table 4.5, the average rating of 2.14 results in an inadequate rating, while the weighted rating of 1.9 results in a satisfactory rating for all measures combined.

For the assessment of mitigating measures, a more qualitative approach can also be used, as shown in table 4.6.

Residual Risk

Residual risk is the assessed risk after mitigation measures have been applied to the inherent risks. For example, an entity with weak AML/CFT controls may not be high risk if the inherent risks arising from its businesses are low (although, over time, criminals may exploit the weaker controls, causing a change in the entity's inherent risk exposure). Similarly, an entity with high inherent risks may not necessarily be high risk if strong AML/CFT controls are applied so that the residual risks are lower. Therefore, evaluating residual risks is an important component in establishing the risk profile of a financial institution. There are various options to estimating residual risk, but a correlation matrix approach is a practical option that can be estimated using the four-level risk-rating methodology described above (table 4.7).

For the example provided in table 4.7, where the weighted inherent risk rating is medium-high and the weighted rating of the mitigating measures is satisfactory, the residual rating assessment would be as follows:

● Total weighted inherent risk rating: medium-high;

● Total weighted mitigating measures rating: satisfactory; and

● **Residual risk: medium.**

TABLE 4.6 Example of a Qualitative Assessment of Compliance

Indicator	1. Strong controls	2. Satisfactory controls	3. Inadequate controls	4. Weak controls	Assigned score
Governance and board	There is an active board, and senior management is involved in monitoring ML/TF risk and approves and regularly updates the institution's ML/TF risk appetite, risk analysis, and AML/CFT policies and procedures.	There is a reasonably active board, and senior management is involved in monitoring ML/TF risk and approves and updates on an irregular basis the institution's ML/TF risk appetite, risk analysis, and AML/CFT policies and procedures.	There is limited involvement of the board or senior managers in monitoring ML/TF risk, and they are sometimes involved in updating the institution's ML/TF risk analysis and significant AML/CFT policies and procedures.	There is no active involvement of the board or senior managers in monitoring ML/TF risk, and they are not involved in the institution's ML/TF risk analysis and AML/CFT policies and procedures.	
Compliance function	The compliance function is independent, has sufficient and skilled resources to fulfill its role in a timely manner, and is managed by an experienced person.	The compliance function is independent, generally has adequate resources to fulfill its role, and is managed by an experienced person.	The compliance function is not entirely independent, does not have appropriately skilled resources, and is not managed by an experienced person.	The compliance function is not independent, does not have sufficient resources, and is not managed by a suitably experienced individual.	
AML/CFT framework	The institution has an adequate and effective AML/CFT framework in place and no compliance issues.	The institution has an adequate AML/CFT framework in place, and only minor shortcomings are identified.	The institution has an adequate AML/CFT framework in place, but there are several shortcomings.	The institution has significant deficiencies in its AML/CFT framework.	
Average (weighted) score for control level					
Adjusted risk level based on combination of factors or supervisory judgment					
Narrative on control-level score					

Source: World Bank.

Note: AML = anti-money-laundering. CFT = combating the financing of terrorism.

TABLE 4.7 Example of a Matrix for Estimating Residual Risk

| Inherent risk rating | Mitigating measures rating | | | |
	Strong	Satisfactory	Inadequate	Weak
Low	Low	Low	Medium	High
Medium-low	Low	Medium	High	High
Medium-high	Medium	Medium	High	Very high
High	Medium	High	Very high	Very high

Source: World Bank.

As indicated in the FATF guidance, the residual risk assessment should not take a purely quantitative approach based solely on numerical risk scores (FATF 2018). Where supervisors have significant concerns about the potential impact of ML/TF risk that an entity poses to the system, they should have the ability to reflect such concerns in the residual risk assessment. Also, they should acknowledge that no matter how robust AML/CFT controls are, inherent risks cannot be mitigated entirely. Therefore, the regulated entities will always have to manage the remaining residual risks in line with the risk appetite of the institution (FATF 2018, para. 66).

Other Risk Factors

In order to develop a more comprehensive risk profile of an institution, supervisors should not limit their assessment to a calculated residual risk rating. In some circumstances, they will have to adjust the residual risk rating. For instance, recent changes in the compliance structure of the institution may not yet have been incorporated in the calculated residual risk. In some cases, the supervisor will also need to apply professional judgment to adjust the residual risk rating.

Moreover, other complementary factors can contextualize the residual risk analysis, including the following:

- Corporate and structural factors, such as

    - Ownership structure;

    - Subsidiaries and branches, both domestic and abroad;

    - Management framework;

    - Years in operation;

    - Enforcement measures; and

    - Compliance incidents.

- Key financial indicators and other statistics, such as

    - Total assets;

    - Total deposits;

    - Number of customers;

    - Number of employees;

    - Net income or loss;

    - Solvency ratio;

    - Liquidity ratio; and

    - Asset and deposit growth rates.

Taken together, these factors plus residual risk analysis provide a more comprehensive basis for documenting institutional risk profiles.

World Bank: Inherent and Residual Risk Assessment Model

The World Bank's institutional risk-scoring tool is broadly similar to the simplified model described in table 4.8. It was developed to guide supervisors in their risk-based planning of

TABLE 4.8 Indicators in the World Bank's Institutional ML/TF Risk-Scoring Tool

	Indicator	Importance of indicator (coefficient) (−) Negative correlation with risk (+) Positive correlation with risk 5-Very high 1-Normal	Institutional scores for indicators (5-high, 4-medium-high, 3-medium, 2-medium-low, 1-low)							
			Bank 1	weighted score	Bank 2	weighted score	Bank 3	weighted score	Bank 3	weighted score
Inherent risk indicators	Size	1	5	5	2	2	4	4	3	3
	Corporate governance	−4	4	−16	3	−12	5	−20	3	−12
	Clarity and diversity of ownership	−2	3	−6	2	−4	5	−10	3	−6
	Risk appetite	5	3	15	5	25	3	15	5	25
	High-risk clients	5	5	25	5	25	2	10	3	15
	High-risk products/services (in terms of nature and complexity)	5	5	25	5	25	2	10	4	20
	International operations and transactions	3	5	15	5	15	2	6	3	9
	High-risk geographic locations of operation (domestic or international).	5	4	20	5	25	2	10	3	15
	Reliance on third parties, agents, and remote processess (delivery channels)	3	3	9	3	9	3	9	3	9
				0		0		0		0
				0		0		0		0
				0		0		0		0
				0		0		0		0
	Management's commmittment to AML/CFT	−5	1	−5	2	−10	4	−20	2	−10

(table continues next page)

TABLE 4.8 *(continued)*

AML/CFT control indicators	Indicator	Importance of indicator (coefficient) (−) Negative Correlation with risk (+) Positive Correlation with risk 5 - Very high 1-Normal 1-Normal	Institutional scores for indicators (5-high, 4- medium-high, 3-medium, 2-medium-low, 1-low)							
			Bank 1	weighted score	Bank 2	weighted score	Bank 3	weighted score	Bank 3	weighted score
	Understanding of ML/TF risks	−3	1	−3	2	−6	4	−12	2	−6
	Independence and effectiveness of compliance function	−5	1	−5	2	−10	4	−20	2	−10
	Adequacy of the AML/CFT policy and procedures	−2	1	−2	4	−8	4	−8	2	−4
	Effectiveness of CDD	−3	1	−3	3	−6	4	−12	2	−6
	Effectiveness of monitoring (including MIS)	−4	1	−4	3	−12	4	−16	2	−8
	Effectiveness of STR analysis and reporting	−4	1	−4	2	−8	4	−16	2	−8
	Effectiveness of report keeping	−3	1	−3	3	−9	4	−12	2	−6
	Effectiveness of internal audits	−4	1	−4	3	−12	4	−16	2	−8
	Effectiveness of training activities	−3	1	−3	3	−9	4	−12	2	−6
				0		0		0		0
				0		0		0		0
				0		0		0		0
	Inherent risk score (0 to 100)		72.0		85.6		28.0		61.4	
	Residual risk score (0 to 100)		70.5		74.2		19.1		56.5	

Source: World Bank risk-based approach toolkit.

Note: AML = anti-money-laundering. CFT = combating the financing of terrorism. ML = money-laundering. TF = terrorism financing.

PREVENTING MONEY LAUNDERING AND TERRORIST FINANCING

AML/CFT supervision activities. The main difference is that it further divides the four inherent risk factors into their components and assigns a weight to each component and risk-mitigating measure to arrive at an overall weighted score for inherent risk and residual risk. As under the simplified method, the mitigating measures have the effect of reducing residual risk.

Using Risk Assessment Outputs in Planning Supervisory Activities

Irrespective of the model used, it is important for supervisors to develop the risk profiles of each financial institution and the sector as a whole. These risk profiles serve as the basis for developing supervisory strategies and actions, including prioritization, planning, and resourcing of the annual calendar of on-site inspections and other supervisory outreach and activities.

This risk assessment can also be used to develop a sectoral risk analysis, including a sectoral risk heat map for tracking the evolution of risks over time. Such a heat map can further inform the supervisor's strategies and plans.

The scope and depth of on-site supervision will be based on the risk profiles of the financial institutions and the sectoral risk assessment. For entities with a high score for risk, enhanced supervisory attention is required (for example, full-scope or targeted inspections).

For entities with a low score, other supervisory activities can be planned, such as periodic compliance meetings or thematic inspections. This aspect of supervising lower-risk sectors and entities requires careful attention, as it may mislead supervisors on the exact nature of their role vis-à-vis activities deemed to generate fewer concerns. Lower risk does not mean no risk, and supervisors need to be able to detect any significant new risks within lower-risk sectors and entities. While supervisors may devote fewer resources to lower-risk areas, they should still devote sufficient resources to verifying and monitoring the understanding of risk in those areas, while allocating greater supervisory resources to higher-risk sectors. The FATF guidance given in box 4.2 provides useful insights on how supervisors should address lower-risk sectors and entities.

BOX 4.2 Extract from FATF Guidance: Supervisory Treatment of Lower-Risk Sectors and Entities

While most supervisory resources should be dedicated to the higher money-laundering and terrorism financing (ML/TF) risk areas, supervisory' strategies should also set out the supervisory approach for areas of lower ML/TF risk. Within a risk-based supervision framework, it is expected that there will be areas and segments of regulated entities that are assessed to be of lower ML/TF risk. ... The sound assessment of risks at a sectoral or subsectoral level does not necessarily require an assessment of each entity in the sector. ... Risk analysis can be undertaken with varying degrees of detail, depending on the type of risk and the purpose of the risk assessment, as well as based on the information, data, and

(box continues on next page)

BOX 4.2 (*continued*)

resources available (for example, keeping in mind the nature, scale, and complexity of the relevant entities/sectors).

It should be clear that lower-risk entities are still subject to supervisory attention commensurate with the level and nature of risk they present. The latter may entail the application of the supervisory tools by a combination of less frequent supervisory cycles, sample testing, and/or reactive interventions. Supervisory authorities are not expected to cover all lower-risk ML/TF entities under a fixed inspection cycle over time, particularly where there are large populations of lower-risk ML/TF entities.

Monitoring of lower-risk entities may allow for limited application of on-site tools. For example, one possible supervisory approach for lower-risk entities is to center them on the detection of any material risk events or escalations in risk profiles among the lower-risk entities, so that supervisors can intervene effectively to mitigate risks. In such scenarios, the nature of the materialized risks and desired supervisory outcomes should guide the application of an appropriate set of tools (either on-site, off-site, or a combination) ....

Supervisory authorities should regularly test their understanding and assumptions of the level of ML/TF risk and the adequacy of controls in the entity/sector .... Supervisors should also have the capacity to carry out supervisory activities on a responsive or reactive basis, where intelligence has been received that would merit supervisory intervention (for example, intelligence from returns or questionnaires, from other supervisors, from media reports or whistleblowers, or from law enforcement or the financial intelligence unit and suspicious transactions reports).

Supervisors should also ensure that education and outreach extend to lower-risk sectors to enable them to implement risk-based, proportionate measures and to help identify and report any ML/TF risks that may arise. With reference to national financial inclusion objectives, supervisors can also play a role in (a) reducing requirements for lower-risk entities that do not mitigate risk sufficiently to justify the effort they consume; and (b) reassuring other regulated entities that provide financial services to lower-risk entities that those lower-risk entities are adequately supervised.

Source: Extracted, with minor edits, from FATF 2021, 31–32.

The illustration in figure 4.1 is a scenario-based output from the World Bank's institutional risk-scoring tool.

At the early stages of a risk-based supervision approach, the risk scores of an institution may need to be based mostly on off-site supervision inputs and outputs. However, these risk assessments should be done in a dynamic way and be subject to periodic updates and refinements based on up-to-date information from off-site and on-site supervision activities. For example, after each on-site visit, the ratings of an institution should be reviewed and updated as necessary.

FIGURE 4.1 Output of the World Bank's Institutional Risk-Scoring Tool

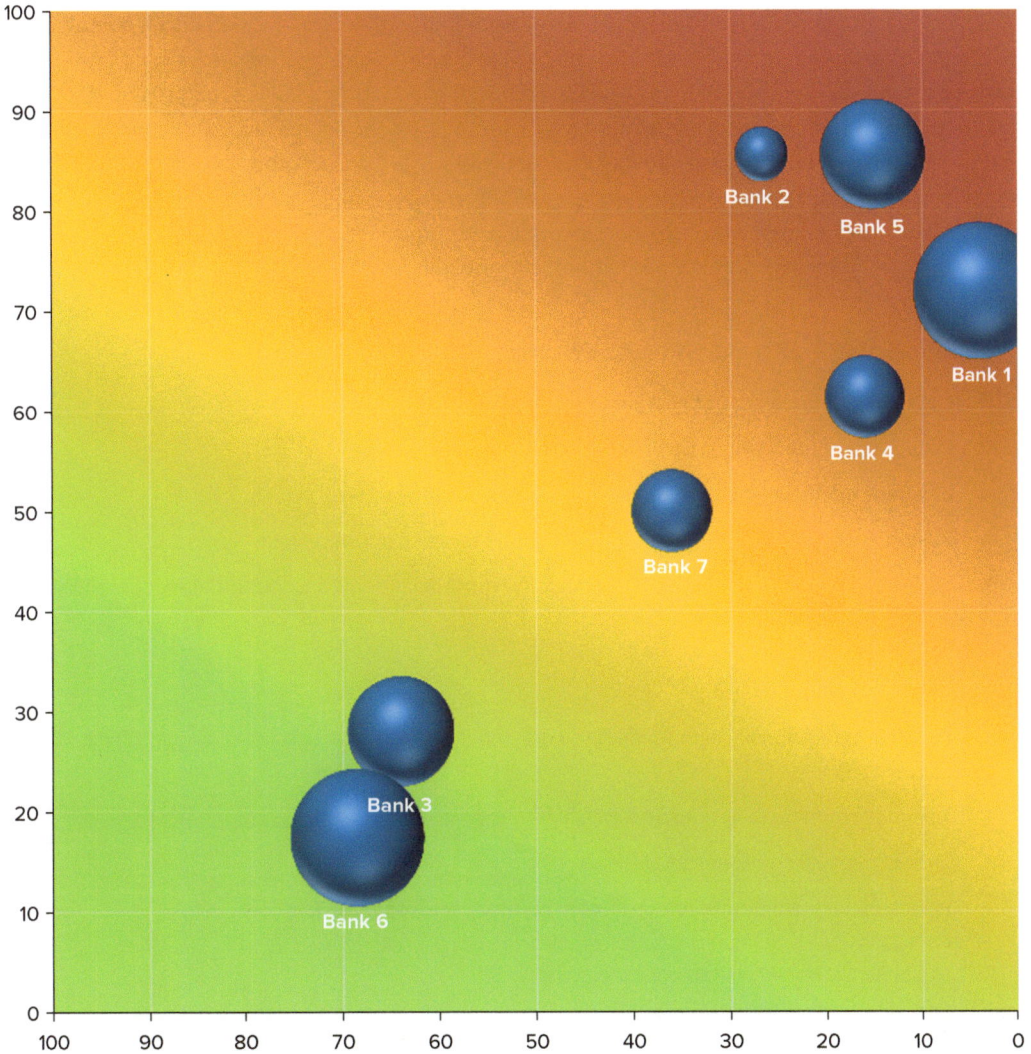

Source: World Bank risk-based approach toolkit.

Note: Color mapping = residual risk. Bubble size = size of the institution. AML = anti-money-laundering. CFT = combating the financing of terrorism.

This overall risk map of a sector can be an important bottom-up input into the sectoral risk assessment. Supervisors can use the map—combined with top-down inputs from the national risk assessments, typologies, and information from other authorities such as the FIU—to build a robust understanding of ML/TF risks in a sector and to develop risk-based supervision policies and strategies at the sectoral level.

Documenting Risk Profiles

Supervisors should document the risk profile of each financial institution or financial sector. Where the assessment is of an institution, supervisors can provide a brief summary of the institution, followed by a summary of its inherent risks, mitigating measures, and residual risk. In addition, other relevant issues that may affect the risk profile of the institution can also be described. These issues can include, for instance, (proposed) changes in ownership, senior management, audit and compliance functions, mergers, acquisitions, or new product lines. This description can also take into account, as appropriate, the results of other areas of supervision, the internal control environment, and the culture of compliance. The following can serve as a guide:

- Background information on the financial institution, including

  - Ownership and control, corporate structure, (foreign) branches, and subsidiaries;

  - Sector, size, and financial position;

  - Business model, including client base and main business lines;

  - Management issues, including recent changes and risk appetite; and

  - Regulatory and supervisory history, including enforcement measures and other compliance issues.

- ML/TF risk profile, including

  - Principal inherent risks with respect to customers, products and services, geography, and delivery channels;

  - Adequacy of mitigating measures;

  - Overall residual risk assessment; and

  - Trends in the institution's inherent risks, controls, and residual risks.

- Other significant issues and events, including

  - Quality and history of STRs;

  - Compliance and audit coverage of AML/CFT and management response;

  - Open-source information (for example, reported ML/TF cases involving the institution or its clients);

  - Home or host supervisory issues (where applicable); and

  - Enforcement measures and regulatory measures by other (supervisory) authorities.

OTHER SUPERVISORY ACTIVITIES

Risk profiles and sectoral risk assessments are important not only for identifying financial institutions for on-site inspections but also for selecting institutions for outreach activities, such as compliance meetings, roundtable discussions, and seminars or conferences.

Compliance Meetings

Compliance meetings with a financial institution help supervisors to understand the AML/CFT frame-work of the institution. Although on-site inspections are the main tool for assessing the effectiveness of the AML/CFT framework of the institution, compliance meetings are also a useful tool for discuss-ing an institution's ML/TF risk and AML/CFT compliance issues. Such meetings help supervisors to assess how well senior management and the managers of the compliance function understand the risks assumed by the institution and its AML/CFT obligations. These meetings are useful for inform-ing the off-site risk assessment of an institution.

Compliance meetings should be tailored to each institution and should take into account both its risk profile and all previous supervisory activities. The following issues can be addressed in a compli-ance meeting:

- The role of the board of directors and senior management in preparing and approving the business-wide ML/TF risk assessment and AML/CFT policies and procedures;

- The resources dedicated to implementing AML/CFT policies and procedures; and

- Specific issues such as the STR decision-making process or progress made on the remediation of previously identified shortcomings.

Depending on their specific objectives, supervisors can meet with directors, senior managers, compliance officers, or auditors. These compliance meetings can be scheduled on a periodic basis or on a case-by-case basis. They can help to raise the awareness of the board of directors and senior management by helping them to understand the rationale for the commitments and resources needed to fulfill AML/CFT requirements and strengthen their personal commitment to providing necessary AML/CFT resources. In some jurisdictions, supervisors can also observe the board meetings of an institution to collect information about its corporate governance and decision-making processes.

Outreach to Sector Representatives

Supervisors should also ensure that all financial institutions have a consistent understanding of ML/TF risks and AML/CFT obligations. This understanding can be attained through outreach to sector representatives, such as the banking association or any other sector association. Outreach programs allow supervisors to provide useful guidance on the interpretation and effective implementation of AML/CFT requirements.

The supervisor can, for instance, hold periodic meetings with representatives of a sector. These meetings can have multiple purposes. They can be used to discuss general compliance issues encountered by financial institutions, which will improve the information of the supervisors and provide a sense of issues that the sector encounters. They can also be used to discuss proposed guidance, questionnaires used for off-site supervision, or emerging risks.

Supervisors also need to raise awareness and clearly define supervisory expectations on the implementation of AML/CFT compliance controls. This awareness raising can be done in various ways. Instruments such as guidance, publications about good and bad practices, questions and answers, or feedback on (anonymized) inspection results or sanitized cases can be used to support these goals. In addition, conferences and seminars, whether organized by the supervisor or by the industry, are an important outreach tool.

These types of outreach are useful in the following:

- Outlining the legal and regulatory framework across a sector;

- Clarifying the interpretation of the requirements of the AML/CFT laws and regulations and explaining how to implement them in practice;

- Sensitizing institutions in assessing and mitigating ML/TF risks and in designing and implementing AML/CFT controls; and

- Raising awareness of risks and new legal requirements related to AML/CFT.

It is also a good practice to publish the main characteristics of the supervisory framework, including the design and method of off-site and on-site supervision and the method of implementation of enforcement actions.

EXAMPLES OF OFF-SITE AML/CFT SUPERVISION SYSTEMS AND PROCESSES IN SOME JURISDICTIONS

Box 4.3 provides examples of off-site AML/CFT supervisory regimes from several jurisdictions.

BOX 4.3 Examples of Off-Site Anti-Money-Laundering and Combating the Financing of Terrorism (AML/CFT) Supervisory Frameworks

Colombia. The Superintendencia Financiera de Colombia (SFC) has incorporated AML/CFT supervision within its broader integrated supervision framework, which addresses both prudential and financial risks and AML/CFT risks (IMF and GFILAT 2018). The AML/CFT component of the framework is based largely on the risk management system for money laundering and terrorism financing (ML/TF), SARLAFT, which is the basic risk-based AML/CFT regulation issued to supervised entities. The risk-based framework does not specifically address terrorism financing risk, and the results of the off-site risk analysis are used for planning on-site inspections.

The current risk-profiling model is based on an assessment of inherent risks associated with clients (individuals and legal entities), products and services (as reported by financial institutions that have been scheduled for on-site inspections), economic sectors, and the geographic location of customers. In addition, the SFC assesses controls and compliance through a questionnaire completed by institutions scheduled for inspections. On-site inspections verify the adequacy of these controls. The questionnaire covers, among

(box continues on next page)

BOX 4.3 (*continued*)

other issues, risk management, organizational structure, board and management oversight, audits, resources, budgets and training, red flags, and identification and reporting of suspicious activity.

Malaysia. Each supervisor has developed a risk analysis tool to assess the inherent risk of each sector using a wide range of information (FATF and APG 2014). This information includes the findings of the national risk assessment, sector-by-sector threat and vulnerability assessments, and periodically produced lists of strategic products at risk. The results of the risk analysis feed into the supervisory authorities' ongoing risk assessment process within each sector. The overall ML/TF risk serves as a key input in determining the intensity of supervision.

Bank Negara Malaysia (BNM) has adopted a supervisory risk-based framework (SuRF) to assess the safety and soundness of licensed financial institutions. This framework enables BNM to evaluate an institution's risk profile, quality of risk management processes, governance, compliance, and financial condition. It allows BNM to focus attention and efforts on areas or activities of higher risks and to assess ML/TF risks consistently across various entities, including risks arising from all activities or entities within a financial group (subsidiaries and branches), both domestic and foreign.

BNM uses a dedicated AML/CFT supervisory framework to complement SuRF, which provides greater detail in the assessment of ML/TF risks. The intensity and frequency of the ML/TF assessment are based on several factors, such as the size and complexity of the institution, type of customers, products, geographic exposure, and channels of delivery.

In addition, BNM supervisors conduct thematic assessments of ML/TF issues, which complement the ongoing supervisory reviews conducted under SuRF. Thematic assessments are carried out simultaneously across an industry and are focused on a specific area.

Macao SAR, China. With respect to the banking sector, Autoridade Monetaria de Macau (AMCM) has devised a risk-rating mechanism for banks by identifying potential ML/TF threats and assessing the quality of AML/CFT prevention (APG 2017). To gain insight into these threats, surveys have been conducted to obtain information on the scope of business and perceived risks within banks. The annual sector survey also collects comprehensive information, including the nature and scale of high-risk transactions, exposure to AML/CFT–deficient jurisdictions, customer structures, products, and delivery channels. The risk profiles of individual banks are updated constantly on completion of each on-site inspection or other major triggers. Under this risk-based approach, lower-risk institutions within the banking, other-financial-institution, and insurance sectors are monitored mainly through off-site surveillance, supplemented by less frequent inspections and thematic reviews.

The AMCM rates banks using a five-level scoring tool to assist with monitoring. The tool rates banks in five categories by identifying their inherent ML/TF threats and assessing the quality of AML/CFT prevention, which includes risk management, preventive measures, ongoing due diligence, and CFT.

ANNEX 4A EXAMPLE OF A QUESTIONNAIRE TO COLLECT INHERENT ML/TF RISK DATA

Supervisors can use the examples below as potential subfactors of the main inherent risk factors (customers, products, transactions, geographic exposure, and delivery channel) to collect information from financial institutions. For each subfactor, supervisors should determine whether it is necessary to collect this information and then determine the best analytical variable to use (for example, number of customers, number of transactions, and volume of assets, deposits, or transactions).

General information	
Name of institution	
License number	
Type of license	
Date of license	
Number of foreign branches	
Jurisdictions of foreign branches	
Number of majority subsidiaries	
Jurisdictions of majority subsidiaries	
Total assets	

Number of customers, by risk category		
Risk category	*Domestic*	*Nondomestic*
Low risk		
Medium risk		
High risk		
Unacceptable risk		
Not yet classified		

Customers		
Indicator	*Number*	*Volume of assets and deposits*
Total		
Newly accepted in year xxxx		
Exited or terminated in year xxxx		
Type of customer		
Retail customers		
-Of which domestic		
-Of which nondomestic		
Small and medium enterprise customers		

(table continues next page)

-Of which domestic		
-Of which nondomestic		
Corporations		
-Of which domestic		
-Of which nondomestic		
High-net-worth individuals		
-Of which domestic		
-Of which nondomestic		
Other types of customer		
-Of which domestic		
-Of which nondomestic		
Customers located in free trade zone		

Retail customers, by jurisdiction	
Jurisdiction	*Number of customers*
Jurisdiction A	
Jurisdiction B	
Jurisdiction C	
Jurisdiction D	
Jurisdiction E	
Jurisdiction F	
Other jurisdictions	

Corporate customers and beneficial owners, by jurisdiction		
Jurisdiction	*Number of customers*	*Number of beneficial owners*
Jurisdiction A		
Jurisdiction B		
Jurisdiction C		
Jurisdiction D		
Jurisdiction E		
Jurisdiction F		
Other jurisdictions		

Type of entity of corporate customers	
Type of customer	*Number*
Trust	
Foundation	

(table continues next page)

Limited partnership	
Limited liability partnership	
Entity with nominee shareholders	
Entity with bearer shares	

Number of customers in high-risk industries	
Type of customer	*Number*
Art trading	
Precious metals and stones, jewelers	
Crowdfunding	
Oil and gas	
Extraction industries	
Commercial real estate	
Not-for-profit	
Crypto assets	
Gambling	
Adult entertainment	
Scrap metal	
Other types of customers	

Assets of politically exposed persons		
Type of customer	*Number*	*Volume of assets and deposits*
Domestic customers		
Domestic politically exposed persons		
Foreign customers		
Foreign politically exposed persons		
International organizations		

Number of institutions with respondent accounts, by jurisdiction	
Jurisdiction	*Number of respondent institutions*
Jurisdiction A	
Jurisdiction B	
Jurisdiction C	
Jurisdiction D	
Jurisdiction E	
Jurisdiction F	
Other jurisdictions	

Products		
Indicator	Number	Volume
Back-to-back loans		
Cash deposits above [threshold]		
Cash withdrawals above [threshold]		
Forex (domestic currency)		

Trade finance		
Indicator	*Number*	*Volume*
Total transactions		
Total number of customers with trade finance facilities		
Number of customers with trade finance facilities per jurisdiction		
Jurisdiction A		
Jurisdiction B		
Jurisdiction C		
Jurisdiction D		
Jurisdiction E		
Jurisdiction F		
Other jurisdictions		

Fund transfers		
Indicator	*Number*	*Volume*
Domestic		
International		

International fund transfers				
Jurisdiction	*Number incoming*	*Volume incoming*	*Number outgoing*	*Volume outgoing*
Jurisdiction A				
Jurisdiction B				
Jurisdiction C				
Jurisdiction D				
Jurisdiction E				
Jurisdiction F				
Other jurisdictions				

Delivery channels	
Indicator	*Number*
Customers accepted through face-to-face contact	
Customers accepted via non-face-to-face channels	
Customers referred by entities in the group	
Customers referred by other AML/CFT entities	
Customers referred by non-AML/CFT entities	

ANNEX 4B EXAMPLE OF A QUESTIONNAIRE TO OBTAIN INFORMATION ON AML/CFT CONTROLS

Supervisors can adapt this questionnaire to other financial sectors. The questions can vary by sector, taking into account the size, maturity, and complexity of the sector. Depending on the method of analysis used and the available resources, the supervisor has to determine whether to ask questions with preset answers or open-ended questions that allow the institution to provide an explanation. The last option will require resources to evaluate all the answers.

General information	
Name of institution	
License number	
Type of license	
Date of license	
Name and contact details of contact person	
Position of contact person	
Name and contact details of responsible person	
Position of responsible person	

Business-wide risk analysis		
Question	*Yes – No – Not applicable*	*Explanation or description*
Does your institution have a process and methodology in place for a business-wide risk analysis?		
When was the last business-wide risk analysis conducted?		
How often is the business-wide risk analysis conducted?		
Are the risks analyzed when new products are developed or business lines are expanded?		
Does the risk analysis also include branches?		
Is the business-wide risk analysis based on inherent risks?		

(table continues next page)

Does the business-wide risk analysis describe the residual risks?		
Are the results of the business-wide risk analysis incorporated in the anti-money-laundering/combating the financing of terrorism (AML/CFT) policies and procedures		
What is the role of the board in the business-wide risk analysis?		
What is the role of compliance in the business-wide risk analysis?		
Has the board determined a risk appetite with respect to money laundering/terrorism financing (ML/TF)?		
Other questions		
Role of the board		
Has the board formally approved the AML/CFT policy and compliance program?		
If so, when did the board approve the latest version?		
Has the board designated any of its members responsible for AML/CFT issues?		
If so, who and when?		
What types of reports does the board receive on the implementation of the AML/CFT policies?		
From whom and how often are such reports received?		
Other questions		
Policies and procedures		
How are the AML/CFT policies and procedures communicated within the institution?		
How often are the AML/CFT policies and procedures reviewed and updated?		
Do the AML/CFT policies and procedures address the following topics:		
-Customer acceptance		
-Review of customers		
-Customer exit		
-Transaction monitoring		
-Reporting of suspicious transactions		
-Reliance on third parties		
-Targeted financial sanctions		
Does the institution communicate changes to AML/CFT policies or procedures to employees? If so, describe how.		
Other questions		
Customer due diligence		
Is customer due diligence done before accepting the customer?		
Do the customer due diligence procedures address the following?		
-Identifying and verifying the identity of the customer		
-Identifying and verifying the identity of the beneficial owners		

(table continues next page)

-Obtaining insight into the ownership and control structure		
-Determining the nature and purpose of the relationship		
-Establishing the source of funds		
-Determining the risk profile of the customer		
Are the following issues taken into account when assessing the risks of a customer?		
-Ownership and control structure		
-Complexity of the structure		
-Jurisdictions where the customer resides		
-Jurisdictions where the beneficial owner resides		
-Jurisdictions where the customer is active		
-Source of funds		
-Negative news		
Do the procedures include enhanced due diligence?		
Is enhanced due diligence applied when the customer or beneficial owner is related to a high-risk jurisdiction?		
Is enhanced due diligence applied when the customer or beneficial owner is a politically exposed person?		
In what other situations is enhanced due diligence applied?		
-Describe the enhanced due diligence measures		
Do the procedures include simplified due diligence?		
When is simplified due diligence applied?		
-Describe the simplified due diligence measures		
How often are customer files reviewed, in case of the following?		
-Low risk		
-Medium risk		
-High risk		
-Involvement of a politically exposed person		
Other questions		
Politically exposed persons		
What system is used for screening politically exposed persons?		
Are customers and beneficial owners screened at acceptance?		
What is the periodicity for screening existing customers and beneficial owners?		
Other questions		

Sanctions screening		
What system is used for screening against the sanctions list?		
Which lists are screened?		
Are customers and beneficial owners screened at acceptance?		
What is the periodicity for screening existing customers and beneficial owners?		
Other questions		
Transaction monitoring		
Does the institution use an automated or manual transaction monitoring system?		
In the transaction-monitoring process, does the institution take the following into account in its business rules?		
-High-risk jurisdictions		
-High-risk industries		
-Customer segments		
-Customer risk		
-Customers or beneficial owners who are politically exposed persons		
-Terrorism financing		
-Proliferation financing		
Are the business rules reviewed periodically?		
When were the business rules reviewed last?		
How many business rules are active in the systems?		
How many alerts were generated last year?		
How many alerts were false positives?		
How many alerts were investigated further by an analyst?		
How many alerts were escalated to compliance?		
How many alerts were closed by compliance as false positives?		
How many alerts were reported to the financial intelligence unit?		
How many full-time-employees are involved in the transaction-monitoring process?		
Other questions		
Suspicious transaction reports		
Is the institution registered with the financial intelligence unit?		
How many suspicious transactions were reported last year?		
What tipping-off measures are in place?		
Who has the final decision on whether to send a suspicious transactions report to the financial intelligence unit?		
Other questions		

Record keeping		
Is there a records-retention policy?		
How long is customer due diligence and transaction information maintained?		
How long are suspicious transaction reports maintained?		
How are records are maintained? Paper, electronically, on-site, off-site?		
What are the security measures for record keeping?		
Can the institution obtain records relating to clients of foreign branches and subsidiaries?		
Can such information include information related to suspicious transaction reports?		
Other questions		
Compliance		
Has the board formally established a compliance function?		
What is the position of the head of compliance?		
Does the compliance function have direct access to the board?		
Does the compliance function report directly to the board?		
If not, to whom does compliance report within the institution?		
Is there a group compliance function?		
Does each foreign branch or subsidiary have a compliance officer?		
What is the relation of group compliance to other compliance functions in the institution?		
How many full-time employees does the compliance function have?		
How many of those are involved in AML/CFT?		
Does compliance have a compliance-monitoring plan?		
What is the role of compliance in reporting suspicious transactions to the financial intelligence unit?		
Other questions		
Audit		
Does the institution have an internal audit function?		
Does the audit function have direct access to the board?		
Do the audit function managers report directly to the board?		
If there is no internal audit, does the institution have an external audit function?		
Does the internal or external audit review and test the AML/CFT program and customer due diligence policies and procedures?		
If yes, when was the last AML/CFT–related audit?		
What were the scope and result of this audit?		
Is there a specific AML/CFT audit plan?		

(table continues next page)

How much time and resources are devoted to AML/CFT–related audits per year?		
Does internal or external audit review the compliance function?		
When was it last reviewed? What were the findings?		
Other questions		
Employees		
Does the institution have policies and procedures that include measures to ensure the integrity of employees?		
Does the institution screen prospective employees?		
If yes, what checks does the institution conduct?		
Does the institution screen existing employees?		
If yes, when does the institution conduct this screening?		
Other questions		
Training		
Is there an AML/CFT training program in place for employees?		
What type of AML/CFT training program (type, frequency, participants) has been implemented for employees?		
When was the last AML/CFT training delivered?		
Does the institution retain records of the training sessions, including attendance records and relevant training materials used?		
Is the AML/CFT training mandatory for all employees?		
Are there consequences for not attending AML/CFT training programs?		
Have the board and senior management participated in AML/CFT training?		
What type of training have the compliance officers attended regarding ML/TF methods and typologies, customer due diligence, transaction monitoring, and suspicious transactions reporting?		
Other questions		

NOTES

1. As an example, risk surveillance (a supervisor's monitoring of relevant data and information, including information from reports of suspicious transactions and currency transactions, where available) is useful for detecting emerging risks in the sector being supervised as well as indicating significant AML/CFT control issues in regulated entities.

2. As set out in FATF Recommendation 1, regulated entities must assess the ML/TF risks facing their businesses. Regulated entities' risk assessments may help to inform supervisors' view of risk and enable them to obtain information on specific categories of risk (for example, products, services, customers, delivery channels, and geographic locations) relevant to the entity.

3. A cluster of financial institutions is a group of intuitions with similar characteristics.

4. The French financial sector supervisor (Autorité de Contrôle Prudentiel et de Resolution) has a dedicated division in charge of press reviews that feeds the off-site supervision teams with regular press reviews, on request. Regular press reviews can be dedicated to specific issues (for instance, tax havens) or specific financial institutions (for example, a financial institution's litigation in other jurisdictions or negative information on its shareholders).

REFERENCES

APG (Asia-Pacific Group on Money Laundering). 2017. "Macao SAR, China, Mutual Evaluation Report." APG, Sydney, December. https://www.fatf-gafi.org/media/fatf/content/images/APG-Mutual -Evaluation-Report-Macao-China-2017.pdf.

FATF (Financial Action Task Force). 2018. "Guidance on Counter Proliferation Financing: The Implementation of Financial Provisions of United Nations Security Council Resolutions to Counter the Proliferation of Weapons of Mass Destruction." FATF, Paris. https://www.fatf-gafi.org /publications/fatfrecommendations/documents/guidance-counter-proliferation-financing.html.

FATF (Financial Action Task Force). 2021. "Guidance on Risk-Based Supervision." FATF, Paris, March. https://www.fatf-gafi.org/publications/documents/Guidance-RBA-Supervision.html.

FATF (Financial Action Task Force) and APG (Asia-Pacific Group on Money Laundering). 2015. "Anti-Money Laundering and Counter-Terrorist Financing Measures—Malaysia, Fourth Round Mutual Evaluation Report." FATF, Paris; APG, Sydney. https://www.fatf-gafi.org/media/fatf /documents/reports/mer4/Mutual-Evaluation-Report-Malaysia-2015.pdf.

IMF (International Monetary Fund) and GAFILAT (Financial Action Task Force of Latin America). 2018. "Mutual Evaluation Report of the Fourth Round—Republic of Colombia." IMF, Washington, DC. https://www.fatf-gafi.org/media/fatf/documents/reports/mer-fsrb/GAFILAT-Mutual-Evaluation -Colombia-2018.pdf.

CHAPTER 5

On-Site Risk-Based AML/CFT Supervision

OVERVIEW

A risk-based approach to supervision of anti-money-laundering and combating the financing of terrorism (AML/CFT) means that a financial institution does not have to be examined annually or with a set frequency. Risk-based supervision allows supervisors to deploy resources more efficiently and to prioritize higher-risk institutions or higher-risk areas. The scope, intensity, and objectives of inspections should be tailored to the risk profiles of the institution or sectors and (emerging) risks in the jurisdiction. This approach allows supervisors to pay enhanced attention to higher-risk institutions or activities and less intense attention to lower-risk institutions or activities. For instance, large, complex banks involved in higher-risk activities (for example, private banking) would be subject to more frequent and intensive on-site examinations.

On-site risk-based supervision of AML/CFT is not an autonomous process, disjointed from the rest of oversight. On the contrary, on-site and off-site inspections are two sides of the same coin. As indicated in the Financial Action Task Force (FATF) guidance, on-site inspections offer supervisors an opportunity to conduct a more thorough review of the entities' controls through the performance of sampling tests and off-site work. Similarly, they are useful for validating the risk profile of an entity so that it can be adjusted as needed. Relatedly, an off-site review can provide an opportunity to revalidate the regulated entities' risk assessment prior to an on-site inspection. So, off-site and on-site inspections go hand in hand (FATF 2021, par. 68).

The supervisor's AML/CFT supervision framework should provide the foundation for the types of inspections that can be conducted using a risk-based approach. The examination program should incorporate a review of the institution's AML/CFT measures and implementation. This chapter addresses the steps required to conduct a risk-based AML/CFT on-site examination. It discusses the types of on-site examinations that can be conducted and how to plan and scope examinations. It also provides an overview of the specific procedures for AML/CFT examinations and how to develop and communicate the findings and conclusions.

RISK-BASED ON-SITE EXAMINATIONS

Under a risk-based approach to AML/CFT supervision, it is very important to establish a clear process for off-site and on-site processes. It does not make sense to conduct off-site examinations to collect information on inherent money-laundering and terrorism financing (ML/TF) risks and levels of AML/CFT compliance from all institutions and also to conduct on-site examinations based on a set frequency. A key objective of the off-site process is to determine the frequency, types of inspection, scope, duration, and resourcing of subsequent on-site examinations.

The AML/CFT supervision framework should describe the types of on-site inspections to be conducted under a risk-based approach. The type of inspection generally determines the range of AML/CFT obligations that will be inspected. Full-scope inspections address all or most AML/CFT obligations, whereas limited-scope or targeted inspections focus on one or several specific AML/CFT requirements or risk areas. Thematic inspections focus on one or several specific AML/CFT requirements or risk areas, but they are conducted in a specific sector or subsector or across sectors.

On-site examinations are conducted to verify compliance with the applicable AML/CFT legal obligations of a financial institution, taking into account its risk profile as determined through off-site processes and other relevant information. In an on-site examination, the supervisor assesses whether the institution has effectively implemented AML/CFT controls in relation to, among others, the level of inherent ML/TF risks and the size and complexity of the institution. The on-site examination also confirms that the information provided to the supervisor through off-site reporting is accurate.

The on-site inspection team should meet with the off-site team as part of the preparation process. The purpose of the meeting is to discuss issues of concern, such as changes in ownership, management, or business model, geographic expansion, inherent risks, compliance issues, and any outstanding corrective measures, among others.

An effective AML/CFT on-site examination program depends on many factors, including adequate resources, tools, and a well-trained staff of examiners. In addition, staff need to have full and complete access to all information at an institution, including information on customers and transactions.

Full-Scope Examinations

Full-scope on-site AML/CFT examinations are the most resource-intensive form of supervisory activities and are generally conducted at financial institutions that are involved in higher-risk activities and have the highest ML/TF risk profile. These examinations are intended to assess the full range of AML/CFT obligations, including policies, procedures, compliance systems, and controls. They review whether the AML/CFT compliance framework is commensurate with the institution's size, complexity, and ML/TF risks and is compliant with the legal requirements. The duration of the inspection depends on factors such as the degree of risk, size and complexity of the institution, and available resources.

Limited-Scope or Targeted Examinations

Limited-scope or targeted examinations are conducted on institutions that have deficiencies in a specific area of AML/CFT obligations or that have a business line with high inherent ML/TF risks. They are generally less resource intensive and may also be conducted as a follow-up to specific issues arising from an off-site review or prior examination. Targeted examinations focus on a specific area of concern (for example, customer due diligence, politically exposed persons, suspicious transactions, transaction monitoring, and functioning of compliance). These examinations may be scheduled on an ad hoc basis. A trigger for an ad hoc examination can also be an incident reported by the institution—for instance, a report that the compliance system is not operating as intended.

Thematic Examinations

Supervisors can carry out thematic examinations of several institutions in a sector or an entire sector as well as across sectors. The topics for a thematic inspection can focus on emerging or contemporary ML/TF risks facing financial institutions (for example, virtual assets), specific types of customers (for example, politically exposed persons or cash-intensive businesses), specific products and services (for example, correspondent banking or trade financing), or combinations of types of customers and geographic exposures (for example, customers active in areas vulnerable to terrorism). Thematic inspections can also focus on a certain element of the AML/CFT process (for example, transaction monitoring or screening for terrorism funding).

These thematic examinations provide supervisors with important information they can use to give supervisory guidance or to focus on the whole sector. The outcomes of the thematic examinations may be fed back to the sector by means of seminars and publications of good and bad practices.

Follow-up Examinations

Follow-up examinations can be conducted any time after an examination has been conducted or enforcement measures have been imposed. Follow-up inspections assess whether an institution has successfully addressed supervisory directives and recommendations for corrective action and whether previously identified deficiencies in the AML/CFT process or violations of AML/CFT requirements have been solved. The timing and focus of follow-up examinations may be determined by the gravity of the deficiencies identified and the resulting recommendations and remediation actions required.

Examination of Foreign Branches and Subsidiaries

Some institutions based in one jurisdiction may also have branches and (majority-owned) subsidiaries in other jurisdictions. Hence, the AML/CFT supervisor of the home jurisdiction should have the ability to plan and conduct cross-border examinations of foreign branches and subsidiaries in coordination with their host supervisors. These examinations are intended to verify whether the institution is applying group-wide AML/CFT controls and complying with the requirements of both home and host jurisdictions. Permission from the host jurisdiction is necessary to conduct these examinations and is generally obtained under supervisory memoranda of understanding or similar agreements. Such examinations may be conducted jointly with the host-jurisdiction supervisor.

In a cross-border context, home-jurisdiction supervisors should require access to and review of customer and transaction information in the host jurisdiction to test the implementation of AML/CFT requirements. Access should not be restricted by secrecy or data protection laws or practices, and the home supervisor should observe the protocols for safeguarding the use of confidential information obtained through this process. The host-jurisdiction supervisors should extend their full cooperation and assistance to home-jurisdiction supervisors to enable them to review compliance with group-wide AML/CFT policies, procedures, and controls.

STRUCTURES OF AML/CFT SUPERVISION UNITS

There is no preferred institutional arrangement or supervisory model for AML/CFT oversight. In fact, the choice of supervisory model is often influenced by the structure of the financial sector and by legal, cultural, historical, and political economy trade-offs. In practice, the choice of model varies widely across countries. Some supervisory authorities have specialized AML/CFT units in charge of all aspects of AML/CFT supervision. Such a specialized unit conducts AML/CFT on-site inspections separately or jointly with units that focus on other areas of supervision. Other supervisory authorities have an integrated structure whereby prudential or conduct supervisors perform the AML/CFT component of supervision. In this instance, the AML/CFT component may be examined by the general supervisor or by a supervisor with knowledge and expertise in AML/CFT supervision. A supervisory authority can also have a system with a specialized AML/CFT unit that conducts off-site supervision, shares the results with the prudential or conduct supervision units, and joins those units during on-site inspections conducted specifically to address AML/CFT issues.

In some jurisdictions, AML/CFT supervision is conducted by an authority—for example, the financial intelligence unit (FIU)—other than the prudential or conduct supervision authority. In this case, effective cooperation and information sharing between the sectoral and AML/CFT supervisor are essential.

The model used is often informed by the availability of supervisory resources, including specialized skills, as well as by the size and complexity of the sector. All models have advantages and disadvantages. However, in any model, clear objectives and a mandate, AML/CFT supervisory knowledge and expertise, a high degree of operational and financial independence, adequate supervisory resources, and effective enforcement powers are essential. Jurisdictions that have designated the AML/CFT supervisor outside of the sectoral supervisory authority and those that have created specialized AML/CFT supervisory units within the sectoral supervisory authority should pay attention to coordination between the two authorities or units. In jurisdictions with an integrated structure, equal attention should be paid to AML/CFT supervision, and adequately experienced staff should be available for AML/CFT oversight.

The staffing of on-site examinations depends on several factors, including how the AML/CFT supervision function is organized within the supervisory authority. Irrespective of how AML/CFT supervision is organized, on-site examinations should be conducted by supervisors with a robust understanding of possible ML/TF risks and AML/CFT issues. They should also be knowledgeable about the AML/CFT legal framework and its interpretation.

PLANNING AND SCOPING RISK-BASED AML/CFT ON-SITE EXAMINATIONS

Examination Notification

Supervisors generally notify management in advance of a proposed examination. This notification informs the institution of the scope and purpose of the examination, the dates of the examination, the documents and information that will be required, and the meetings that will be held with management and staff. Part of the notification will be a request for information, such as business-wide ML/TF risk assessments, AML/CFT policies and procedures, and compliance monitoring and audit reports for examiners to analyze before the on-site visit. The advantage of prior notification and the request for information is that the institution has time to prepare all of the necessary information in advance and to arrange for the appropriate staff to be available for the examiners to interview. This preparation facilitates the examination process.

An alternative approach is to conduct an unannounced inspection, in which examiners do not provide prior notice that an inspection will occur. This approach is generally used when there are indications of violations of AML/CFT obligations or reasonable grounds to suspect that the institution, including any of its managers and staff, is involved in illicit activities. In such cases, advance notice may not be appropriate because the supervisor wants to safeguard evidence. In this case, of course, the institution will not have prepared any information, and key staff may not be available immediately.

Surprise examinations are an important tool that should be at the supervisor's disposal. Although prior notice is recommended in most cases, it should not be binding on the supervisors, and institutions should be aware that prior notice is at the discretion of the supervisory authority. In addition, while inspecting an institution, supervisors can always make surprise visits to its departments or branches and conduct surprise interviews with staff. Surprise examinations can be more difficult to organize in the case of cross-border on-site visits, when home supervisors decide to inspect a branch in a host jurisdiction. In that case, the host supervisor may have a different practice in relation to examination notification.

When circumstances warrant, the information and meetings requirements can change during the examination. The institution should make physical arrangements, including providing adequate workspace and access to necessary information, systems, and staff.

Information Request

The following list is an example of the types of information that should be obtained and reviewed prior to the start of an on-site inspection. Some information will be available within the supervisory authority, for instance, as part of the off-site process. Other information will need to be obtained from the institution. The types of information include:

- The risk profile of the institution, which is developed as part of the off-site process, previous examination reports, supervisory recommendations, and corrective actions taken;

- The history of supervision and enforcement actions with respect to AML/CFT and other supervision topics;

- Where relevant, foreign supervisors' reports, particularly for financial groups and cross-border operations;

- The most recent business-wide ML/TF risk assessment of the financial institution, including information on the institution's risk appetite, which should at least address inherent risks and compliance measures;

- The corporate structure, including information on ownership and management;

- The current organizational chart, including information on positions of the audit and compliance functions;

- The latest AML/CFT compliance programs, including policies, procedures, work instructions on client due diligence and suspicious transactions reports (STRs), and the AML/CFT training program;

- Internal audit reports on AML/CFT issues and compliance reports, including the history of STRs;

- Actions taken with respect to the United Nations and domestic sanctions (for example, assets frozen or number of potential vs. actual matches on sanctions lists);

- External audit reports and management's responses to any previously identified AML/CFT issues;

- Information on the number of customers, refused businesses, and closed accounts;

- Lists of customers[1] and alerts from the transaction-monitoring process to facilitate the selection of customers' files and transactions to be tested during the examination; and

- Any information in relation to the loss or restriction—if any—of correspondent banking relationships.[2]

Some information, such as qualitative and quantitative information on STRs and reporting behavior, might have to be obtained from other authorities. Depending on the focus of the inspection, the on-site inspection team may also meet with the FIU to discuss possible concerns about the institution (for example, issues concerning the number and quality of STRs). This information can provide useful insights into an institution's monitoring, analysis, and reporting regime.

Audit reports covering AML/CFT issues can yield important information for the examination. It is also important to review the correspondence between the institution's management and its auditors, especially to determine if any remedial action has been taken to correct deficiencies found by the auditor.

Reviewing this information up front will facilitate the interviews with staff of the institution and the examination of systems and files. The information can provide a preliminary view of the AML/CFT compliance systems and processes in place. Reviewing the policies is very important to determine, for instance, if there are systems for enhanced due diligence and monitoring when higher risks are involved or if simplified due diligence can be applied for lower risks. Assessing the effectiveness of the compliance processes is part of the actual on-site inspection, where examiners can test and verify the implementation of the processes.

The evaluation of off-site and other information will assist the examination team to determine more precisely the specific objectives and scope of inspections and, in particular, to ascertain areas that require more intense review. The preliminary assessment of this information will also allow the supervisors to amend the duration of the inspection, the staff resources required, and the assignment of examiner responsibilities and tasks.

MANAGEMENT OF THE ON-SITE EXAMINATION

Supervisory authorities should establish on-site AML/CFT examination procedures to ensure effective and efficient processes. The examination procedures should reflect the risk, size, complexity, and systemic importance of a sector. The process should be linked closely to off-site AML/CFT processes. Of course, examination planning should remain flexible to accommodate unplanned cases.

Detailed inspection procedures should be documented in, for example, an AML/CFT examination manual. The manual should include processes for the following:

- Developing the annual calendar of inspections;

- Undertaking unplanned inspections triggered by risk events or new information;

- Planning the examination of individual financial institutions and financial groups;

- Conducting on-site examinations;

- Writing the report; and

- Taking follow-up actions after the examination.

The on-site examination generally includes a kick-off meeting with management as well as an exit meeting. The kick-off meeting is held to inform the institution's managers of the objectives and process of the inspection. The exit meeting provides management with the preliminary key findings. During the exit meeting, management should preferably already have committed to making improvements or to taking corrective actions where needed. To improve the accuracy of the findings, the examination team should be receptive to any reasonable clarifications and corrections of fact that management offers. During the exit meeting, timelines with respect to the examination report and possibilities for the institution to provide comments should also be discussed.

The duties and responsibilities of the examination team should be clearly assigned. The examination team leader carries the primary responsibility for planning and overseeing inspections, including coordinating report writing and follow-up action. The team leader is the key person to liaise with other departments of the supervisor, the institution's management and compliance officer, internal or external auditors, the FIU, and other relevant authorities (for instance, law enforcement or the public prosecutor in case of suspicions that the institution or its managers and staff are involved in illicit activities). In particular, the team leader has the following responsibilities:

- *Examination planning, organization, and implementation.* The team leader, with input from the inspection team, is responsible for planning and scoping the examination (see box 5.1 for details on inspection planning), setting the objectives, identifying and assigning inspection activities and tasks, establishing the list of information to be requested, and ensuring that the inspection meets the agreed-on objectives.

- *Assignment of responsibilities of the examination team.* The team leader (in consultation with the management of the AML/CFT supervision unit) forms the examination team in accordance with the expertise and skills necessary to carry out the inspection and assigns tasks and responsibilities to team members accordingly. Meetings should be held with the team throughout the planning process to ensure that each team member understands the objectives of the inspection as well as his or her individual tasks and responsibilities.

- *Examination plan.* The team leader makes changes to the scope of an inspection or changes to the examination plan in light of new information arising during an inspection.

- *Guidance for the examination team.* The team leader oversees the conduct of inspections, provides guidance and support to the team, and coordinates the process of requesting and receiving information.

- *Kick-off and exit meetings.* The team leader organizes and leads the kick-off and exit meetings with management of the institution to discuss the objective and process of the inspection and consequently the preliminary findings, conclusions, and recommendations of the examination.

- *Report of examination.* The team leader organizes and overseas preparation of the examination report and is the key contact person with whom the institution's management and compliance officer and the supervisory authority can discuss examination findings, recommendations, enforcement actions, and follow-up processes.

BOX 5.1 Planning Inspections and Associated Resources in Line with the Supervisory Strategy

The inspection plan is an important part of implementing a supervisory strategy for inspections. The inspection plan should list the following:
- The entities that will be subject to planned anti-money-laundering and combating the financing of terrorism (AML/CFT) inspections or reviews during a specified period (that is, inspections to be conducted over one year or several years), which may include follow-up on previous inspections;
- The type and scope of those inspections or reviews, taking into account the level of risk associated with each entity;

(box continues on next page)

BOX 5.1 *(continued)*

- Where relevant, the focus of each inspection or review, taking into account specific risks that have been identified or specific objectives that have been agreed on (for example, fact-finding to inform an ongoing risk assessment); and
- The supervisory resources required for each inspection or review as well as a timeline for each inspection or review.

In addition, the inspection plan should have the following characteristics:

- The approach to be taken on entities with different levels of risk exposure, in line with the supervisory strategy;
- Sufficient flexibility to accommodate or address unplanned inspections triggered by risk events or new information that could not have been foreseen when the plan was agreed on;
- Procedures for adequate documentation and amendments where the risk exposure of an entity included in the plan has changed or a new risk is identified in the course of on-site or off-site supervision; and
- An internal policy that sets out the level at which the plan should be agreed on or approved within the supervisory unit, how progress against the plan can be reviewed, the process for approving changes to the plan, and the extent to which an overview of the plan can be published (for example, number of inspections per risk rating).

Sources: Adapted from guidance from the European Banking Authority and the International Monetary Fund and from FATF (2021, 29).

RISK-BASED EXAMINATION PROCEDURES

Under a risk-based approach to AML/CFT supervision, depending on the type of inspection to be conducted, each examination requires tailored approaches determined by the examination planning process. These tailored approaches are determined by the risk profile of the institution and the objective and scope of the examination.

The following examination procedures apply to full-scope inspections but can be adapted for other types of inspections. In general, inspections follow a two-pronged approach. The first part consists of assessing the existence and design of AML/CFT mitigating measures against the inherent risks of the institution. The second part consists of assessing the actual and effective implementation of AML/CFT controls.

An essential part of the examination is to assess the AML/CFT systems and controls regarding (a) corporate governance and role of the board and senior management in AML/CFT issues; (b) the AML/CFT compliance framework; (c) audit and compliance functions; (d) AML/CFT policies, procedures, and controls, including customer due diligence, record keeping, and STR systems; and (e) AML/CFT resources, budget, training, and technology. These examination procedures are elaborated below.

Corporate Governance: Role of the Board and Senior Management in AML/CFT Issues

Supervisors should verify whether the governance of an institution includes the active involvement of the board and senior management in AML/CFT issues. Active involvement is a prerequisite for an adequate AML/CFT compliance framework. Corporate governance is reviewed to determine whether the top level of the institution is involved in setting the risk appetite, the assessment of ML/TF risks, and the approval of risk-based AML/CFT policies, procedures, and controls. The examination should also ascertain whether the board is accountable for the overall management of the institution in a transparent manner that imbues sound ethical values, accountability, and a strong culture of compliance generally and for AML/CFT, in particular. The board should set the tone for compliance from the top. The board should concern itself not only with the interests of the shareholders but also with those of other stakeholders—including its customers, the sector, and society in general—to ensure that negative AML/CFT issues do not adversely affect their interests.

In practice, on-site examiners should meet with board members and senior managers to ascertain whether they know and understand the bank's ML/TF risks, including those arising from new technologies or from the use of structures that impede transparency. These interviews are excellent opportunities to determine whether the bank's board receives adequate and timely information (for example, from the compliance function) in relation to the abuse of its financial services. In addition, reviewing the minutes of board meetings can yield insights on the nature of AML/CFT issues discussed and capacity of the board to redress any flaws brought to its attention.

AML/CFT Compliance Framework

Examiners should examine the adequacy of an institution's AML/CFT compliance framework to determine whether it is appropriate and proportional to the institution's risk profile as well as the size and complexity of its operations. The AML/CFT compliance framework should enable the institution to identify and assess the inherent ML/TF risks. Examiners should review how well the inherent ML/TF risks are assessed and mitigated. Supervisors should also review the process for updating the business-wide risk assessment, both periodically and when trigger events occur, such as changes in the organization or the legislation. As part of this assessment, examiners should review the role of management, business, and compliance in developing and reviewing the business-wide risk assessment (for what should be expected from banks in the context of business-wide risk assessments, see appendix A).

The quality of the compliance framework should be reviewed on two levels: AML/CFT controls at the management level and at the business level. At the management level, the supervisor should assess whether the risk appetite has been determined, the ML/TF risks have been sufficiently analyzed, and AML/CFT policies and procedures have been approved by the board or senior management. At the level of the business, the supervisor should analyze whether the ML/TF risks and mitigating measures are communicated effectively throughout the organization and whether mitigating measures are indeed implemented, especially in important areas of risk.

Examiners should establish whether senior management and the board receive effective communication from the management information system regarding the level of AML/CFT compliance, compliance issues, and trends in ML/TF risks being assumed by the institution. Similarly, examiners should ascertain if the policies and procedures are communicated effectively to other relevant business lines. It can be instructive to interview customer relationship managers in larger firms to ascertain the culture and compliance with the rules throughout the institution.

Examiners should also take into account whether the AML/CFT compliance framework addresses issues such as foreign branches, subsidiaries, mergers and acquisitions, and new business lines or product development.

Audit and Compliance Functions

The supervisor should ascertain the roles of the audit and compliance functions. Both the audit and compliance functions should have a reasonable degree of independence from the operational areas of the institution. These functions should be led by senior staff who report directly to the board. Hence, the examiners should review the adequacy of arrangements for reporting to the board and senior management, as appropriate.

The supervisor should examine whether the audit function is adequately resourced and independent and whether it tests compliance with the institution's AML/CFT procedures, policies, and controls, including the compliance function. Independent testing can generally be carried out by an internal audit department, external auditors, consultants, or other qualified independent parties.

The supervisor also should check the independence, quality, and resources of the AML/CFT compliance function. A board-approved AML/CFT compliance program should include the appointment of an AML/CFT compliance officer at the management level to ensure that the AML/CFT program is being implemented effectively. The core functions of the compliance officer are to oversee compliance with internal policies and controls and the applicable laws and regulations. The compliance officer should be highly knowledgeable about AML/CFT issues and should contribute to the development of AML/CFT systems and controls, including staff training. Interviewing AML/CFT compliance officers is therefore warranted.

Also, examiners should ascertain whether audit and compliance take a risk-based approach to their activities, giving enhanced attention to higher-risk areas.

AML/CFT Policies, Procedures, and Controls

This part of the examination assesses the effectiveness and implementation of the AML/CFT policies, procedures, and controls and whether they are proportional to the ML/TF risks of the institution. Key components are (a) customer due diligence, including enhanced and simplified measures, and ongoing monitoring; (b) suspicious transactions reporting; and (c) record keeping. Examiners should establish whether the procedures are risk based and effective.

To test the effective implementation of the policies and procedures, examiners should select customer files and transactions for review. This selection can be based on a combination of risk factors, such as customers in combination with products, services, transactions, geographic locations, and delivery channels. The size of the sample generally depends on the size of the institution, the ML/TF risks, and other factors, such as past breaches of laws and regulations. The size of the sample should be determined during the planning phase of the examination. Supervisors should develop a sampling procedure that captures an adequate representation of the risks posed by customers.

With respect to transaction testing, on-site examiners should keep in mind that the purpose of such controls is to verify whether the procedures and internal controls are implemented effectively. Under no circumstances should the examiner seek to detect whether the bank's clients are engaged in ML/TF operations. The on-site inspection must not be converted into investigative work; this task is the responsibility of the competent authorities (the FIU or law enforcement authorities). Of course, during their inspection, examiners can encounter transactions that they deem to be suspicious. In that case, they have a duty to check whether the bank is aware of them and has taken appropriate action. However, the inspector should not undertake additional research to determine whether or not the operation qualifies as an ML/TF operation.

Box 5.2 provides a list of examination questions and topics to guide examiners in their on-site processes; it should be adjusted according to the scope of the examination and the risk profile of the institution.

BOX 5.2 List of Possible Questions for Assessing Compliance with Customer Due Diligence Obligations

- Has the board approved the anti-money-laundering and combating the financing of terrorism (AML/CFT) or customer due diligence policy?
- Does the AML/CFT or customer due diligence policy adequately address the risks identified in the business-wide risk assessment?
- Are the policy and procedures in line with the AML/CFT legislation?
- Have the policy and procedures been disseminated to management and relevant employees and, if so, how?
- Are the policy and procedures reviewed periodically and adjusted, taking into account changes in risk or legislation?
- Do the customer due diligence procedures provide for the following?
  - Customer acceptance;
  - Customer rejection (but not based solely on United Nations sanctions);
  - Closure of accounts and business relationships;
  - Risk-based customer due diligence measures; and
  - Periodic or event-driven reviews.
- Are there adequate customer due diligence procedures for identifying and verifying the identity of business relationships and for customers that conduct an occasional transaction, and do these procedures address the following?
  - Customers that are natural persons or legal persons or arrangements;
  - Ongoing monitoring that is adequate for detecting unusual activities and changes in a customer's risk profile;
  - The purpose of the relationship and background of the customer; and
  - The frequency or triggers for updating customer due diligence information.
- Do customer due diligence procedures identify and verify the identity of beneficial owners, and do they gain insight into the ownership and control structure of a customer that is a legal person or a legal arrangement?
- Does the institution establish a risk profile of the customer that takes into account the customer due diligence information obtained, including source of funds?
- Does the institution apply simplified customer due diligence when lower-risk customers have been identified? Are simplified measures compliant with regulatory requirements where this is permitted?
- Have customers been identified as higher risk, and is that identification in line with the risk profile of the institution?
- Where higher-risk customers are identified, are enhanced customer due diligence measures applied? Are these measures proportional to the identified risks?
- Do customer due diligence policies and procedures adequately cover the identification of customers who are politically exposed persons, and are extended due diligence measures applied, including establishing the source of wealth?

(box continues on next page)

- Are extended due diligence measures applied with respect to correspondent relationships, including payable-through accounts?
- Do customer due diligence procedures cover business relationships established through or with the participation of third-party intermediaries?
- Are any of the customer due diligence procedures outsourced or conducted through third or related parties?
- Is customer due diligence conducted by using information from electronic identification databases (where available)?
- If suspicion was raised when applying customer due diligence procedures, were suspicious transaction reports filed with the financial intelligence unit?
- Do specific customer due diligence measures exist for certain categories of higher-risk customers? For example,
  - Legal arrangements, such as trusts;
  - Private banking customers;
  - Companies with nominee shareholders or bearer shares;
  - High-net-worth customers;
  - Cash-intensive businesses;
  - Casinos and gambling outlets;
  - Offshore entities;
  - Customers from high-risk jurisdictions; and
  - Customers that deal in virtual assets.

Customer Due Diligence

This part of the inspection seeks to ascertain whether the institution has risk-based customer due diligence policies and procedures that comply with legal requirements and are implemented effectively. Basel Core Principle (BCP) 29 on abuse of financial services provides a useful framework on what is expected from supervisors in relation to customer due diligence. As specified in Essential Criterion 5, the supervisor determines that banks establish customer due diligence policies and processes that are well documented and communicated to all relevant staff. The supervisor also determines that such policies and processes are integrated into the bank's overall risk management and that appropriate steps are taken to identify, assess, monitor, manage, and mitigate risks of ML/TF with respect to customers, countries, and regions as well as to products, services, transactions, and delivery channels on an ongoing basis.

The customer due diligence management program, on a group-wide basis, has the following essential elements:

- A customer acceptance policy that identifies business relationships that the bank will not accept based on identified risks

- A customer identification, verification, and due diligence program on an ongoing basis that encompasses verification of beneficial ownership, understanding of the purpose and nature of the business relationship, and risk-based reviews to ensure that records are updated and relevant

- Policies and processes to monitor and recognize unusual or potentially suspicious transactions

- Enhanced due diligence on high-risk accounts (for example, escalation to the bank's senior management of decisions on entering into business relationships with these accounts or maintaining such relationships when an existing relationship becomes high-risk)

- Enhanced due diligence on politically exposed persons (including, among other things, escalation to the bank's senior management level of decisions on entering into business relationships with these persons)

- Clear rules on what records must be kept on customer due diligence and individual transactions and how long they should be held; such records should be kept for at least a five-year period.

Suspicious Transactions Reporting

The examiner should review the adequacy of the systems used to monitor, detect, and report suspicious transactions. Monitoring for unusual and suspicious activities should be risk-based and consistent with the risk profile and enhanced monitoring of higher-risk areas. A key focus of the examination is to assess the robustness of the internal monitoring and reporting processes and the quality of the STRs filed with the FIU. The examiner should assess whether a manual or automated detection system is appropriate, depending on the risk profile, size, and complexity of the institution, and whether technological support for detecting suspicious transactions is appropriate. The review should also assess controls to prevent tip-offs as well as controls to safeguard the confidentiality and security of STR-related information.

The examiner should determine the following:

- Are processes manual or automated, and are they in line with the institution's size, risk profile, complexity, and so forth? Do the monitoring systems generate automated alerts? How are false positives identified?

- How often are monitoring systems reviewed for accuracy and effectiveness, including a periodic review of business rules and alerts to ensure that they reflect the business model?

- Are procedures and processes in place to analyze alerts and decide to file or not to file an STR? Is this process adequate?

- Is there a procedure and process for enhanced monitoring of high-risk clients, including politically exposed persons?

- What is the role of management, compliance, and internal audit in overseeing the effectiveness and integrity of the STR regime, including management information systems to inform senior management and the board about STR issues?

- What are the internal security and confidentiality protocols for handling STRs?

- Are there measures in place to prevent tip-offs?

- Is there effective training of staff to identify and deal with STR issues?

- Are specific procedures in place for dealing with monitoring and reporting concerning insiders and related parties of the bank (for example, staff and board)? How are staff accounts monitored?

- What are the procedures for reviewing business relationships for which STRs have been filed?

- Is the transaction-monitoring system capable of monitoring across all branches and accounts of a business relationship and for related transactions of a customer?

Record Keeping

To ensure that the institution complies with the regulatory requirements for recording information, the examiner should determine whether record-keeping procedures and systems are in place with respect to following issues:

- Are the following records retained?

  - Customer due diligence information;

  - Accounts and transaction records; and

  - Business correspondence.

- Is the retention period in line with the legal requirement, and did it start at the beginning of a one-off transaction or closure of a business relationship?

- Is there a security system, including physical storage, backup and recovery, and cybersecurity?

- Is there a retrieval system for complying with requests for information from competent authorities in a timely manner?

- Are records sufficient for reconstructing accounts for use by competent authorities?

- Does a policy cover outsourcing arrangements for record keeping?

AML/CFT Resources

An important part of the inspection is to assess whether the institution has adequate resources to support implementation of its AML/CFT compliance framework. Examiners should focus on assessing whether the institution devotes sufficient resources to the business and to compliance for AML/CFT purposes, taking into account the risk profile and size of the institution.

Examiners should establish that there is an ongoing employee training program to ensure that all employees are kept informed of ML/TF risks and AML/CFT requirements. Examiners need to assess the substance of the AML/CFT training program to determine whether it is sufficiently tailored to the type of institution and its risk profile. This review should focus on the following:

- Adequacy of the training facilities, taking into account the institution's size, risk profile, and number of staff;

- Appropriate training for all staff, including management and the board;

- Training addressing higher-risk business activities and processes;

- Adequacy of web-based training and e-learning facilities; and

- Training for cross-border branches and subsidiaries.

Part of the examination relates to the institution's processes for assessing the integrity of employees, during recruitment and ongoing or periodically. It should assess whether the institution has screening procedures to ensure high standards and to avoid any conflicts of interest. The inspection with respect to processes should focus on the following:

- Screening procedures for employees, including consultants, and more stringent screening for employees who will be working in high-risk areas;

- A policy prohibiting employees from managing their own accounts or accounts on behalf of related parties and additional controls on the ability of employees to access their own accounts; and

- A policy on penalties for violations of internal rules and legislation by employees.

OTHER EXAMINATION PROCEDURES

In addition to the examination procedures related to the general AML/CFT compliance framework described above, specific AML/CFT topics may need to be evaluated in some cases. For instance, the supervisor may want to assess whether the institution has adequately assessed specific inherent risks related to geography or delivery channels. Specific examination procedures will also be relevant for certain high-risk customers, such as correspondent relationships.

Geographic Risk

Examiners need to ascertain whether the institution's AML/CFT framework takes adequate account of geographic risk exposure, both domestic and cross-border, with respect to its client base and branch and subsidiary network. Such an assessment is important for determining whether the institution adequately identifies and assesses the risks when establishing or acquiring foreign branches or subsidiaries.

The examination of geographic risk exposure should undertake the following:

- Assess whether the institution's policy and procedures take into account FATF-listed jurisdictions and United Nations–sanctioned jurisdictions as well as other reliable sources, such as the national risk assessment;

- Determine whether the institution's geographic risk assessment captures high-risk domestic regions;

- Assess whether the institution assesses the jurisdiction's risks with respect to its branches and subsidiaries;

- Assess whether the institution takes geographic risk into account when assessing or reviewing business relationships and monitoring transactions; and

- Assess whether enhanced customer due diligence measures are implemented for business relationships in higher-risk jurisdictions.

Delivery Channels

ML/TF practices can proliferate amid digital financial platforms that facilitate anonymity in transactions, jeopardizing the overall integrity of the financial system. Fintech activities carry important risks to integrity, such as identity theft and online extortion (for example, ransomware attacks). The use of crypto assets, which are increasingly popular in emerging markets, raises important concerns. Several high-profile cases of criminal activities have surfaced in recent years,[3] calling for the authorities' attention and prompting the FATF to issue a new recommendation specifically for virtual asset services providers.[4]

In this context, the role of AML/CFT supervisors is essential. Examiners need to ascertain whether the institution's AML/CFT framework takes adequate account of the high inherent risk of certain delivery channels, including the risks associated with new technologies for delivering services to customers.

The examination of delivery channels should undertake the following:

- Determine that the ML/TF risk assessment addresses risks from non-face-to-face situations where there are no specific safeguards and that an ML/TF risk assessment is conducted before new technologies for delivering services are introduced;

- Determine that the institution assesses the risks of the use of new technologies and platforms to initiate business relationships or conduct transactions, particularly when there is non-face-to-face contact without specific safeguards;

- Assess whether compliance and audit have a role in these processes prior to introducing new technologies; and

- Assess whether the institution takes delivery channel risks into account when assessing or reviewing business relationships, including enhanced customer due diligence measures for business relationships when there is no face-to-face contact without specific safeguards.

Correspondent Relationships

Large international banks typically act as correspondents for thousands of other banks around the world. These respondent banks may receive a wide range of services, including cash management, international funds transfers, payable-through accounts, and foreign exchange services. With respect to the role assigned to the supervisor in relation to correspondent relationships, BCP 29, Essential Criterion 6, stipulates that, in addition to normal due diligence, banks should have policies and processes regarding correspondent banking. Such bank policies and processes should include (a) gathering sufficient information about their respondent banks to understand the nature of their business and customer base and how they are supervised; and (b) having rules against establishing or continuing correspondent relationships with banks that do not have adequate controls against criminal activities, are not supervised effectively by the relevant authorities, or are considered to be shell banks. Supervisors are expected to verify that this is the case in practice.

In recent years, large international banks have terminated, restricted, or threatened to terminate correspondent relationships with respondent banks across the globe. This loss of correspondent relationships—commonly known as de-risking—seriously damages the provision of domestic and cross-border payments.

In line with FATF Recommendation 13, a jurisdiction's AML/CFT legislation needs to have specific customer due diligence obligations with respect to correspondent relationships. Even though these requirements are for the correspondent banks, not the respondent banks, supervisors in jurisdictions with respondent banks whose accounts are or may be terminated or restricted can take measures to strengthen the AML/CFT supervisory regime to meet the FATF standards and address the national and sectoral ML/TF risks. The following are some of these measures:

- Enhance transparency of the supervisory framework and make available information on AML/CFT enforcement measures imposed on institutions;

- Ensure that the respondent banks have no business relationships with shell banks, wherever located; and

- Strictly supervise the AML/CFT compliance framework of respondent banks and ensure that they meet their AML/CFT obligations, including enhanced customer due diligence measures on nested correspondent accounts and on customers who directly access payable-through accounts.

For banks whose accounts have been terminated, supervisors should investigate the exacerbating factors and circumstances and take the necessary supervisory and corrective measures where deficiencies are identified.

In developing a risk-based AML/CFT supervision plan, supervisory authorities should be aware that "de-risking can frustrate AML/CFT objectives and may not be an effective way to fight financial crime and terrorism financing. By pushing higher-risk transactions out of the regulated system into more opaque, informal channels, they become harder to monitor" (World Bank 2016). Supervisory authorities have a key role to play in strengthening the AML/CFT regime and providing guidance on the AML/CFT requirements to ensure their consistent implementation.

EXAMINATION FINDINGS AND THE EXAMINATION REPORT

Examiners should determine the level of compliance with each specific requirement being examined, based on a general classification of how the findings will be assessed. For instance, table 5.1 presents an example of a classification of compliance with the requirement to identify and verify the identity of a customer.

TABLE 5.1 Example of an Assessment of Compliance with an AML/CFT Requirement

Customer due diligence: identification and verification of the identity				
The identification of a client and the verification of the identity of the client should be done on the basis of documents, data, or information obtained from a reliable and independent source.				
Expected behavior	**Compliant**	**Largely compliant**	**Partially compliant**	**Not compliant**
The institution has policies and procedures for identifying and verifying the identity of customers, and those procedures are implemented adequately. Evidence of this verification is recorded in the customer files.	There are clear procedures for verifying the identity that describe the documents to be used and in which cases a certified copy or an apostille is required. Procedures are applied in practice, and documents are present in the examined customer files.	There are mostly clear procedures for verifying the identity that describe the documents to be used. Procedures are not always applied in practice, and required documents are not always present in the examined customer files.	The procedures only give some examples of documents that can be used to verify the identity of customers. In several examined customer files, incorrect documents are found or ones not duly certified.	The procedures do not describe the documents to be used. In the examined customer files, there are hardly any documents indicating that the identity of the customer has been verified.

Source: World Bank.

Based on the examination results, supervisors should reach sound conclusions with respect to the effectiveness of the AML/CFT compliance framework of the institution and determine whether there are deficiencies and breaches of law. The examination should provide supervisors with the essential elements for writing an examination report that the institution can use to improve its AML/CFT compliance systems and practices. The examination report should clearly show that the objectives of the inspection were achieved and provide a sound basis for addressing the findings and identified deficiencies. For internal purposes, the examination report should provide a proper basis for determining enforcement actions for noncompliance with AML/CFT requirements. This report should follow the enforcement and sanctions policy and procedures of the supervisory authority.

Developing Conclusions and Recommendations

When developing conclusions for the examination report, the examiners should take account of all pertinent findings arising from the inspection and determine the following:

- Is the AML/CFT compliance system proportional and adequate in relation to the institution's risk profile, size, and complexity?

- Are the board of directors and senior management fully engaged in overseeing implementation of the AML/CFT program and knowledgeable about their institution's risks and compliance obligations?

- Does the institution adequately identify and assess the inherent ML/TF risks with respect to customers, products, services, geographic exposure, and delivery channels?

- Does the institution have adequate AML/CFT policies, procedures, and controls in line with legal requirements and implement these policies, procedures, and controls effectively?

- Is the audit function independent, and does it execute AML/CFT–related audits in compliance with the applicable AML/CFT laws and regulations?

- Is the AML/CFT compliance function competent, and does it have the necessary resources and authority to carry out its responsibilities?

- Is there an adequate training program supported by the compliance function that takes into account the risk profile, size, and complexity of operations?

Examiners should also determine whether deficiencies or violations previously identified by the supervisor or through compliance monitoring or an audit have been remedied. They should also assess the overall level of compliance, as shown in table 5.2.

TABLE 5.2 Example of an Assessment of the Overall Level of AML/CFT Compliance

Assessed level of compliance	Description
Compliant	Level of compliance exposes the institution to low risks due to no or minor gaps; no administrative sanction or other measures; no notable impact on reputation
Largely compliant	Level of compliance exposes the institution to moderate risks due to several gaps; limited administrative sanction or other measures; some reputational risk

(table continues next page)

TABLE 5.2 *(continued)*

Assessed level of compliance	Description
Partially compliant	Level of compliance exposes the institution to significant risks due to major gaps; major administrative sanctions or other measures, including a fine; major reputational risk
Not compliant	Level of compliance exposes the institution to serious risks due to material gaps; significant administrative or criminal sanctions, including fines; loss of operating license, grave reputational impact

Source: World Bank.

The assessment of findings should be the basis for recommending enforcement measures and sanctions. Additionally, the risk profile of the institution should be updated.

Structure of the Examination Report

As indicated, at the end of the on-site examination, the key preliminary findings should be discussed with the management of the institution. These discussions and management's commitments should be documented in the final examination report.

The supervisory authority or the AML/CFT supervision unit should determine the structure for the examination report based on several factors. Nevertheless, the examination report should follow a consistent, agreed-on format. Furthermore, the type, scope, objectives, and findings of the examination should generally determine the content and length of the report.

The following basic outline provides a guide for drafting the report:

● Background of the institution, including the type of institution, type and date of license, corporate structure, markets, and business model;[5]

● Summary of the ML/TF risk profile as determined by the off-site risk assessment, subject to the discretion of the supervisory authority, which may not want to disclose detailed information on its risk assessment of the institution;

● Description of the legal basis, objective, type, scope, and duration of the examination and names of the examiners;

● Summary of key findings and recommendations of the examination;

● Description of the examination procedures that were applied;

● Description of findings for each area examined, supported by deficiencies found in customer or transaction files; and

● Clear recommendations for corrective measures, action plan, and timelines.

World Bank's Data Collection Tool for Supervisory Activities

The World Bank has developed a basic supervision data tool to support the supervisory authorities in keeping the summary records of the on-site supervisory activities and conducting strategic analyses based on these records. This simple tool asks the authorities to record the following systematically:

- Examination dates and total time spent for an examination;

- Examination team;

- Focus and characteristics of the examination (full, partial, thematic);

- Inherent and residual risk levels before and after the examination;

- Ratings for examination areas (customer due diligence, STR, governance, and compliance function);

- Findings of the examination (policies, procedures, and effectiveness aspects);

- Recommendations and relevant deadlines; and

- Sanctions (as a result of the examination).

The outputs of the tool aim to support the authorities in undertaking the following activities:

- Track the on-site supervision activities in all institutions

- Monitor the general trends about efficiency of AML/CFT controls;

- Track the recommendations and progress made by the institutions; and

- Track trends in inherent and residual risks in the sector.

Monitoring and analyzing such kinds of data on supervision activities can eventually inform strategic decisions such as planning staff and other resources, determining focus areas for future supervision, identifying common deficiencies at the institutions, and developing guidance and training material accordingly. Annex 5A presents the entry fields and some outputs of this data collection tool.

ANNEX 5A WORLD BANK'S AML/CFT SUPERVISION DATA COLLECTION TOOL

○ AML/CFT Supervision Data App
File View

DATA ENTRY FORM

- ⌂ Home
- ✎ Data Entry Form
- ▤ Manage Cases
- ⅃⅃ Charts and Graphs
- ⚙ Configuration
- ⚙ New User
- ⚙ Manage Users
- ⚙ DataImport
- ⇄ Import History
- ⚙ Logout

Data Entry Form

GENERAL INFO

Database Record Number (DRN) *	0016	❶
Entry Date (MM/DD/YYYY) *	7/24/2020	❶
Entry made by *		❶
Country/State of Inspection (if applies)		❶
Sector *	Select ▾	❶
Inspected Institution *	Select ▾	❶
Start & End Dates (MM/DD/YYYY) *	7/24/2020 7/24/2020 ❶	
Inspection Report Date (MM/DD/YYYY)* & Ref. No. *	7/24/2020 Ref No	❶
Inspected Permises *		❶

INSPECTION TEAM

Inspector	Days for Prep.	Days for Inspection	Days for Reporting	Total	
Lead *					❶

+ Add More

| | Total * | | | | | ❶ |

INSPECTION PLANNING

Last AML/CFT Inspection Completion Date	AML/CFT Inspection Date	

	Inherent Risk Level	Residual Risk Level
Risk Rating from Last Inspection *	Select ▾	Select ▾
Risk Rating from Off-site Supervision/Monitoring *	Select ▾	Select ▾

Is the Inspection: ❶

Standalone	☐
As part of Prudential	☐

Is the Inspection: ❶

Full fledged	☐
Partial focused	☐
Thematic (holistic)	☐

Risk Based Inspection Plan

Short Narrative

Upload Supporting documents   [upload]

(continues next page)

ANNEX 5A *(continued)*

DATA ENTRY FORM

INSPECTION RESULTS

	Rating for Policies/Procedure ⓘ	Rating for Effectiveness ⓘ	Findings ⓘ
Board's and Management's Comments.	Select ▾	Select ▾	Findings
Compliance Office and Unit	Select ▾	Select ▾	Findings
Customer Due Diligence	Select ▾	Select ▾	Findings
Record Keeping (including MIS)	Select ▾	Select ▾	Findings
Monitoring (including MIS)	Select ▾	Select ▾	Findings
Suspicious Transaction Reporting	Select ▾	Select ▾	Findings
Internal Contorl and Audit	Select ▾	Select ▾	Findings
Training and Staff Knowledge	Select ▾	Select ▾	Findings
Others	Select ▾	Select ▾	

	Rating for Policies/Procudures	Rating for Effectiveness	
Overall Compliance	Select ▾	Select ▾	ⓘ

	Inherint Risk Level	Residual Risk Level	
Overall Risk Level	Select ▾	Select ▾	ⓘ
Risk Profile Summary	Short Narrative		

CORRECTIVE ACTIONS

	Yes/No	Explaination ⓘ	Amount	Currency ⓘ
Warning Letter	☑			
Administrative Fine	☑			Select ▾
Criminal Fine	☐			
Suspension of License	☐			
Revokation of License	☐			
Temporary ban for officials	☐			
Permanet ban for officials	☐			
Reffered to prosecution (for criminal charges).	☐			

RECOMMENDATIONS

Recommendation	Mapping	Deadline
	Select ▾	7/24/2020

+ Add More

ATTACHMENTS

Inspection Report	upload
Other Supporting documents	upload

Save As Draft   Save Case

Inspection results

Overall ratings

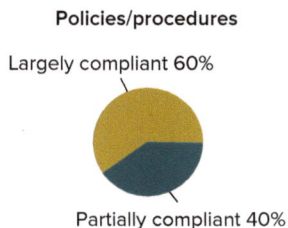

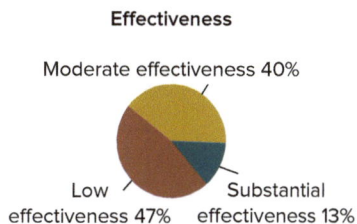

Policies/procedures

Largely compliant 60%

Partially compliant 40%

Effectiveness

Moderate effectiveness 40%

Low effectiveness 47%

Substantial effectiveness 13%

Board and management's commitment

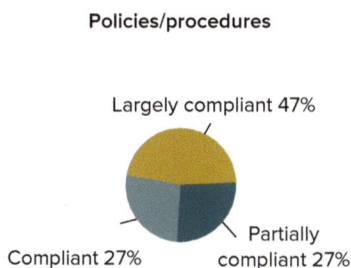

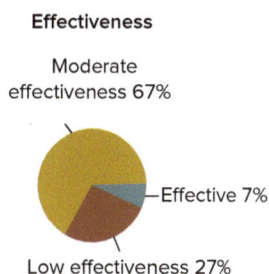

Policies/procedures

Largely compliant 47%

Compliant 27%

Partially compliant 27%

Effectiveness

Moderate effectiveness 67%

Effective 7%

Low effectiveness 27%

Monitoring (including MIS)

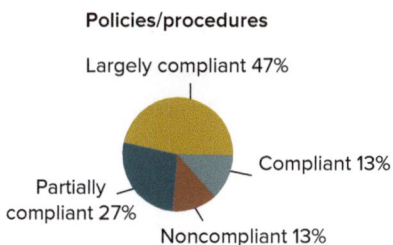

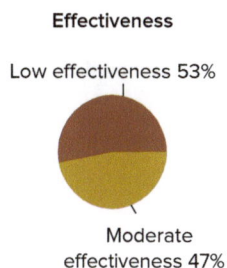

Policies/procedures

Largely compliant 47%

Compliant 13%

Partially compliant 27%

Noncompliant 13%

Effectiveness

Low effectiveness 53%

Moderate effectiveness 47%

Suspicious transaction reporting

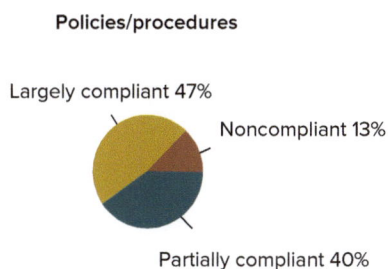

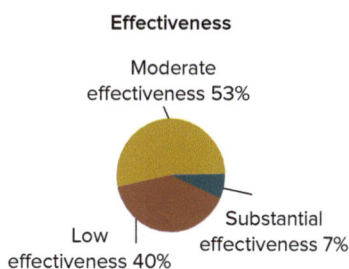

Policies/procedures

Largely compliant 47%

Noncompliant 13%

Partially compliant 40%

Effectiveness

Moderate effectiveness 53%

Substantial effectiveness 7%

Low effectiveness 40%

NOTES

1. Instead of asking the full list of customers, which might become overwhelming in the case of systemically important banks, examiners are advised to select certain types of customers that may present a particular risk, for example, nonresidents, politically exposed persons, cash-intensive businesses, and so forth.

2. The home supervisor should treat the termination or restriction of a correspondent account as a warning sign, as it may suggest serious concerns from the correspondent bank about the quality— or lack thereof—of the AML/CFT regime of its respondent.

3. See, for example, the case of Crypto Capital Corporation in Poland, which held bank accounts in a small rural bank and laundered illegal proceeds through a cryptocurrency exchange firm. For further details, see Faccia and others (2020).

4. See the new interpretive note to FATF Recommendation 15, as amended in October 2021 (FATF 2021, 76).

5. If this is not the institution's first on-site examination, and no changes have occurred in the background of the institution, the examination report could simply refer back to a prior examination report.

REFERENCES

Faccia, Alessio, Narcisa Roxana Mosteanu, Luigi Pio Leonardo Cavaliere, and Leondardo Jose Mataruna Dos Santos. 2020. "Electronic Money Laundering, the Dark Side of Fintech: An Overview of the Most Recent Cases." In *Proceedings of the 2020 12th International Conference on Information Management and Engineering*, 29–34. Osaka: ICIME.

FATF (Financial Action Task Force). 2021. "Guidance on Risk-Based Supervision." FATF, Paris. https://www.fatf-gafi.org/publications/documents/Guidance-RBA-Supervision.html.

World Bank. 2016. "Brief: De-risking in the Financial Sector." *Understanding Poverty* (blog), October 7. https://www.worldbank.org/en/topic/financialsector/brief/de-risking-in-the-financial-sector.

CHAPTER 6

Sanctions and Enforcement Measures

OVERVIEW

A robust system of enforcement measures and sanctions—whether criminal, civil, or administrative—for failure to comply with anti-money-laundering and combating the financing of terrorism (AML/CFT) requirements is a fundamental requirement of an effective AML/CFT system. Specifically, jurisdictions need to ensure that remedial actions and effective, proportionate, and dissuasive sanctions are applied in practice. An effective, proportionate, and dissuasive sanctioning regime is critical for compliance with AML/CFT laws and regulations. It also sends a clear signal of the (political) determination of the authorities to combat money laundering and terrorism financing (ML/TF) in their jurisdiction.

This chapter provides insight into the level of compliance with the relevant Financial Action Task Force (FATF) recommendations. It also outlines a range of sanctions and enforcement measures that authorities can implement in their supervised sectors as well as some contextual factors of an effective framework and issues related to the publication of sanctions. This chapter also gives examples of sanctions that have been handed down in some jurisdictions and outlines the basic requirements for processing enforcement measures and sanctions.

COMPLIANCE WITH THE FATF STANDARD

This section describes the importance of establishing an AML/CFT sanctioning regime in accordance with international standards. Recommendation 35 states that jurisdictions should have a range of effective, proportionate, and dissuasive sanctions for failure to comply with the preventive measures. In addition, Recommendation 27 requires that supervisors have powers to impose sanctions for failure to comply with the AML/CFT requirements. These powers include a range of disciplinary and financial sanctions, including the power to withdraw, restrict, or suspend the financial institution's license, where applicable. The FATF guidance on effective supervision and enforcement provides a comprehensive guide on remedial actions and sanctions (FATF 2015a). Also, according to Basel Core Principle (BCP) 29 on abuse of financial services (which refers to the FATF recommendations), supervisors should have adequate powers to take action against a bank that does not comply with its AML/CFT obligations.

Deficiencies in the sanctioning regime and low levels of effective implementation will lead to poor compliance with FATF Recommendation 35. As shown in figure 6.1, more than half of the 119 assessed jurisdictions are largely compliant or compliant with FATF Recommendation 35.

However, when looking separately at jurisdictions that are members of the FATF and jurisdictions that are members of an FATF-style regional body (FSRB), figure 6.2 shows that 41 percent of the 89 assessed FSRB members are partially compliant or noncompliant with this requirement, whereas 80 percent of the 30 assessed FATF members are largely or fully compliant.

FIGURE 6.1 FATF Assessments of Compliance with Recommendation 35, 2021

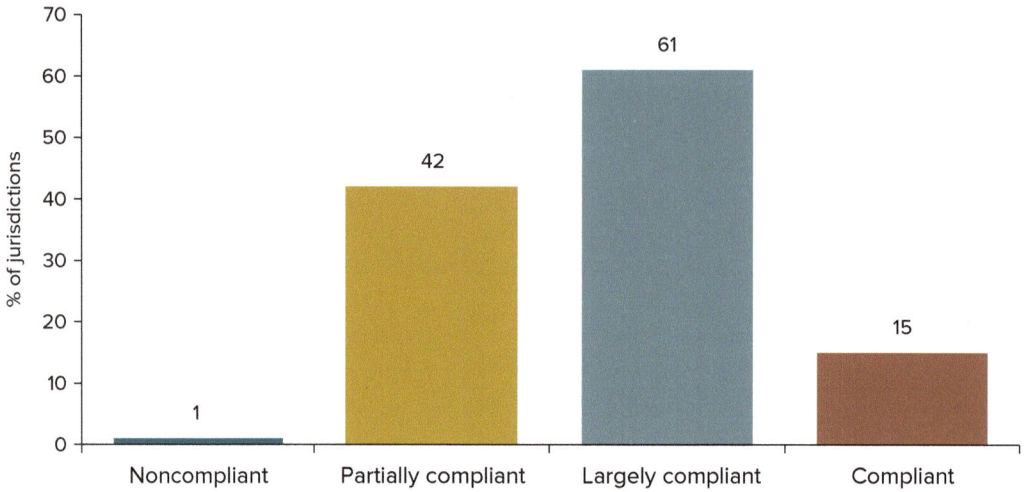

Source: Financial Action Task Force (FATF) consolidated assessment ratings, updated November 8, 2021.

FIGURE 6.2 FATF Assessments of Compliance of FATF and FSRB Members with Recommendation 35, 2021

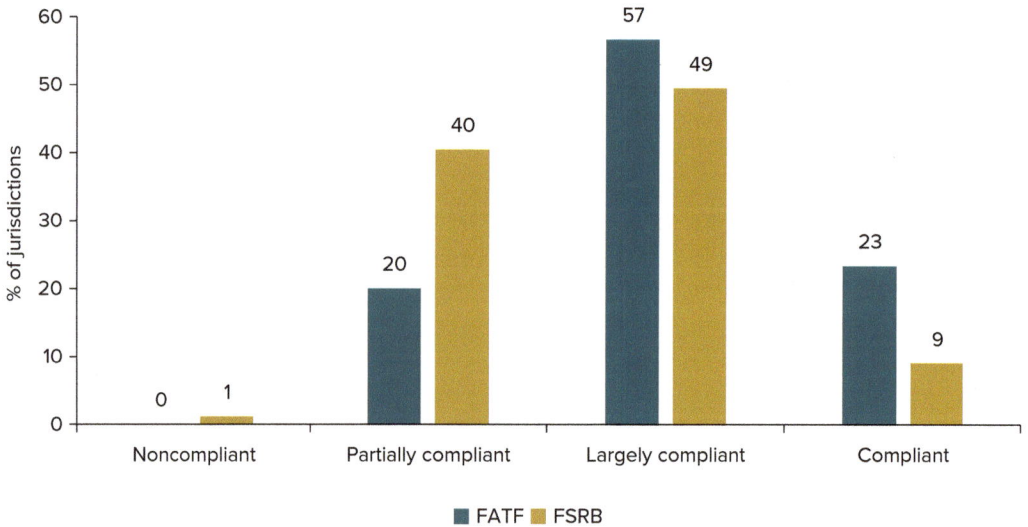

Source: Financial Action Task Force (FATF) consolidated assessment ratings, updated November 8, 2021.
Note: FSRB = FATF-style regional body.

CONTEXTUAL FACTORS OF AN EFFECTIVE ENFORCEMENT AND SANCTIONING REGIME

A strong system of sanctions is critical to combating ML/TF. Even the most well-designed AML/CFT laws and regulations will not be effective if they are not adequately enforced. Specifically, sanctions support the broad goals of AML/CFT in the following ways:

- Safeguarding the integrity and soundness of the financial system by deterring banks and other financial institutions from wittingly or unwittingly engaging in criminal activities;

- Supporting the investigation and prosecution of ML/TF and related predicate crimes; and

- Promoting sound governance and ethical practices in the financial sector and broader economy.

Every jurisdiction should have a sanctioning regime that is based on and takes account of the legislative system, jurisprudence, legal practices and traditions, and systems of government. In addition, all jurisdictions should implement a legal, regulatory, and institutional framework that enables enforcement actions to be taken for failure to comply with the AML/CFT requirements. Factors such as context and risks in the jurisdiction are important to consider when setting up a sanctioning regime:

- *Jurisdiction context.* The size, structure, and complexity of the jurisdiction as well as its financial and economic sectors may influence the nature and complexity of the legal framework and requirements for the enforcement and sanctioning regime. Jurisdictions with a common-law system will differ from those with a civil law regime. In addition, the constitutional structure of government will determine enforcement and sanctions, for instance, at the national or federal level vs. state or other government administrative level. With regard to the size and complexity of institutions, some jurisdictions with very large internationally active banks have applied multi-million-dollar sanctions. Jurisdictions with much smaller financial sectors and institutions may apply proportionately smaller penalties for noncompliance.

- *Risk.* National and sectoral ML/TF risk assessments can determine the level and nature of sanctions to be applied. For instance, jurisdictions with very high exposure to terrorism and terrorism financing may apply proportionately stiffer penalties for CFT noncompliance. Similar approaches can be taken for AML noncompliance by jurisdictions faced with, for instance, serious drug, corruption, and human trafficking crimes. Penalties should adhere to the principle of dissuasiveness, with tougher penalties for serious threats. Jurisdictions can, as a matter of policy, take a risk-based approach to enforcement and sanctions, with more severe sanctions for noncompliance in cases of higher risk. Sanctions should also be applied against boards of directors and management, controlling owners, and other employees of regulated entities, depending on their level of responsibility in committing the breach, especially if the breach is intentional or serious.

Additionally, establishing an effective enforcement and sanctioning regime requires jurisdictions to meet several basic and universal preconditions. Each jurisdiction should clearly designate the authority or authorities with the power to apply sanctions for noncompliance with AML/CFT requirements. In some jurisdictions, both the financial or AML/CFT supervisor and the financial intelligence unit (FIU) are legally vested with the authority to impose sanctions. In other jurisdictions, the FIU, not the supervisor, has the power to enforce AML/CFT requirements. In yet other jurisdictions, the supervisor has AML/CFT sanctioning power over the institutions it supervises. Irrespective of national arrangements, the supervised entities should have a clear understanding of who is the sanctioning authority (or authorities). Where there is more than one possible sanctioning authority, it is important to have effective coordination to avoid applying different levels and types of sanctions for similar offenses. In addition, it is important to avoid the risk of "double jeopardy," where an institution is sanctioned twice for the same offense. This situation can arise even where only one AML/CFT sanctioning authority is designated but where the prudential supervisor is separate and can also use its prudential supervision powers to apply sanctions for AML/CFT purposes.

The nature and range of sanctions themselves should rest on a strong legislative basis, including where the law allows for the publication of sanctions. In some jurisdictions, this basis is found in the financial sector laws, while in others, the AML/CFT legislation itself contains the specific sanctioning provisions. Sometimes, sanctioning powers contained in both types of legislation can be applied for AML/CFT purposes, and it is therefore important to establish policies and procedures for determining which powers will be used and in what circumstances. The legal framework should adhere to the principle of proportionality and dissuasiveness through a range of possible actions, including warning letters, restrictions, cease-and-desist powers, monetary fines, and license suspension and revocation. The legal framework should also allow for an appeal process where there are reasonable grounds for challenging the actions of the sanctioning authority. This process can be administrative (for example, an appeals board) or judicial through the normal court system.

It is also paramount that supervisors have operational independence to enforce their decisions. The irrevocability of the supervisory mandate helps to assure this independence, as does the adoption of a regime of legal protections that prevents supervisors from being exposed to any kind of external interference or from being sued for acts performed in good faith in the exercise of their duties. It is, of course, essential to the professionalism and impartiality of the decision-making process that the persons in charge of imposing remedial measures and sanctions are of high professional and ethical standards, skills, and integrity. They should also be subject to strict confidentiality requirements.

A jurisdiction needs to have a strong tradition of respect for the rule of law and a framework of good governance. The absence of these elements may compromise the application of sanctions in a fair, consistent, and legal way. Banks and other financial institutions are influential institutions in most jurisdictions and are sometimes owned or controlled by politically exposed persons or their associates. In this environment, the supervisor or sanctioning authority should ensure institutions' operational independence and integrity.

RANGE OF POSSIBLE SANCTIONS AND REMEDIAL MEASURES

The objectives of enforcement measures and sanctions are generally twofold. On the one hand, some measures are aimed at remediation.[1] These types of measures instruct a financial institution to remediate the deficiencies within a set time frame. On the other hand, some sanctions, such as fines, are aimed at punishment. Generally, it should be possible to impose both types of sanctions at the same time for the same infringement.

The range of sanctions that jurisdictions can impose on noncompliant financial institutions should be as broad as possible. According to FATF guidance, "Supervisory authorities should have access to a range of remedial actions and sanctions that can be applied based on the level and nature of identified deficiencies or gaps in the regulated entity's AML/CFT controls and risk management system. This range could include warnings, action letters, orders, agreements, administrative sanctions, penalties, fines, and other restrictions and conditions on an entity's activities that may be progressive in severity, requiring entities to remedy AML/CFT deficiencies and any breach of AML/CFT obligations or failure to mitigate risks in a timely manner" (FATF 2021, para. 84) According to the Basel Core Principles for Effective Banking Supervision, an effective regime allows supervisors to make a graduated response depending on the nature of the problem or failure.

The sanction imposed in a given case varies according to each jurisdiction's legal and constitutional regime and the particular circumstances of the case. No single model of sanctions, therefore, can be generally applied. Some jurisdictions use a large array of measures that range from reprimands to license withdrawals. Others emphasize administrative sanctions and focus less on financial penalties.

In deciding on a sanction, supervisors should be aware of the tension between the sanctions for AML/CFT infringements and their impact on the viability of financial institutions. Heavy fines, in particular, may have an impact on an institution's financial situation and continuity. Supervisors should be able to impose sanctions with respect to AML/CFT, but nevertheless be wary of the prudential effects.

According to the Basel Committee on Banking Supervision, deficiencies in banks' AML/CFT systems could have prudential consequences. For example, AML/CFT deficiencies could result in significant regulatory actions or criminal penalties that may lead to reputational damage affecting the bank's operations, such as depositor outflows, loss of counterparties, or loss of market access, including loss of correspondent banking relationships. Additionally, failures in AML/CFT may lead to the revocation of a banking license or the termination of deposit insurance in some jurisdictions (BCBS 2020, annex 5, para. 6). Enforcing compliance with AML/CFT requirements is not an easy exercise, and multiple aspects, sometimes conflicting, should be considered. Box 6.1 provides some insights from the FATF on how to apply remedial measures and sanctions in the context of risk-based supervision.

BOX 6.1 Extract from FATF Guidance: Applying Remedial Actions and Sanctions in the Context of Risk-Based Supervision

In assessing the appropriate remedial actions or sanctions to apply in a risk-based supervision approach, supervisors should consider the following:

● The nature of findings: deficiencies in relation to higher-risk areas—including those identified in a national, sectoral, or supervisory risk assessment—could be prioritized for remedial action or sanctions as appropriate;

● The impact or harm that the identified deficiency or gap in terms of money-laundering and terrorism financing (ML/TF) risk exposure of the entity, sector, and the public (for example, whether it is a systemic breakdown, isolated incident, or other egregious activity, such as failing to report large volumes of suspicious activity or other required reports and the length of time the identified deficiency or gap in the regulated entity's risk management system remained outstanding or uncorrected; supervisors may consider the scope of the deficiency in terms of the probability of the risks materializing, given the entity's size, nature, geographic reach, and volume of business conduct);

(box continues on next page)

BOX 6.1 *(continued)*

● Using the power to withdraw, restrict, or suspend the entity's license (or equivalent for those registered), where applicable, for example, in situations where the entity has been determined by legal process to have engaged in criminal activity related to ML or TF, a severe and systematic violation of anti-money-laundering and combating the financing of terrorism (AML/CFT) measures, or similarly applicable sanctions or prohibition of directors and senior managers; and

● Publishing the results of the supervisory actions and providing information on the relevant entities' deficiencies to help address risks across the sector, as other entities take note of the consequences of similar failings.

Source: Extract, with minor edits, from FATF 2021, para. 85.

Effective, Proportionate, and Dissuasive Sanctions

The sanctions should be effective, proportionate, and dissuasive. To be effective, the type and severity of sanctions applied should be consistent with or proportional to the nature and gravity of the offense committed. Similarly, to be dissuasive, stiffer penalties are required for serious and repeat offenses. For example, a small fine or a warning letter to a financial institution is not a dissuasive sanction for serious breaches. Effectiveness can be assessed over time with respect to the impact of sanctions on the level of compliance by an institution to determine whether the sanctioning regime is achieving the desired results regarding compliance and risk mitigation.

There is no requirement to establish a regime encompassing all three types of sanctions (criminal, civil, and administrative). The type of sanctions available will be determined by the legal system and conventions of each jurisdiction and by the type of offenses prescribed by law. As the FATF puts it, supervisors should avoid taking a "zero-tolerance" or "zero-failure" approach. A sanctioning regime based only on criminal measures will not suffice, because it does not meet the proportionality test. The application of a criminal sanction like imprisonment for failure to comply with AML/CFT obligations could, for example, be disproportionate to the nature of the breach and, as a result, probably would not (easily) be invoked. In contrast, the failure to file suspicious transactions reports (STRs) intentionally or to comply with the obligations related to supervising terrorism financing or prohibiting tip-offs may attract more severe sanctions, including criminal penalties. In practice, several jurisdictions have established a wide range of civil, administrative, and criminal sanctions that can be combined.

To ensure that sanctions are proportionate, supervisory and AML/CFT laws provide for a range of enforcement actions to suit the circumstances. Should the deficiency detected be relatively minor, an informal action might be warranted, such as a warning letter to the institution's management. In other instances, more formal action may be necessary, and the severity of the sanction imposed will depend on the seriousness of the violation and the level of culpability. The principle of proportionality requires that the sanction reflects the nature of the violation: multiple and repetitive failures should carry higher sanctions than a single failure.

Box 6.2 describes an action taken by authorities in the United States and the United Kingdom.

BOX 6.2 Anti-Money-Laundering and Sanctions Violations: An Example from the United States and the United Kingdom

HSBC Holdings, a UK corporation headquartered in London, and HSBC Bank USA, a federally chartered banking corporation headquartered in McLean, Virginia—together known as HSBC—agreed to forfeit US$1.256 billion and enter into a deferred prosecution agreement with the US Justice Department for violating the Bank Secrecy Act, the International Emergency Economic Powers Act, and the Trading with the Enemy Act (US Department of Justice 2012). According to court documents, HSBC Bank USA failed to maintain an effective anti-money-laundering (AML) program or to conduct appropriate due diligence on its foreign correspondent account holders, a violation of the Bank Secrecy Act. The HSBC Group illegally conducted transactions on behalf of customers in Burma, Cuba, the Islamic Republic of Iran, Libya, and Sudan, violating the Emergency Economic Powers Act and the Trading with the Enemy Act. All of these jurisdictions were subject to sanctions enforced by the Office of Foreign Assets Control (OFAC) at the time of the transactions.

HSBC agreed to forfeit US$1.256 billion as part of its deferred prosecution agreement with the Department of Justice and agreed to pay US$665 million in civil penalties—US$500 million to the Office of the Comptroller of the Currency (OCC) and US$165 million to the Federal Reserve—for its AML program violations. The OCC penalty also satisfied a US$500 million civil penalty imposed by the Financial Crimes Enforcement Network (FinCEN). The bank's US$375 million settlement agreement with OFAC was satisfied by the forfeiture to the Department of Justice. The United Kingdom's Financial Services Authority pursued a separate action.

A four-count felony criminal information also was filed in federal court in the Eastern District of New York, charging HSBC with willfully failing to maintain an effective AML program, willfully failing to conduct due diligence on its foreign correspondent affiliates, and violating both the Emergency Economic Powers Act and the Trading with the Enemy Act. HSBC waived the federal indictment, agreed to the filing of the information, and accepted responsibility for its criminal conduct and that of its employees.

According to court documents, from 2006 to 2010, HSBC Bank USA severely understaffed its AML compliance function and failed to implement an AML program capable of adequately monitoring suspicious transactions and activities from HSBC Group affiliates, particularly HSBC Mexico, one of the bank's largest Mexican customers. It failed to monitor billions of dollars in purchases of physical US dollars, or "banknotes," from these affiliates. Despite evidence of serious money-laundering risks associated with doing business in Mexico, from at least 2006 to 2009, HSBC Bank USA rated Mexico as "standard" risk, its lowest AML risk category. As a result, HSBC Bank USA failed to monitor more than US$670 billion in wire transfers and more than US$9.4 billion in purchases of physical US dollars from HSBC Mexico during this period, when HSBC Mexico's own lax AML controls made it the preferred financial institution for drug cartels and money launderers.

Range of Sanctions

The range of sanctions for AML/CFT noncompliance should include the power to impose disciplinary and financial sanctions:

- Written warnings (in a separate letter or an examination report), including regular reports from the institution on the measures it is taking;

- Orders to comply (for example, cease-and-desist orders or an order subject to a penalty) with specific instructions (possibly accompanied by daily or monthly fines for noncompliance);

- Orders to engage outside independent professionals to review AML/CFT systems and recommend corrective actions;[2]

- A temporary ban on any person discharging managerial responsibilities in an institution or any other natural person held responsible for the breach from exercising managerial functions in a financial institution;

- Fines for noncompliance;

- Imposition of conservatorship, restrictions, suspension, or withdrawal of the license; and

- Imposition of criminal penalties, where appropriate.

With respect to banks, BCP 11, Essential Criterion 4, also sets out specific sanctioning and remedial measures that supervisors can employ (although these measures are not directed explicitly at cases of AML/CFT noncompliance). The following measures, among others, are relevant to AML/CFT failures:

- Restricting the current activities of the bank;

- Withholding approval of new activities or acquisitions;

- Restricting or suspending payments to shareholders or share repurchases and restricting asset transfers;

- Barring individuals from banking and replacing or restricting the powers of managers, board directors, or controlling owners; and

- Facilitating a takeover by or merger with a healthier institution, providing for the interim management of the bank, and revoking or recommending revocation of the banking license.

For very serious offenses, especially where there are major deficiencies, supervisors should have the authority to assume control of an institution that is failing to meet critical and essential AML/CFT requirements. An example is when an institution and its senior management have been grossly negligent or deliberately involved in ML/TF activities. In such cases, the supervisor should have the authority to impose conservatorship on an institution, assume control of it, close it down and have its license revoked, sell its operations, or merge it with another institution.

The supervisor should also be empowered to refer the case to the relevant criminal and judicial authorities for investigation and possible prosecution. Although the administrative and criminal processes are separate and distinct, a criminal conviction registered against an institution for ML/TF would clearly be cause for a supervisor to reevaluate the institution's directors and senior management in relation to fit and proper criteria.

In some legal systems, it may not be feasible to apply criminal sanctions to legal persons and arrangements, as doing so may entail imprisonment. In such cases, the severity of civil and administrative sanctions against legal persons and arrangements should be as severe as those applied to natural persons.

Box 6.3 provides an example of the sanctioning regime in France that illustrates the broad range of sanctions available for AML/CFT issues.

BOX 6.3 France: ACPR

The Autorité de Contrôle Prudentiel et de Resolution (ACPR) is an independent administrative authority chaired by the governor of the Banque de France, the French central bank, which is in charge of supervising the banking and insurance sectors, including with regard to anti-money-laundering and combating the financing of terrorism (AML/CFT).

The ACPR uses a range of remedial actions, depending on the breach (ACPR n.d.):

- *Follow-up letter.* In the context of off-site controls, the financial institution must provide explanations and documentation, possibly within a time limit.
- *Action letter.* Following the on-site inspection, a letter is transmitted systematically to the financial institution detailing the authority's findings and addressing recommendations within a specified timetable.

The ACPR also has administrative enforcement powers that are distinct from sanctions. These powers are a means of escalating enforcement when the nature of the deficiencies is more serious and the financial institution has the ability to correct these deficiencies by itself.

To enforce AML/CFT compliance, the ACPR issues cease-and-desist orders and requires the correction within a specific time period. At the end of the time period, a new on-site inspection is undertaken to ensure that the remedial measures have taken place; if they have not, the ACPR has the power to escalate to sanctions measures. Such administrative enforcement measures may be brought to the attention of the parent undertakings on a consolidated basis.

In addition, sanctions may include a warning, a reprimand, a prohibition on conducting certain operations for a maximum period of 10 years and any other restrictions on the conduct of its activity, the temporary suspension of senior managers for a maximum period of 10 years, the compulsory resignation of senior managers, the partial or total withdrawal of the license or authorization, and expulsion from the list of authorized entities. Instead of, or in addition to, these sanctions, a financial penalty of up to €100 million (€1 million for bureaux de change) may also be handed out.

The decisions taken by the Sanctions Committee are published in the official register of the ACPR and may be made public in any publication, newspaper, or media

(box continues on next page)

Sanctions to Be Applied to Directors and Senior Management

Where there has been a failure to comply with AML/CFT requirements, sanctions may be applied not only to the financial institution but also to its directors, senior management, controlling owners, and other employees of regulated entities.

Where directors and senior management facilitate or are responsible for AML/CFT violations by the institution, whether by commission or omission including negligence, they should be held accountable and subject to appropriate sanctions. Serious and deliberate violations of directors and senior management should be escalated to the law enforcement and prosecution authorities.

The scope of application is to directors and senior management only, on the assumption that compliance failures at the lower ranks of the organization are their ultimate responsibility. Nevertheless, since the tipping-off prohibition extends to all employees, there should be sanctions for all employees who breach this obligation. In the United Kingdom, for example, a financial penalty of £25,600 was imposed on the money-laundering reporting officer at Sonali Bank UK who, in successive years, failed to put in place an adequate compliance monitoring system, despite the warnings of internal auditors (Financial Conduct Authority 2016).

EXAMPLES OF ENFORCEMENT MEASURES AND SANCTIONS IN SOME JURISDICTIONS

Remedial Measures

Enforcement measures are intended to instruct the financial institution to remediate deficiencies expeditiously. Remedial measures aim to strengthen the AML/CFT compliance system of an institution and, more generally, to foster a culture of compliance. Where applicable, remedial measures should include action plans with well-defined timelines and follow-up action by the supervisor to ensure compliance.

When applying remedial measures, it is very important that supervisors clearly communicate their expectations and requirements to the financial institution with respect to the deficiencies and required measures. Major issues should always be brought to the attention of the board and senior management, who should be held accountable for implementing the remedial measures required.

The example in box 6.4 summarizes an agreement to remedy AML/CFT deficiencies in a bank in the United States.

BOX 6.4 Example of an Enforcement Action in the United States, July 2018

The most recent examination of the New York branch of United Bank Ltd., conducted by the Federal Reserve Bank of New York, identified deficiencies relating to the branch's risk management and compliance with federal and state laws, rules, and regulations relating to anti-money-laundering (AML) compliance under the Bank Secrecy Act.

Corporate governance and management oversight. Union Bank's board of directors and the New York branch's management agreed to, within 60 days of the agreement, submit jointly a written plan to enhance oversight by the management of Union Bank and its New York branch of the branch's compliance with the Bank Secrecy Act's AML requirements and with regulations issued by the Office of Foreign Assets Control of the US Department of the Treasury and acceptable to the New York Federal Reserve Bank.

Compliance review. Union Bank and its New York branch agreed to, within 30 days of the agreement, retain an independent third party acceptable to the New York Federal Reserve Bank to (a) conduct a comprehensive compliance review and (b) prepare a written compliance report of its findings, conclusions, and recommendations.

Compliance program. Union Bank and the New York branch agreed to, within 60 days of submission of the compliance report, jointly submit a written, revised Bank Secrecy Act AML compliance program acceptable to the New York Federal Reserve Bank.

Customer due diligence. Union Bank and the New York branch agreed, within 60 days of submission of the compliance report, to submit jointly a written revised customer due diligence program for the branch acceptable to the New York Federal Reserve Bank.

Suspicious activity monitoring and reporting program. Union Bank and the New York branch agreed, within 60 days of submission of the compliance report, to submit a written program reasonably designed to ensure the identification and timely, accurate, and complete reporting by the branch of all known or suspected violations of law or suspicious transactions to law enforcement and supervisory authorities, as required by applicable suspicious activity reporting laws and regulations acceptable to the Federal Reserve Bank.

Source: New York Federal Reserve Bank, https://www.federalreserve.gov/newsevents/pressreleases/files/enf20180712a1.pdf.

Examples of Civil and Administrative Sanctions

Box 6.5 presents examples of civil and administrative sanctions that can be applied in some jurisdictions to financial institutions that fail to meet their AML/CFT obligations.

BOX 6.5 Examples of Civil and Administrative Sanctions across Jurisdictions

United States. The Financial Crimes Enforcement Network (FinCEN), the US financial intelligence unit (FIU), is authorized to assess civil money penalties against a financial institution, nonfinancial trade or business, or a partner, director, officer, or employee of a financial institution or nonfinancial trade or business for violations of the anti-money-laundering (AML) law. These violations can include failures in record keeping, reporting, or maintaining an adequate AML program. FinCEN may assess a civil fine of not less than two times the amount of the transaction up to US$1 million against a financial institution that violates the AML requirements of due diligence on correspondent and private banking or the prohibition on correspondent shell banks (FATF 2015b).

The Republic of Korea. Korea's FIU delegated its supervisory authority to the Financial Supervisory Service and other entrusted agencies, including the power to impose administrative sanctions. The entrusted agencies have the power to issue corrective orders, give warnings or cautions to a financial institution or casino, and partially or fully suspend a license. Additionally, the entrusted agencies can apply administrative sanctions to senior management (reprimand warning, cautionary warning, and caution) and employees (removal, suspension, salary reduction, reprimand, and caution). Entrusted agencies do not have the ability to impose monetary sanctions, but Korea's FIU can impose them on request by the entrusted agencies. Monetary sanctions can be (and are) applied concurrently for each identified violation. With the recent increase in the level of monetary sanctions, each violation can be penalized by ₩100 million (€77,044). If 100 counts are identified as breaching customer due diligence requirements, the maximum monetary fine can be ₩100 million multiplied by 100 counts, that is, ₩10 billion (€7.7 million) (FATF 2020).

Malta. Findings of anti-money-laundering and combating terrorism financing (AML/CFT) supervisory examinations undertaken by the Financial Intelligence Analysis Unit (FIAU) or by the Malta Financial Services Authority and Malta Gaming Authority that indicate AML/CFT shortcomings are referred to the FIAU's Compliance Monitoring Committee. The Compliance Monitoring Committee is an internal FIAU committee, composed of FIAU officials from the compliance section (the three most senior officers) and legal section (the manager of the legal section or his or her representative) as well as the director and deputy director of the FIAU. The committee is responsible for reviewing potential breaches of AML/CFT obligations and, where breaches subsist, for imposing administrative penalties or requesting remedial action. The officers carrying out the supervisory examination are invited to present their findings and the subject person's submissions in front of the Compliance Monitoring Committee. The committee may decide to impose a reprimand, a monetary sanction, or both. Concurrently and independently of an administrative sanction, subject persons may be required to rectify their shortcomings and, if deemed necessary, the committee may request that the subject person provide an action plan (FATF 2019b).

Examples of Criminal Sanctions

Box 6.6 provides examples of criminal sanctions that can be applied in some jurisdictions to financial institutions that fail to meet their AML/CFT obligations.

BOX 6.6 Examples of Criminal Sanctions across Jurisdictions

United States. Prosecutors have powers to investigate and sanction financial institutions that do not comply with US anti-money-laundering (AML) law. The Department of Justice has authority to bring criminal actions against financial institutions that breach their statutory and regulatory obligations. It also has criminal authority to pursue money-laundering violations and the ability to prosecute unlicensed money-transmitting businesses (FATF 2015b).

British Virgin Islands. Administrative anti-money-laundering and combating terrorism financing (AML/CFT) breaches are handled either by the Financial Services Commission or by the Financial Intelligence Agency. If, during this time, it is found that there is some criminal element to the breach, the matter is turned over to the police. Conversely, if the police encounter cases that may reveal a breach in the AML/CFT framework, this information is passed on to the police financial investigation unit for further investigation. The police can, through established memoranda of understanding, share information with the Financial Intelligence Agency and the Financial Services Commission (FATF 2015b).

Hong Kong SAR, China. The Custom and Excise Department relies primarily on criminal investigations and prosecutions to sanction money service operators. Five money service operators were convicted between 2012 and 2017. Fines were imposed in four cases for a total of HK$270,000 (US$34,400), and a 200-hour community service order was imposed in one case (FATF 2019a).

Other Sanctions

In addition to administrative and criminal sanctions, competent authorities may take further measures should the breach be particularly serious. They can, for instance, combine fines with administrative and other disciplinary measures. The most severe disciplinary sanction a competent body can impose is the withdrawal of a license, which effectively terminates the activity of the financial institution.

Such measures must be applied independently of any sanctions that the courts may impose. The supervisor must be vested with the authority to file an application with a prosecutor when there are reasonable grounds to believe that the financial institution or its board members and senior management participated in ML/TF activities. In the case of a serious offense, the supervisor must have direct access to the prosecutor and be able to have the case prosecuted as a criminal matter, notwithstanding the supervisor's ability to impose specific administrative or civil sanctions.

Furthermore, in some jurisdictions, stockholders of publicly traded financial institutions have brought lawsuits against members of the boards of directors and have succeeded in recovering monetary damages from individual members of the board.

PUBLICATION OF SANCTIONS

The question of whether imposed sanctions should be made a matter of public knowledge is not addressed in either the FATF recommendations or the Basel Core Principles. However, the FATF guidance indicates that supervisors should consider publishing the results of the supervisory actions and providing information on the relevant entities' deficiencies to address risks across the sector, as other entities take note of the consequences of similar failings. The FATF guidance also stipulates that making supervisory sanctions public when appropriate may improve the transparency of enforcement (FATF 2021, para. 44).

Practices vary widely across jurisdictions. Some jurisdictions do not communicate publicly about sanctions for AML/CFT breaches, whereas others do. In the European Union (EU), for instance, the authorities of EU member states are required to publish on their official website all decisions to impose an administrative sanction or measure for breach of the national AML/CFT provisions; once the sanctioned institution is informed of that decision. there is no possibility of appeal (European Parliament 2018).

Publication of sanctions can be regarded as part of the "dissuasive" element of a sanctioning regime. It is the responsibility of each jurisdiction to determine, in light of its own legal regime and other circumstances, if sanctions are to be published. There are pros and cons to public disclosure, and each jurisdiction has to balance the pros and cons of publishing, including the names of offending institutions.

If sanctions are publicly disclosed, they have a deterrent function. In other words, other financial institutions become more cautious and more inclined to comply fully with AML/CFT requirements if they know that a failure to comply will be published. Publication, therefore, promotes stricter adherence to AML/CFT regulations within the financial sector. Furthermore, the publication of sanctions can be used as leverage. To some extent, the possibility of either making a sanction publicly available or keeping it confidential enhances the supervisor's authority by reinforcing its power.

Disclosing the name of a financial institution that has been sanctioned can also be a means of reinforcing supervision internationally. If the name of the financial institution is disclosed in its home jurisdiction, supervisors in other jurisdictions in which the institution operates may decide to take prompt action and conduct on-site inspections of its branches. If a parent bank is not compliant, there are reasonable grounds to believe that its subsidiaries and branches abroad also fail to apply the AML/CFT policy correctly.

Conversely, there are several possible disadvantages to disclosing the name of a financial institution for violating AML/CFT regulations. Doing so can tarnish the reputation of the institution or, indeed, the sector as a whole and thus undermine public and investor confidence in the jurisdiction's financial system. For that reason, in jurisdictions where the financial sector has been seriously weakened by a financial crisis in the past, authorities may be reluctant to disclose the names of institutions that breach AML/CFT regulations. Indeed, for entities in a weak financial situation, the publication of sanctions may create new stress and impede their financial recovery. They may not be able to access the interbank market for their own refinancing, and foreign banks may decide to terminate their correspondent relationships with them. Some jurisdictions also believe that the public disclosure of AML/CFT failures—in addition to the other administrative, civil, and financial penalties imposed on a financial institution—is in effect a "double penalty," because it sanctions the institution twice for the same violation.

Some jurisdictions favor an approach whereby decisions to disclose sanctions are made on a case-by-case basis, depending on their seriousness and frequency of occurrence. Other jurisdictions may choose not to publish sanctions or may limit themselves to publishing limited or general information or only an anonymized decision.

Whatever their choices about the disclosure of specific sanctions, the authorities should adhere to the legal basis for such decisions and, where disclosure is permissible, should establish a clear policy on whether to publish or not.

Boxes 6.7 and 6.8 present examples of sanctions imposed in Bermuda and Luxembourg, respectively.

BOX 6.7 Example of Sanctions Imposed on Sun Life Financial Investments: Bermuda

The Bermuda Monetary Authority imposed civil penalties totaling US$1.5 million on Sun Life Financial Investments Ltd. pursuant to the provisions of section 20 of the Proceeds of Crime (Anti-Money Laundering & Terrorist Financing Supervision & Enforcement) Act 2008 (BMA 2017). It also restricted the company's investment business license pursuant to section 20 of the Investment Business Act 2003.

The civil penalties were imposed for the company's failure to comply adequately with the following requirements of the Proceeds of Crime Regulations 2008:

1. Apply customer due diligence measures;

2. Conduct ongoing monitoring of business relationships;

3. Cease transactions where it is not possible to apply customer due diligence measures;

4. Apply enhanced due diligence; and

5. Establish and maintain appropriate and risk-sensitive policies and procedures.

Some of the findings represented failings of the company to remediate similar findings from an on-site review conducted in 2013. The Bermuda Monetary Authority viewed these breaches as serious because of their extent and duration and because they demonstrated systemic weaknesses in the company's internal anti-money-laundering and combating terrorism financing (AML/ATF) controls. The regulations have been in effect since 2009. This case highlights the importance of licensees having in place up-to-date AML/CTF policies and procedures that are appropriate, effective, and fully implemented in order to avoid the risk of financial products being used as a vehicle for money laundering or terrorism financing.

BOX 6.8 Example of an Administrative Sanction Imposed on a Credit Institution: Banque Internationale à Luxembourg S.A.

On March 16, 2020, the Commission de Surveillance du Secteur Financier (CSSF) imposed an administrative fine amounting to €4.6 million on the credit institution Banque Internationale à Luxembourg S.A. (CSSF 2020). The fine was imposed on the basis of the provisions of Article 2-1, paragraph (1) and Article 8-4, paragraphs (1), (2), and (3) of the amended Law of November 12, 2004, on anti-money-laundering and combating terrorism financing (AML/CTF), following two on-site inspections carried out by the CSSF between October and November 2017 and between July and September 2018 on the premises of the bank. These inspections identified certain weaknesses in the bank's processes for monitoring a small segment of customers whose inherent risk was generally considered to be high. The bank reacted promptly to remediate the identified weaknesses. The amount of the fine imposed was proportional to the turnover of the bank, in line with applicable rules.

OVERVIEW OF THE STEPS TO BE FOLLOWED FOR EFFECTIVE SANCTION PROCEEDINGS

This section provides an overview of the principal steps that supervisors or designated authorities should consider taking when there has been a serious breach of AML/CFT regulations and before sanctions, whether disciplinary or administrative, are undertaken. It also describes the basic stages for processing sanctions. These guidelines are based on what are considered best practices; they are not a "one-size-fits-all" solution. They do not address violations of the AML/CFT law punishable by criminal sanctions, which are a matter for law enforcement.

General

Neither the FATF recommendations nor the Basel Core Principles provide guidance on the procedures to adopt for the imposition of AML/CFT sanctions. However, the FATF guidance recommends that supervisors consider transparency, consistency, and proportionality in applying remedial actions or sanctions, while taking into account the specifics of the particular entity, the nature and significance of the risk mitigation failures, and the deficiency or gap identified.

Each jurisdiction, according to its own legal regime, is responsible for establishing its own procedures. In some jurisdictions, the procedures for preparing and applying AML/CFT sanctions are established by a single authority, which is vested with the power both to monitor AML/CFT compliance and to enforce sanctions.

Thus, while there is no single model, as a general principle, each jurisdiction should establish clear policies and procedures before taking any action against a financial institution failing to meet its legal and regulatory AML/CFT obligations. This systematic approach is key to ensuring an effective enforcement regime as well as to safeguarding the rights of offenders. In developing an enforcement policy, supervisors should keep in mind that, in a risk-based approach that gives financial institutions a certain degree of discretion in the application of AML/CFT measures, it might not always be evident that a violation has occurred and what its severity is. Supervisors should therefore avoid a zero-tolerance approach. Too much sanctioning pressure may drive institutions to defensive, rules-based measures, which can eventually weaken the effectiveness of AML/CFT measures

Moreover, the national framework and processes for applying sanctions for AML/CFT infringements can determine the efficiency and effectiveness of the sanctioning regime. Where more than one authority is involved and where the supervisory and sanctioning authorities are different, effective coordination of activities is critical. Where this coordination is absent, sanctions may not be applied in a timely manner or at all, possibly giving rise to disagreement about whether or not to apply sanctions and what type of sanctions to apply, which may cause delays.

Another issue to consider where the supervisory authority is different from the sanctioning authority is the potential for political interference and bureaucratic delays in the application of sanctions. Whereas the AML/CFT supervisor (for example, a central bank) may enjoy a high degree of autonomy and adequate resources, the sanctioning authority (for example, a ministry of finance or the FIU) may be more prone to political interference or have fewer resources. These issues may be a source of interagency conflict and friction, which could undermine the effectiveness of the sanctioning regime.

Another issue can arise where different authorities supervise and sanction. For instance, when a supervisor conducts a full-scope examination and finds breaches in broad-based requirements such as corporate governance, risk management, and internal audit that cover both prudential and AML/CFT requirements, the supervisor may wish to apply one sanction addressing all of these issues, as this approach could be reasonable and efficient in the specific case. But if the AML/CFT sanctions can only be applied by another authority, this situation may create confusion and inefficiencies; the financial institution should not be sanctioned twice for the same underlying offense, which would violate the principle against double jeopardy.

For purposes of this handbook, the steps laid out in this section generally assume that the supervisory authority and the sanctioning authority are the same.

Notification of the Outcomes

Sanctions are usually triggered by an on-site visit that has identified serious deficiencies in the institution's AML/CFT framework. In many jurisdictions, a draft inspection report is discussed with the management of the institution before the on-site inspection process is finalized. In that case, management can provide comments on factual inaccuracies or make other comments on the findings. The inspection team consequently assesses the validity of the comments and addresses them in the final report of findings.

Following finalization, the report is sent to the relevant department or committee of the supervisory authority for a decision on further actions. In some jurisdictions, the role of the inspection team is limited to identifying deficiencies, whereas in other jurisdictions the inspection team is also responsible for proposing possible enforcement measures and timelines. Each observation made by the inspection team must be substantiated by precise facts so that the sanctioning department or committee clearly understands the seriousness of the breach and determines appropriate sanctions.

If the institution has to take remedial actions, the AML/CFT supervision department usually sends a follow-up letter to the institution detailing the main conclusions of the on-site inspection report and highlighting the strengths and weaknesses of the internal AML/CFT framework, such as policies, procedures, and controls, customer due diligence and monitoring systems, staff resources, and training. The document describes in detail the most serious deficiencies detected during the on-site inspection. It also provides comments and recommendations or instructions on what needs to be improved and describes the prompt action that should be taken to address all of the main deficiencies, often within certain timelines. Instructions may consist of a range of issues, for instance:

- Developing a business-wide risk assessment for all business lines;

- Reviewing and updating AML/CFT policies and related procedures

- Strengthening customer due diligence measures;

- Remediating customer files and reviewing previous transactions for unusual and suspicious activity;

- Appointing an AML/CFT compliance officer; and

- Implementing targeted training programs for staff.

The financial institution is generally asked to respond to the supervisor's instructions. These letters are sent to the board, which has overall responsibility for the institution. In some jurisdictions, a copy of the letter is also sent to the supervisory board and the (external or internal) auditors, who should be made aware of any deficiencies in the institution's internal organization.

Follow-up Procedures

It is important for the supervisor to follow up the instructions and recommendations to ensure that the institution corrects all of the deficiencies identified. To this end, the supervisor will make systematic checks and hold frequent meetings with the institution's representatives to ascertain whether concrete measures have been adopted and the degree of progress made toward compliance. It is critical that supervisors show vigilance in their oversight of the problems by periodically checking the institution's progress in complying with the instructions and recommendations. The supervisor can, for example, give the institution orders to comply with specific AML/CFT requirements and can request regular reports describing measures that the institution is taking to address the deficiencies in its AML/CFT compliance framework. Periodic review meetings follow, and, if necessary, there is a follow-up on-site inspection. If the problems escalate or if management of the institution does not take corrective actions (in time), there should be a progressive escalation of enforcement or remedial measures. Box 6.9 presents examples from two jurisdictions.

BOX 6.9 Examples from Malaysia and Singapore

Malaysia. Following an on-site examination, Bank Negara Malaysia (BNM) provides banks with extensive feedback as well as recommendations that address key anti-money-laundering and combating terrorism financing (AML/CFT) deficiencies. Several meetings are organized with the bank's board of directors, the board's audit committee, and the bank's senior management. Following a consultative process, banks establish remediation programs subject to a stringent follow-up process. Banks must report their progress in addressing their deficiencies on a quarterly basis. If the information provided to BNM is not sufficient, further information is requested; if necessary, there will be a follow-up on-site examination.

Singapore. In Singapore, the Monetary Authority of Singapore examination report consists of two key parts. The first is a general description of AML/CFT risks and the measures taken by the bank to address them. The second is a table that includes descriptions of qualitative findings and deficiencies identified in the bank's AML/CFT practices and a remediation plan agreed on by the bank and the supervisor. The plan is subject to a stringent follow-up process to ensure that the bank is taking adequate actions to address the shortcomings.

Hearing

When imposing sanctions, supervisors or the designated authorities normally follow strict rules, especially with respect to the right to a defense. Some supervisory authorities require that the imposition of certain sanctions, such as fines, can only be decided on by a department other than the supervisory department, often the legal department. In this way, an independent review of the findings and deficiencies is guaranteed. These rules are key to a fair and expeditious processing of the case. In a scheduled hearing, the competent authorities review the inspection outcomes, the specific legal and regulatory provisions that have been violated, and the possible sanctions that can be imposed. Normally, the institution has the right to object and to defend itself. At the end of the hearing, the competent authority deliberates the seriousness of the breach and determines the final sanctions, which are usually delivered to the institution in writing and may be subject to publication.

Notification of the Sanction

In the most serious cases, when an institution fails to comply with core AML/CFT obligations (for example, repeated failure to report suspicious transactions to the FIU), the supervisor may decide to proceed directly to the next stage by launching disciplinary proceedings, which may entail sanctions, such as fines and other civil penalties, or other types of measures, such as cautionary warnings or notifications of reprimand. Where it appears that the findings may lead to sanctions, the content of the notification letter should be very detailed and satisfy strict requirements. Each breach should be described concisely and accurately and be supported by concrete facts so that the competent authority can establish the link between the failure and the appropriate sanction. Once all these elements have been provided to the institution, the competent authority will normally ask the institution's management to reply and provide comments.

Sometimes the proper sanction is difficult to determine. In some jurisdictions, as shown above, a wide range of sanctions are available to enforce AML/CFT laws, extending from reprimands to civil and criminal penalties, and the sanctioning authority must make a judicious choice among them. In the most extreme cases, authorities may consider suspending or withdrawing the institution's license and closing it down. Even in cases where a financial institution is found to have participated actively in an ML/TF scheme, the wisest choice may not necessarily be to close it down, given the interests of depositors and the public (see the example in box 6.10). For example, the closure of systemically important banks could have undesirable ripple effects across the financial sector and the economy. In such cases, other options may be considered, such as a sale or merger.

BOX 6.10 Example of Imposing a Large Fine: The Netherlands

ING Bank N.V. in Amsterdam accepted and paid a fine of €775 million to the Public Prosecution Service, which accused ING of violating the Money Laundering and Terrorist Financing (Prevention) Act over a number of years (Public Prosecutor's Office 2018). The bank was also accused of culpable money laundering: between 2010 and 2016, the

(box continues on next page)

accounts of ING customers were used to launder hundreds of millions of euros, and the bank did nothing to prevent it.

The investigation by the Fiscal Information and Investigation Service (FIOD) started at the beginning of 2016 after several criminal investigations revealed that suspected companies or persons held accounts with ING in the Netherlands. These findings suggested that the bank's customer due diligence and monitoring of accounts were insufficient and that unusual transactions were not reported or were reported too late.

De Nederlandsche Bank (DNB), the Dutch central bank, had warned ING several times and taken formal measures. ING was aware of shortcomings in its implementation of the policy from 2010 onward, but did not remedy them sufficiently. Improvement programs were undertaken, but were implemented insufficiently. For example, ING solved incidental issues, but did not recognize or sufficiently address structural problems in the transaction monitoring system. In consultation with DNB and the FIOD, the Public Prosecution Service decided to bring criminal proceedings against the bank.

The interests of law enforcement authorities sometimes differ from those of the supervisory authorities, in that the former value the deterrent effect of closing down an institution, while the latter are concerned with maintaining financial stability. A compromise is often found by removing or discharging officers of the institution or imposing a large fine, while at the same time rehabilitating the institution with new owners and management under the watchful eye of the supervisor.

APPEAL

The system of sanctions must be consistent with the legal guarantees of an accused person's right to a defense. The institution must be able to make its observations known to the supervisor and must have the right to lodge an appeal before a competent authority or jurisdiction. The appeal system itself depends on a given jurisdiction's constitutional arrangements, but some supervisors can set up specialized administrative appeal boards to expedite the process, as judicial processes can take a long time, even if the defendant has access to the courts for final determination. In the United States, for example, three levels of jurisdictions deal with appeals: the Federal District Court in the area where the bank is located; the Federal Circuit Court; and, in the last resort, the US Supreme Court. In France, the Council of State is the only authority empowered to examine appeals against the ACPR's rulings. In Sweden, appeals can be made to the County Administrative Board, the Administrative Court of Appeal, and finally the Supreme Administrative Court, depending on the sanction chosen by the inspection authority, the Finansinspektionen.

NOTES

1. "Effective remedial actions and sanctions application should seek not only to discourage past inappropriate actions and correct weaknesses in processes, procedures, and systems or controls within regulated entities but also to promote changes in behavior to foster a corporate culture of compliance that covers the board, senior management, compliance teams, and all other relevant staff of the relevant entity" (FATF 2021, para. 86).
2. Third parties can help supervisors to monitor entities' remediation efforts. For example, in the United Kingdom, the Financial Conduct Authority can require an entity to engage the services of a "skilled person" to carry out a review and submit a report to it. See https://www.fca.org.uk/about /supervision/skilled-persons-reviews.

REFERENCES

ACPR (Autorité de Contrôle Prudentiel et de Resolution). n.d. "The Disciplinary Procedures." ACPR, Paris. https://acpr.banque-france.fr/en/sanctions/disciplinary-procedures.

BCBS (Basel Committee on Banking Supervision). 2020. "Guidelines on Sound Management of Risks Related to Money Laundering and Financing of Terrorism; Issued in January 2014 and Revised July 2020." BCBS, Paris. https://www.bis.org/bcbs/publ/d505.pdf.

BMA (Bermuda Monetary Authority). 2017. "Bermuda Monetary Authority Fines Sun Life Financial Investments (Bermuda) Ltd $1,500,000 and Restricts Licence." Press release, Bermuda Monetary Authority, City of Hamilton, February 27. https://www.bma.bm/news-and-press-releases /bermuda-monetary-authority-fines-sun-life-financial-investments-bermuda-ltd-1-500-000-and -restricts-licence.

CSSF (Commission de Surveillance du Secteur Financier). 2020. "Sanction administrative prononcée à l'encontre de l'établissement de crédit Banque Internationale à Luxembourg S.A." CSSF, Luxembourg, August 10. https://www.cssf.lu/wp-content/uploads/S_25_B_Banque _Internationale_à_Luxembourg_S.A._160320.pdf.

European Parliament. 2018. "Article 60 Directive (EU) 2018/843 of the European Parliament and of the Council of 30 May 2018 Amending Directive (EU) 2015/849 on the Prevention of the Use of the Financial System for the Purposes of Money Laundering or Terrorist Financing, and Amending Directives 2009/138/EC and 2013/36/EU." European Parliament, Brussels. https://eur -lex.europa.eu/legal-content/EN/TXT/?uri=CELEX:32018L0843.

FATF (Financial Action Task Force). 2015a. "Emerging Terrorist Financing Risks." FATF, Paris. https:// www.fatf-gafi.org/publications/methodsandtrends/documents/emerging-terrorist-financing-risks .html.

FATF (Financial Action Task Force). 2015b. "Guidance for a Risk-Based Approach—Effective Supervision and Enforcement by AML/CFT Supervisors of the Financial Sector and Law Enforcement." FATF, Paris, October. https://www.fatf-gafi.org/media/fatf/documents/reports/RBA -Effective-supervision-and-enforcement.pdf.

FATF (Financial Action Task Force). 2019a. "Anti-Money Laundering and Counter-Terrorist Financing Measures—Hong Kong, China, Fourth Round Mutual Evaluation Report." FATF, Paris. https://www .fatf-gafi.org/media/fatf/documents/reports/mer4/MER-Hong-Kong-China-2019.pdf.

FATF (Financial Action Task Force). 2019b. "Moneyval, Malta, Fifth Round Mutual Evaluation Report." FATF, Paris, July. https://www.fatf-gafi.org/media/fatf/documents/reports/mer-fsrb/Moneyval -Mutual-Evaluation-Report-Malta-2019.pdf.

FATF (Financial Action Task Force). 2020. "Anti-Money Laundering and Counter-Terrorist Financing Measures—Republic of Korea, Fourth Round Mutual Evaluation Report." FATF, Paris. https://www .fatf-gafi.org/media/fatf/documents/reports/mer4/Mutual-Evaluation-Report-Korea-2020.pdf.

FATF (Financial Action Task Force). 2021. "Guidance on Risk-Based Supervision." FATF, Paris, March. https://fatf-gafi.org/publications/documents/Guidance-RBA-Supervision.html.

Financial Conduct Authority. 2016. "Final Notice." Financial Conduct Authority, London, October 12. https://www.fca.org.uk/publication/final-notices/steven-smith-2016.pdf.

Public Prosecutor's Office. 2018. "ING betaalt 775 miljoen vanwege ernstige nalatigheden bij voorkomen witwassen." *Openbaar Ministerie* (blog), September 4. https://www.om.nl/actueel/nieuws/2018/09/04 /ing-betaalt-775-miljoen-vanwege-ernstige-nalatigheden-bij-voorkomen-witwassen.

US Department of Justice. 2012. "HSBC Holdings Plc. and HSBC Bank USA N.A. Admit to Anti-Money Laundering and Sanctions Violations, Forfeit $1.256 Billion in Deferred Prosecution Agreement," Press Release, US Department of Justice, December 11. https://www.justice.gov/opa/pr /hsbc-holdings-plc-and-hsbc-bank-usa-na-admit-anti-money-laundering-and-sanctions-violations.

CHAPTER 7

National and International Supervisory Cooperation

OVERVIEW

For an anti-money-laundering and combating the financing of terrorism (AML/CFT) framework to be effective, a seamless process of national interagency coordination, cooperation, and flow of information is critical. In addition, cooperation between national agencies is of paramount importance to cooperation with international counterparts. Without strong domestic cooperation, international cooperation will be difficult. Recommendation 2 of the Financial Action Task Force (FATF) standards sets out the principal requirements for jurisdictions to coordinate and cooperate their AML/CFT efforts at the national level. Recommendations 36 through 40 establish the main requirements for international cooperation; in particular, Recommendation 40 establishes cooperation requirements for specific AML/CFT authorities. Under the FATF standards, Immediate Objectives 1 and 2 require jurisdictions to demonstrate the effectiveness of their national and international cooperation regimes, respectively. The 2021 FATF guidance on risk-based supervision also provides useful indications on what supervisors should do in the area of cooperation (FATF 2021).

Nationally and internationally, AML/CFT supervisors cooperate with other AML/CFT supervisors and other authorities at both the policy and operational levels. Nationally, cooperation and information exchange between AML/CFT supervisors, other supervisors, financial intelligence units (FIUs), and other competent authorities, including tax authorities and law enforcement, are important to ensure that all stakeholders have a good understanding of, and can act to mitigate, money-laundering and terrorism financing (ML/TF) risks. Areas of cooperation include national risk assessments, legislative drafting, AML/CFT policy and strategy formulation, evaluations, and specific cases of ML/TF. The findings of supervisory operations may assist other authorities in executing their AML/CFT function, while the information of the FIU or law enforcement agencies may assist supervisors in performing their role. Internationally, national representatives, including representatives of national supervisory authorities, often cooperate to combat cross-border ML/TF and predicate crimes, including through information-sharing protocols. They also participate in regional and international projects, including through FATF and FATF-style regional body (FSRB) working groups, and share expertise through training and other programs. Most of this cooperation is carried out pursuant to mutual assistance treaties, memoranda of understanding, and informal channels.

This chapter addresses the various frameworks, both domestic and international, within which cooperation can be achieved. It also addresses operational cooperation between supervisors and other authorities and cooperation at the policy level between AML/CFT stakeholders, including public-private partnerships.

THE IMPORTANCE OF COOPERATION

Arguably, one of the most important elements of an effective AML/CFT framework is the ability and willingness on the part of all stakeholders to cooperate at national and international levels. Consequently, cooperation among AML/CFT stakeholders is a prominent component of the FATF standards and the Basel Core Principles for Effective Banking Supervision, including cooperation between home and host supervisors. Moreover, several FATF recommendations and Basel core principles embed elements of cooperation, such as recommendations on licensing procedures, consolidated supervision, correspondent banking, and FIUs.

Cooperation between public and private sector stakeholders is also embedded in relevant FATF standards and Basel Core Principles. These standards and principles include cooperation on various AML/CFT aspects such as national risk assessments, feedback mechanisms, typologies, legislative drafting, national policy and strategy formulation, training, suspicious transaction reports (STRs), investigations and prosecutions, freezing and confiscation of assets, and targeted financial sanctions.

Effective cooperation, whether domestic or cross-border, has specific prerequisites that include, among others, a sound legal framework, cooperation instruments, adequate rules and procedures, and clear protocols. These elements can significantly enhance supervisors' ability to share information, including by lifting secrecy or confidentiality restrictions. They can also support cooperation mechanisms through the use of mutual legal assistance treaties, memoranda of understanding, supervisory colleges, and technological networking platforms, among others. In addition to setting up these mechanisms, it is important to foster a spirit of cooperation and instill a common purpose and trust among supervisors and other authorities. These mechanisms should not exist only in theory. Instead, competent authorities should be encouraged to use these legal and institutional frameworks for cooperation, including through less formal channels. Without this spirit and willingness of cooperation, formal systems and tools are not effective.

In jurisdictions where the prudential supervisor and the AML/CFT supervisor are different, it is necessary to ensure the effectiveness of coordination and cooperation mechanisms between them. The prudential supervisor overseas a broad range of governance, compliance, and risk management issues, some of which are also relevant for AML/CFT purposes, and the findings of prudential supervisors should be shared with AML/CFT supervisors. In this context, the European Banking Authority has published an opinion on how prudential supervisors should take into account ML/TF risks in the supervisory review and evaluation process (EBA 2020b). The opinion states that combating ML/TF requires certain actions by both AML/CFT and prudential supervisors. For this reason, European Union (EU) law requires prudential supervisors and AML/CFT supervisors to cooperate and exchange information regarding their respective supervisory activities.

NATIONAL COOPERATION

The objective of AML/CFT cooperation is to strengthen national mechanisms to prevent, investigate, and prosecute money laundering, terrorism financing, and associated predicate offenses. At the national level, cooperation refers to the interaction between all public and private AML/CFT stakeholders, including financial and nonfinancial sectors, AML/CFT supervisors, FIUs, agencies that manage official records and registries, tax, law enforcement, prosecutorial and judicial authorities, and immigration, customs, and intelligence agencies. These agencies can also include ancillary parties such as academia (for example, for research), journalists, and social and human development agencies (for example, those involved in financial inclusion and informal sectors).

Interagency cooperation can take place under formal and informal arrangements, depending on legal requirements, conventions, and practice. In some jurisdictions, the duty to cooperate and coordinate on AML/CFT issues is established by law and may be implemented through formal mechanisms, such as a memorandum of understanding or a cooperation agreement. In others, legally established national cooperation and coordination bodies, such as national coordination councils or agencies, already include cooperation in their mandates for participating agencies, including supervisors. Often, the conduct of national risk assessments and other national undertakings, such as the formulation of national policies and strategies, is based on these mandates.

Figure 7.1 shows the role of the AML/CFT national coordination function, the parties involved in a jurisdiction's AML/CFT system, and the interrelationships between them.

FIGURE 7.1 National Coordination Functions and Interrelationships in a Domestic AML/CFT System

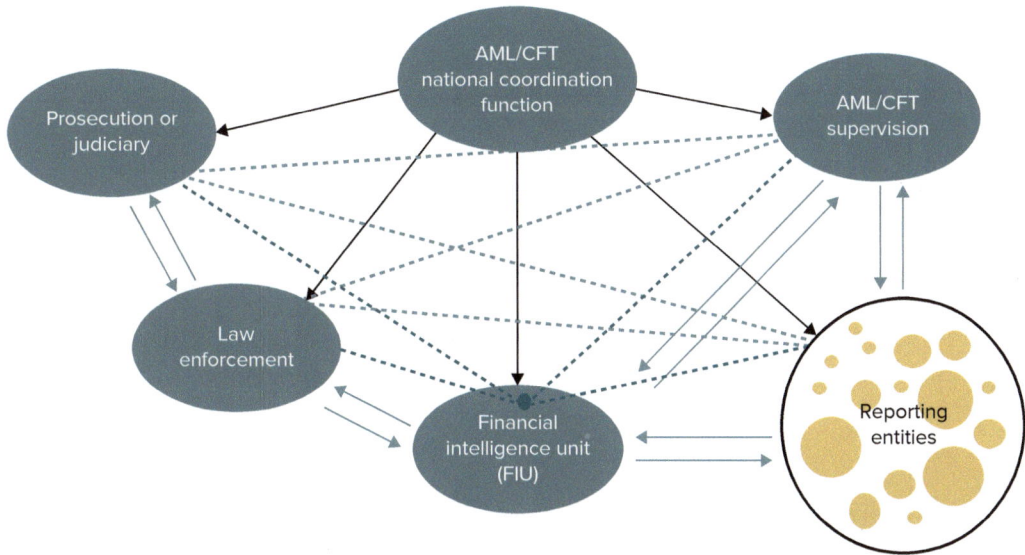

Source: World Bank risk-based approach toolkit.
Note: AML = anti-money-laundering. CFT = combating the financing of terrorism.

Box 7.1 presents an example of national cooperation by way of a national coordination function (FATF 2015).

BOX 7.1 AML/CFT Policy Coordination: Singapore

Singapore has a high-level anti-money-laundering and combating the financing of terrorism (AML/CFT) steering committee that leads the national effort to develop and implement its AML/CFT framework. The committee comprises the permanent secretary of the Ministry of Home Affairs, permanent secretary of the Ministry of Finance, and managing director of the Monetary Authority of Singapore, who are heads of their respective agencies. The committee coordinates a whole-of-government approach to prevent and combat money laundering and terrorism financing (ML/TF) by overseeing the effective implementation of AML/CFT measures by the respective agencies and by identifying and mitigating emerging ML/TF risks (for example, through the national risk assessment exercise). The committee meets three to four times a year, or more often if necessary. It is supported by an interagency committee made up of the key agencies in Singapore's AML/CFT framework.

PUBLIC-PRIVATE PARTNERSHIPS

In several jurisdictions, public-private partnerships have been created to foster information exchange between the public and private sectors and among financial institutions that are part of that partnership. These platforms, which can be formal or informal, aim to provide a conducive environment for feedback and guidance between public and private sectors as well as to share operational intelligence and information on risks and prevent, detect, and disrupt possible threats (FATF 2017). Such partnerships need to be based on mutual trust and have added value for all parties involved. An example is the United Kingdom's Joint Money Laundering Intelligence Taskforce, which is a partnership between law enforcement and the financial sector to exchange and analyze information relating to money laundering and wider economic threats. The taskforce consists of more than 40 financial institutions, the Financial Conduct Authority, and five law enforcement agencies (National Economic Crime Agency n.d.). Another example can be found in Singapore, where the AML/CFT Industry Partnership (ACIP) brings together the financial sector, regulators, law enforcement agencies, and other government entities to identify, assess, and mitigate key and emerging ML/TF risks facing Singapore (MAS n.d.). Currently, at least 18 jurisdictions have established financial information–sharing partnerships (Maxwell 2020).

OPERATIONAL COOPERATION

In general, domestic operational AML/CFT cooperation is intended to share information, intelligence, and evidence and to coordinate actions to prevent, investigate, and prosecute ML/TF offenses and predicate crimes. It also helps to avoid potential overlap or duplication of efforts that can occur, especially in the case of conglomerates, when different supervisors decide to perform inspections simultaneously. Information sharing, pooling of staff, and sharing of resources among the different agencies can bring economies of scale and improve overall effectiveness. Boxes 7.2 and 7.3 present examples of operational interagency cooperation in the United Kingdom and the Netherlands, respectively (Maxwell 2020).

BOX 7.2 United Kingdom: Cooperation and Coordination with Relevant Authorities

The United Kingdom's Financial Crime Network (FIN-NET) facilitates the sharing of financial crime–related information between its members, comprising regulators, law enforcement, and government departments. Established in 1992, in response to the collapse of the Bank of Credit and Commerce International, the network helps to ensure that the right people are communicating with the right people at the right time on an array of financial crime issues, including money laundering and terrorism financing (ML/TF).

FIN-NET has approximately 110 members representing public sector organizations from both UK and overseas authorities. It relies on each member having a single point of contact

(box continues on next page)

that specializes in financial crime matters. Where members have a shared interest in a case, a meeting may be held to ensure that all parties have the full picture, to avoid duplication of effort, and to assist members in collaborating on a joint investigation.

Typically, members make around 180 requests for information each year, which can lead to positive results. FIN-NET is an independent body accountable to a steering group chaired by the UK government's Home Office. The country's Financial Conduct Authority serves as the secretariat and is a member of FIN-NET.

BOX 7.3 Cooperation Partnership: The Netherlands

The Financial Expertise Center (FEC) is a cooperative partnership between authorities with supervisory, control, prosecution, or investigation tasks in the financial sector. The FEC takes preventive and active actions against threats that could affect the integrity of the sector. It also provides education and information. By exchanging insights, knowledge, and skills among FEC partners and observers, the FEC can act effectively and efficiently. A joint approach makes it possible to focus on problem solving and have a broad effect (FEC n.d.).

In addition, the Fiscal Intelligence and Investigation Service, the Public Prosecutor's Office, the Dutch Central Bank, and the Netherlands Authority for Financial Markets cooperate in the monthly steering and guiding committee (FIOD n.d.). In this committee, cases are discussed that might be of interest to either the supervisory or the criminal justice authorities. The basic principle of enforcement is that a person should not be punished twice for the same offense. If a punitive administrative sanction has been issued, authorities are not allowed to take criminal action for that same offense. If supervisory actions reveal criminal or economic offenses (and vice versa), this committee discusses the most effective means of enforcement. Depending on several factors—such as the severity of the offense, criminal intent, recidivism, complexity, and damages—the case is transferred to the criminal justice authorities. It is then, however, still possible to handle the case with administrative powers, which are corrective, not punitive.

Cooperation with the FIU

The supervisor can benefit significantly from information and feedback provided by the FIU to strengthen its supervisory activities and the operational effectiveness of the FIU itself. Various types of information generated by the FIU can be used for supervisory purposes. The reports that the FIU receives from financial institutions provide useful information on their adherence to customer due diligence and STR obligations.

Some FIUs provide feedback to supervisors on the quality of STRs under less structured arrangements (for example, through regular or informal meetings and agency coordination). In other cases, supervisors request information from the FIU on a case-by-case basis—for instance, as part of the on-site examination planning process. In Jersey, for example, the FIU gives exact reports on

STRs submitted by reporting institutions, and this information is fed directly into the supervisor's risk model, which ultimately determines the on-site inspection program. In Canada, the Financial Transaction and Reports Analysis Centre (FINTRAC), the FIU, which is formally responsible for ensuring compliance with the AML/CFT legislation, and the Office of the Supervisor of Financial Institutions (OSFI), which is the regulator and supervisor of financial institutions, have a memorandum of understanding under which OSFI shares with FINTRAC all of the information gained from its AML/CFT assessment program. FINTRAC shares with OSFI information on suspicious transactions and large cash or electronic fund transfer filings and sector statistics on filing trends and effectiveness. Regular meetings are held between the two agencies to discuss trends and emerging issues as well as results of the assessments of individual entities.

Figure 7.2 provides an overview of the various roles and functions that the AML/CFT supervisors and the FIU have in the AML/CFT system of a jurisdiction.

FIGURE 7.2 Roles of the Supervisor and the Financial Intelligence Unit in the AML/CFT System

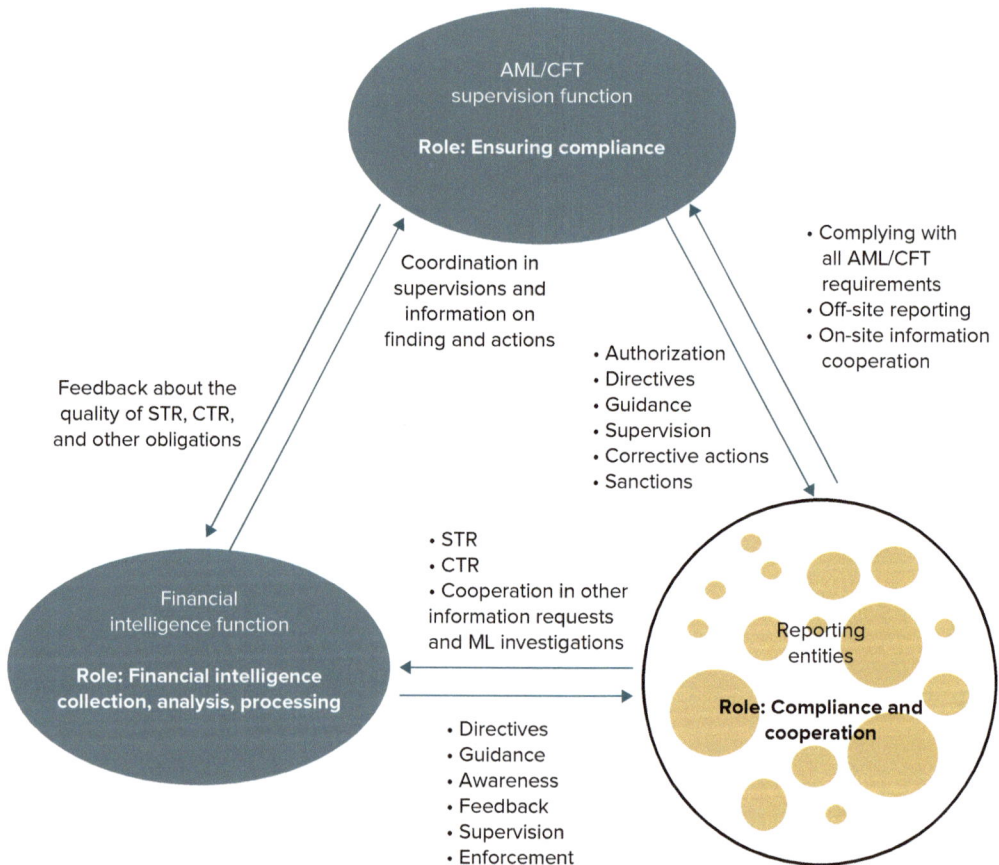

Source: World Bank risk-based approach toolkit.

Note: AML = anti-money-laundering. CFT = combating the financing of terrorism. CTR = currency transactions report. ML = money laundering. STR = suspicious transaction report.

FIU information assists the supervisor in targeting its supervision activities to those institutions where AML/CFT controls may be deficient. Some of the types of FIU information that can assist supervisors in achieving this objective are information on trends and typologies, information in annual or periodic reports, and information in STRs.

Trends and Typologies

Trends and methods of ML/TF provide useful information for the supervisor to understand new and evolving risks that affect financial institutions. They are particularly useful when analyzed along with national risk assessments, and they inform the supervisor's sectoral risk assessments and risk profiles of institutions. Where such typologies include specific information on particular financial sectors, types of customers and products, and geographic locations, they allow for more targeted risk assessments that inform supervisory activities.

Annual or Periodic FIU Reports

FIUs generally publish annual or periodic reports on their activities. These reports often include general statistical information on STRs by sector or type of institution. Sometimes, supervisors also contribute toward the drafting of such reports, providing, for instance, financial sector statistics and their views on compliance by financial institutions with STR requirements. This contribution benefits from such reports by giving supervisors a sectoral and system-wide view of STR levels and trends and any other information that may be reported, such as ML/TF risks. Sometimes, these reports provide information about the quality of reporting by sectors. All of this information is useful for sectoral risk profiling as well as for planning and targeting supervisory activities, such as thematic inspections.

Information on STRs

Information from FIUs to AML/CFT supervisors on the quality of STRs filed by an institution is an important source of information for assessing the compliance of an individual institution with STR requirements. Low-quality STRs may reflect other deficiencies, including weak customer due diligence, inadequate systems for monitoring customers' activities and transactions, and inadequate training of staff. Information on the quality of STRs can greatly assist supervisors in their inspection planning and other activities to identify potential noncompliance and to take corrective action promptly. In turn, these supervisory activities should improve the quality of STRs, strengthening the FIU's capacity to develop high-quality intelligence products.

While the number and quality of STRs will vary from institution to institution, such differences should not lead to definitive supervisory conclusions with respect to their compliance frameworks. While not conclusive, analysis of the number and quality of STRs can provide useful indications with regard to institutions that may be underreporting or those that may be engaged in defensive reporting practices. STR statistics allow supervisors to compare STR reporting practices for peer groups, different sectors, and so forth, which will better inform their understanding of the financial sector's STRs and compliance in general terms.

The analysis of the number and quality of STRs can be correlated. For example, recent sanctions applied to institutions for breaches of their STR obligations may lead to defensive reporting by some institutions, or some institutions may have introduced new automated monitoring systems that are generating a high number of false positives that are not assessed properly prior to filing STRs. This type of analysis will better inform supervisory focus and activities, including on-site inspection planning.

A study by the Bank of Italy and the Italian FIU shows the effect of AML/CFT inspections on the reporting of STRs by banks (Gara and others 2019). According to the study, "Following an inspection, banks are likely to increase the number of STRs they file to the FIU by some 18 percent; also the probability that they file one report increases accordingly, larger banks being more sensitive to supervisors' checks. Crucially, we find that the increase in STRs caused by inspections is not limited to low-quality reports, which would be the case if banks' responses in increasing the reporting effort were only apparent, but spreads to high-quality reports, thus showing that the authorities' on-site controls actually spurred an increase in banks' propensity to identify and report risky transactions. Further analysis has documented that such a positive effect is associated mainly with an actual intervention by the authorities following the inspection, in the form of reprimand letters or stronger action, such as enforcement measures and sanctions."

Supervisory Information for FIU Purposes

Conversely, a flow of information from the supervisor to the FIU may be needed as well. On-site inspections conducted by the supervisor may bring to light unreported suspicious activity. To remedy this situation, jurisdictions may provide the supervisor with the right to ensure that the FIU is informed, either by making a report directly or by having the reporting institution file a belated STR. The channels for sharing information from the supervisor to the FIU are generally the same as the channels for sharing FIU information with supervisors. The channels include both formal (for example, memoranda of understanding) and informal channels, subject to the legislative framework, particularly with respect to the treatment of confidential information.

Impediments to Sharing FIU Information with Supervisors

The ability to exchange information effectively and ensure cooperation between the FIU and supervisors depends largely on the type of information to be shared, the legal framework, and the national institutional cooperation framework. While it is generally easy to share information such as trends and typologies (often this information is published), sharing information related to STRs is not always feasible. Not all jurisdictions have a framework for providing systematic information to supervisors. Legal impediments sometimes prevent FIUs from sharing information with supervisors, for example, when the analysis conducted by the FIU is considered to be criminal intelligence and only sharable with law enforcement authorities (European Commission 2019).

Some jurisdictions take a strict interpretation on the confidentiality of STRs, such that the confidentiality of FIU data also extends not only to the content of STRs but also to information on the *quality* of STRs and reporting behavior of the entity. In addition, some jurisdictions interpret these confidentiality restrictions as preventing supervisors from accessing STR information during the course of their on-site inspections for compliance review purposes, even in the absence of explicit restrictions. Supervisors generally have broad, unfettered legal access to all information held by institutions for supervisory purposes, but some jurisdictions have not ascertained whether the legislation on FIU and STR reporting supersedes the powers of supervisors with respect to access to STR information. In contrast, some jurisdictions, such as the United States, provide supervisors with effective access to STR and other data filed by institutions for purposes of their supervisory and on-site examination function (European Commission 2019).[1]

The strict interpretation of the confidentiality provisions of STRs by certain jurisdictions has prevented some supervisors from reviewing the internal STR data and reports of institutions during on-site inspections, notwithstanding their designation as the competent AML/CFT supervisory authority. This situation limits their ability to assess compliance with this very important requirement, which can adversely affect the quality of financial intelligence generated by the FIU where STR compliance is deficient.

Cooperation with Law Enforcement Authorities

The scope of interagency cooperation between supervisors and law enforcement authorities is very wide. In the course of its supervisory activities, the supervisor might uncover potential breaches of AML/CFT laws by an institution or possible ML/TF by customers or the institution itself that would require investigation and possible prosecution. In such cases, the supervisor, subject to national legal requirements and procedures, may refer such matters to the appropriate law enforcement authority or public prosecutor for investigation. These cases may also involve the need to inform the FIU of its suspicions of ML/TF. The supervisor may, in fact, be obliged to report any suspicions or evidence of wrongdoing. Once such matters are referred to law enforcement, the supervisor may be required to provide further information and assistance to support investigations and prosecutions. Because such a situation deals with criminal conduct, any information that the supervisor gathers should not be covered by any confidentiality provisions. To put matters beyond doubt, however, legislators may choose to include an explicit provision to this effect in the law.

In any event, there is a need for collaboration, coordination, and cooperation between supervisory and law enforcement authorities. When a law enforcement agency is investigating a customer of a financial institution or its officials, it needs to inform the supervisor so that the supervisor does not take action independently. Taking independent action without the knowledge of the law enforcement authority can undermine or disrupt the criminal investigation. In such cases, both authorities should coordinate their activities and support each other. If the supervisory action includes the imposition of administrative sanctions, these sanctions could preclude criminal sanctions from being applied or vice versa.

Similarly, where a prosecutor or law enforcement authority takes action against a financial institution or any of its officials without consulting the supervisor, such action may put at risk the stability of the financial institution and the sector (if it is a systemically important bank). The prosecutor's concern, which is punishing criminal behavior, should be balanced against the supervisor's objective, which is safeguarding the integrity and stability of the financial system. The supervisor should also be able to take preventive measures to safeguard the interests of depositors and the wider public.

Box 7.4 provides examples of cooperation between supervisors and law enforcement in several jurisdictions (FATF 2015).

BOX 7.4 Examples of Cooperation between Supervisors and Law Enforcement

United Kingdom: supervisors with both regulatory and criminal powers. The United Kingdom's Financial Conduct Authority takes regulatory action and imposes substantial fines against firms and individuals for failures in their anti-money-laundering (AML) systems and controls. It does not have the statutory power to investigate stand-alone offenses of substantive money laundering (as opposed to system failures), but it does have the power to prosecute allegations of substantive money laundering in the context of criminal prosecutions (for offenses such as insider dealing) brought in furtherance of its statutory objectives. It also liaises closely with other law enforcement agencies to which it refers stand-alone investigations of substantive money laundering.

British Virgin Islands: enforcement referral from the supervisor. Administrative AML/CFT breaches are usually handled either by the Financial Services Commission or by the Financial Intelligence Agency. If, during this time, it is found that the breach has a criminal element, the matter is turned over to the police. Conversely, if the police encounter cases that may reveal a breach in the AML/CFT framework, this information is passed on to the police financial investigation unit for further investigation. The police financial investigation unit can, through established memoranda of understanding, share information with the Financial Services Commission and the Financial Intelligence Agency.

Denmark: enforcement referral from supervisor. If an inspection by the Finanstilsynets (the Danish Financial Supervisory Authority) reveals a breach, the Finanstilsynets reports its findings to the state prosecutor for serious economic and international crimes. The prosecutor decides on the merits of the case after due investigation of whether to initiate criminal proceedings. The Finanstilsynets issues administrative orders and continues its investigations until all administrative orders have been complied with.

United States: parallel investigations. Prosecutors and the financial intelligence unit have complementary authority to investigate and sanction financial institutions that do not comply with the US anti-money-laundering (AML) law. In addition to the corrective and enforcement actions of supervisors, the US Department of Justice, pursuant to 31 U.S.C. §5322, has authority to bring criminal actions against financial institutions that willfully fail to comply with their statutory and regulatory obligations under the AML law, Title 31 of the Bank Secrecy Act. For example, under this authority, the Department of Justice may pursue criminal charges against a financial institution that willfully fails to comply with its statutory and regulatory requirements for maintaining an AML or customer identification program, reporting suspicious activity, or fulfilling other relevant provisions of the AML law. It does not have any supervisory authority under the Bank Secrecy Act.

The Financial Crimes Enforcement Network (FinCEN) is also authorized to assess civil monetary penalties against a financial institution, nonfinancial trade or business, or a partner, director, officer, or employee of a financial institution or nonfinancial trade or business for willful or negligent violations of the AML law. These violations can include deficiencies in record keeping or reporting and failure to maintain an adequate AML program.

Cooperation among Supervisors, FIU, and Law Enforcement

Coordination and cooperation among supervisors, FIU, and law enforcement agencies (investigative and prosecutorial) is required when supervisors intervene in an institution due to serious AML/CFT violations or where the institution itself is involved in ML/TF activities. In such cases, a coordinated approach is required to ensure that suspicious transactions are duly reported to the FIU and, where appropriate, that funds are seized, frozen, or confiscated, among others. This approach requires careful coordination among the supervisor, the FIU, law enforcement, and the prosecution.

The degree to which supervisory instruments can complement or substitute for the law enforcement action is based on the particular circumstances of each case and domestic legislation. Where, for example, a prosecutorial agency cannot obtain sufficient evidence to bring a criminal case to trial, it may pass the case to the supervisor for civil or administrative action where noncompliance with AML/CFT requirements has been identified. Notwithstanding, a referral to the supervisor can still be made when, under domestic legislation, parallel proceedings can be instituted against an institution or its officers.

COOPERATION AT THE POLICY LEVEL

With all AML/CFT Stakeholders

In line with the FATF standards stating that jurisdictions should have national cooperation and coordination mechanisms at the policy and operational levels, many jurisdictions have established national cooperation and coordination councils or similar arrangements. These bodies organize and conduct national and sectoral risk assessments, which draw on the contributions of all AML/CFT stakeholders, including supervisors and the private sector. Often as a product of national risk assessments, these bodies coordinate the formulation of national and sectoral laws, policies, strategies, and plans of action. Another key element of national cooperation is the development and implementation of national AML/CFT programs by all stakeholders.

With Other Supervisors

In jurisdictions with more than one AML/CFT supervisor, these supervisors also coordinate the development of AML/CFT supervision strategy and policies. This coordination often includes the FIU, whether or not the FIU has an AML/CFT supervision mandate. Some jurisdictions establish supervisory committees or similar groups to ensure supervisory cooperation and sharing of information and experience. Such cooperation involves a risk-based supervision methodology to ensure harmonized approaches to AML/CFT supervision. Cooperation may also entail coordination for the drafting of legislation, regulations, and guidelines.

With the FIU

Cooperation between the AML/CFT supervisor and the FIU at the policy level can take many forms. One area of cooperation involves the formulation of feedback and guidance to the reporting institutions. Such feedback involves ML/TF risks, trends, and methods developed through operational and strategic analysis. Such cooperation can also take the form of joint training or seminars of the FIU and supervisors for the sectors.

With Reporting Entities

Supervisors and other competent authorities are tasked with promoting an understanding of the legal framework and ML/TF risks. They therefore establish guidelines and provide feedback to assist financial institutions in applying AML/CFT measures and promote a clear understanding by financial institutions of their AML/CFT obligations and ML/TF risks.

In Jersey, guidelines to clarify AML/CFT requirements are prepared by the Jersey Financial Services Commission with the assistance of a steering group representing the financial industry. The guidelines give special importance to corporate governance issues (board responsibilities, ML/TF compliance officer's missions, and so forth) and cultural barriers to implementing an effective AML/CFT framework. The guidelines are discussed extensively with the industry.

Ongoing collaboration between supervisors and the private sector they supervise is critical for the effectiveness of an AML/CFT framework. The private sector is on the front line of ML/TF risks and plays an important gatekeeper function. To achieve this collaboration, both supervisors and private sector entities should forge a working environment based on trust and understanding each other's roles. A key requirement is that the private sector is included in the conduct of national risk assessments and that the results are shared with all covered entities.

The importance of supervisor–private sector collaboration is particularly important for understanding and controlling ML/TF risks. In particular, having a common understanding of national and sectoral risks provides institutions with information to develop targeted ML/TF risk identification and assessment mechanisms and to implement risk-based AML/CFT systems (see appendix A). This, in turn, facilitates the supervisor's development and implementation of a risk-based AML/CFT supervisory framework.

AML/CFT training is another important tool for supervisor–private sector collaboration. While training for the staff of an institution is the primary responsibility of the institution, supervisors can organize seminars and workshops or participate in training events organized by sectoral associations. Supervisors should not, as a general principle, provide training to individual institutions. As mentioned, the FIU generally participates in such training events. Supervisors should support the establishment of associations of institutions, associations of compliance officers, or similar initiatives that provide a forum for supervisory cooperation in numerous fields.

INTERNATIONAL SUPERVISORY COOPERATION

General

As indicated by the FATF guidance, many regulated entities routinely operate across national borders and are therefore subject to AML/CFT supervision by several supervisory authorities in multiple jurisdictions. The ML/TF risks in question are frequently cross-border in nature, and failures in systems and controls in one part of the group may indicate weaknesses elsewhere. Therefore, cooperation between supervisors is important to mitigate those risks.

On a regional level, supervisory authorities ensure that AML/CFT cross-border cooperation is promoted and supported.

Cooperation among Supervisors

With the growth and consolidation of international financial groups, the need for effective cross-border supervisory cooperation is increasingly important. Both the FATF recommendations and the Basel Core Principles require international cooperation for supervisors.

The assessment methodology for Recommendation 40 on other forms of international cooperation sets out requirements in Essential Criteria 40.12–40.16 for the exchange of information between foreign financial sector supervisors:

- Financial supervisors should have a legal basis for cooperating with their foreign counterparts (regardless of their nature or status), consistent with the applicable international standards for supervision, in particular, with respect to the exchange of supervisory information related to or relevant for AML/CFT purposes.

- Financial supervisors should be able to exchange with foreign counterparts information domestically available to them, including information held by financial institutions, in a manner proportionate to their respective needs.

- Financial supervisors should be able to exchange the following types of information when relevant for AML/CFT purposes, in particular with other supervisors that have a shared responsibility for financial institutions operating in the same group:

  - Regulatory information, such as information on the domestic regulatory system and general information on financial sectors

  - Prudential information, in particular, for the supervisors of Basel Core Principles, such as information on the financial institution's business activities, beneficial ownership, management, and fit and proper characteristics

  - AML/CFT information, such as internal AML/CFT procedures and policies of financial institutions, customer due diligence information, customer files, samples of accounts, and transaction information.

- Financial supervisors should be able to conduct inquiries on behalf of foreign counterparts and, as appropriate, to authorize or facilitate the ability of foreign counterparts to conduct inquiries themselves in the country, in order to facilitate effective group supervision.

- Financial supervisors should ensure that they have the prior authorization to disseminate information or to use it for supervisory and nonsupervisory purposes, unless the requesting financial supervisor is under a legal obligation to disclose or report the information. In such cases, at a minimum, the requesting financial supervisor should promptly inform the requested authority of this obligation.

Specifically, with respect to bank supervisors, Basel Core Principle 3 requires jurisdictions to put in place laws, regulations, or other arrangements that provide a framework for cooperation and collaboration with relevant domestic authorities and foreign supervisors. These arrangements reflect the need to protect confidential information. With respect to banking groups, Basel Core Principle 13 requires home and host supervisors of cross-border banking groups to share information and cooperate for effective supervision of the group and group entities and effective handling of crisis situations. Supervisors require local operations of foreign banks to adhere to the same standards as those required of domestic banks.

Multinational Supervision

ECCB

The Eastern Caribbean Central Bank (ECCB) was established in October 1983. It is the monetary authority for a group of eight island economies: Anguilla, Antigua and Barbuda, Dominica, Grenada, Montserrat, St. Kitts and Nevis, St. Lucia, and St. Vincent and the Grenadines. The ECCB conceives of its mission as balancing prudential supervision with AML/CFT supervision to ensure an integrated approach (ECCB n.d.). The AML/CFT supervision framework includes the following:

- The AML/CFT legislation in Eastern Caribbean Currency Union member jurisdictions, which transfers the AML/CFT regulatory and supervisory authority for licensed financial institutions to the ECCB

- The multilateral memorandum of understanding between AML/CFT supervisory authorities in the Eastern Caribbean Currency Union, which provides a framework for cooperating in the supervision of licensed financial institutions and for implementing an effective AML/CFT system for the financial institutions for which the central bank has regulatory responsibility

- Implementation of an AML/CFT risk-based on-site examination manual

- Development and implementation of the ML/TF prudential return and the ML/TF risk assessment tool

- Partnership with key stakeholders to ensure ongoing training on emerging AML/CFT issues.

The ECCB established an AML supervisory unit within the Bank Supervision Department in April 2018 to focus primarily on developing and implementing the AML/CFT risk-based supervision framework for licensed financial institutions. The ECCB executed a multilateral memorandum of understanding in August 2018 that provides a framework for mutual cooperation in the supervision of compliance with the legal obligations for licensees to establish and implement an effective AML/CFT system. The ECCB has been named as the AML/CFT supervisory authority in three territories and continues to encourage its member governments to amend the necessary AML/CFT legislation to name the ECCB as the AML/CFT supervisory authority for its licensees (EECB 2019).

European Union

The European Banking Authority (EBA) is responsible for leading, coordinating, and monitoring AML/CFT efforts across the entire EU financial sector (EBA 2020a). The EBA discharges its functions in this field by the following:
- Leading the development of AML/CFT policy and supporting its effective implementation by competent authorities and financial institutions across the EU to foster an effective risk-based approach to AML/CFT with consistent outcomes

- Coordinating across the EU and beyond by fostering effective cooperation and information exchange between all relevant authorities in a way that supports the development of a common understanding of ML/TF risks, strengthens risk-based AML/CFT supervision, ensures that emerging risks are dealt with promptly across the single market, and ensures that oversight of cross-border financial institutions is effective
- Monitoring the implementation of EU AML/CFT policies and standards to identify vulnerabilities in competent authorities' approaches to AML/CFT supervision and to take steps to mitigate them before ML/TF risks materialize (figure 7.3).

FIGURE 7.3 Role of the European Banking Authority in Coordinating AML/CFT Efforts in the European Union

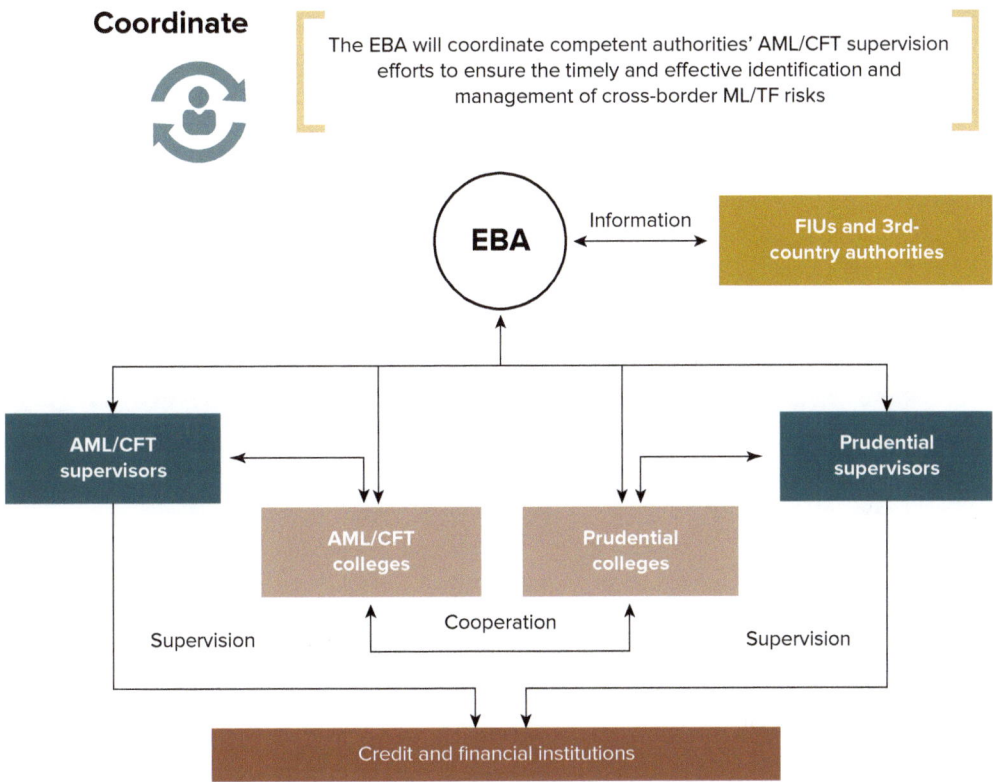

Coordinate

The EBA will coordinate competent authorities' AML/CFT supervision efforts to ensure the timely and effective identification and management of cross-border ML/TF risks

Source: EBA 2020a.

Note: AML = anti-money-laundering. CFT = combating the financing of terrorism. FIU = financial intelligence unit. ML = money laundering. TF = terrorism financing.

The EBA monitors the implementation by EU authorities of EU AML/CFT standards to identify vulnerabilities in their approaches to AML/CFT supervision and to take steps to mitigate them before ML/TF risks materialize. It does not have direct supervision or enforcement powers. However, it does foster effective cooperation and information exchange between all relevant authorities in a way that supports the development of a common understanding of ML/TF risks, strengthens risk-based AML/CFT supervision, ensures that emerging risks are dealt with promptly across the single market, and ensures effective oversight of cross-border financial institutions (EBA 2020a).

NOTE

1. The examination manual of the US Federal Financial Institutions Examination Council Bank Secrecy Act (BSA)/AML allows on-site examiners to have access to STR data: "FinCEN Query is the system used to access all BSA reports. BSA/AML examination planning should include an analysis of BSA reports that the bank has filed, such as Suspicious Activity Reports." See https://bsaaml.ffiec.gov /manual.

REFERENCES

EBA (European Banking Authority). 2020a. "Anti-Money-Laundering and Countering the Financing of Terrorism." Factsheet, European Banking Authority, Paris, February. https://eba.europa.eu/sites /default/documents/files/document_library/News%20and%20Press/Press%20Room/Press%20 Releases/2020/EBA%20acts%20to%20improve%20AML/CFT%20supervision%20in%20Europe /AML%20CFT%20Factsheet.pdf.

EBA (European Banking Authority). 2020b. "Opinion of the European Banking Authority on How to Take into Account ML/TF Risks in the Supervisory Review and Evaluation Process." European Banking Authority, Paris, November 4. https://eba.europa.eu/sites/default/documents /files/document_library/Publications/Opinions/2020/935606/Opinion%20on%20how%20to%20 take%20into%20account%20MLTF%20risks%20in%20SREP.pdf.

ECCB (Eastern Caribbean Central Bank). 2019. "2018–2019 Annual Report: Annual Report and Statement of Accounts for the Financial Year Ended 31 March 2019." ECCB, St. Kitts. https://www .eccb-centralbank.org/documents/5.

ECCB (Eastern Caribbean Central Bank). n.d. "Anti-Money Laundering and Combating the Financing of Terrorism Risk Based Supervision Framework." ECCB, St Kitts. https://www.eccb-centralbank .org/files/_ECCB_AML_CFT_Superviso...%20(1).pdf.

European Commission. 2019. "Report from the Commission to the European Parliament and the Council Assessing the Framework for Cooperation between Financial Intelligence Units." European Commission, Brussels, July 24. https://ec.europa.eu/info/sites/info/files/report _assessing_the_framework_for_financial_intelligence_units_fius_cooperation_with_third _jurisdictions_and_obstacles_and_opportunities_to_enhance_cooperation_between_financial _intelligence_units_with.pdf.

FATF (Financial Action Task Force). 2015. "Guidance for a Risk-Based Approach—Effective Supervision and Enforcement by AML/CFT Supervisors of the Financial Sector and Law Enforcement." FATF, Paris, October. https://www.fatf-gafi.org/media/fatf/documents/reports /RBA-Effective-supervision-and-enforcement.pdf.

FATF (Financial Action Task Force). 2017. "Guidance on Private Sector Information Sharing." FATF, Paris. https://www.fatf-gafi.org/publications/fatfrecommendations/documents/guidance -information-sharing.html.

FATF (Financial Action Task Force). 2021. "Guidance on Risk-Based Supervision." FATF, Paris. https://www.fatf-gafi.org/publications/documents/Guidance-RBA-Supervision.html.

FEC (Financial Expertise Center). n.d. "The Financial Expertise Centre." FEC, Amsterdam. https://www.fec-partners.nl/nl.

FIOD (Fiscal Intelligence and Investigation Service). n.d. "How Does the FIOD Work?" FIOD, Amsterdam. https://www.fiod.nl/hoe-werkt-de-fiod/.

Gara, Mario, Francesco Manaresi, Domenico J. Marchetti, and Marco Marinucci. 2019. "The Impact of Anti-Money-Laundering Oversight on Banks' Suspicious Transaction Reporting: Evidence from Italy." Questioni di Economia e Finanza (Occasional Paper) 491, Economic Research and International Relations Area, Bank of Italy, Rome, April. https://www.bancaditalia.it/pubblicazioni /qef/2019-0491/QEF_491_19.pdf.

MAS (Monetary Authority of Singapore). n.d. "AML/CFT Industry Partnership." MAS, Singapore. https://www.mas.gov.sg/regulation/anti-money-laundering/amlcft-industry-partnership-acip.

Maxwell, Nick J. 2020. "Survey Report: Five Years of Growth in Public–Private Financial Information-Sharing Partnerships to Tackle Crime." Future of Financial Intelligence Sharing Research Programme, Royal United Services Institute, London. https://www.future-fis.com /uploads/3/7/9/4/3794525/five_years_of_growth_of_public-private_partnerships_to_fight _financial_crime_-_18_aug_2020.pdf.

National Economic Crime Agency. n.d. "Improving the UK's Response to Economic Crime." National Economic Crime Agency, London. https://www.nationalcrimeagency.gov.uk/what-we-do /national-economic-crime-centre.

APPENDIX A
Institutions' Business-Wide Risk Assessment and Risk Mitigation Processes

OVERVIEW

The Financial Action Task Force (FATF) recommendations have set standards for jurisdictions to apply a risk-based approach to implementing national anti-money-laundering and combating the financing of terrorism (AML/CFT) measures. These standards include obligations for all AML/CFT stakeholders, including government agencies, the financial intelligence unit (FIU), law enforcement agencies, supervisors, financial institutions, and designated nonfinancial businesses and professions.

First and foremost, jurisdictions should identify, assess, and understand their money-laundering (ML), terrorism financing (TF), and proliferation financing risks. The AML/CFT supervisor should also assess the risks of the sector as a whole and the risks of each institution under its supervision. This assessment evaluates several qualitative and quantitative factors, including the national risk assessment; the size and complexity of the institutions under supervision; the institutions' inherent ML/TF risks related to risk factors such as customers, products, services, and transactions; geography; delivery channels; and the quality of institutions' AML/CFT systems and compliance track record. Information from FIUs and other competent authorities such as law enforcement is also useful, particularly with respect to the reporting of suspicious transactions and current and emerging risks facing the sectors.

Based on the assessments of institutional and sectoral risks, the supervisor can develop its supervisory strategies, priorities, and action plans more effectively. This process includes developing and resourcing the annual plan of inspections, training, and so forth. The supervisor needs to update the institutions' risk assessments periodically using information obtained in its off-site supervision as well as the outcome of on-site examinations.

This appendix describes the risk assessment and risk mitigation efforts that financial institutions should undertake and the adverse consequences of noncompliance. More specifically, it addresses the assessment of business-wide risks, inherent ML/TF risks, and risk mitigation measures, including policies, procedures, and controls for both institutions and financial groups.

UNDERSTANDING RISK ASSESSMENT AND MITIGATION BY FINANCIAL INSTITUTIONS

With respect to financial institutions, the key AML/CFT requirements are contained in Recommendation 1 (risk assessment), in Immediate Objective 4 for effectiveness (understanding and mitigating risks), and in other more specific risk-based obligations such as Recommendation 10 on customer due diligence and Recommendation 18 on AML/CFT policies, procedures, and controls, including group-wide programs. This appendix deals in more detail with a bank's obligations because the supervisor needs to have a thorough understanding of those obligations to enable it to conduct effective supervision.

In addition to the FATF recommendations, the Basel Core Principles of Effective Banking Supervision and the "Guidelines on Sound Management of Risk Related to Money Laundering and Financing of Terrorism" of the Basel Committee on Banking Supervision (BCBS) require banks to have adequate policies and processes, including customer due diligence rules, to prevent them from being used for criminal activities (FATF 2020). This requirement should be a specific part of a bank's general obligation to have sound risk management programs in place to address all kinds of risks, including ML and TF risks. In this context, having "adequate policies and processes" requires other measures in addition to the implementation of effective customer due diligence rules. These measures should also be risk based and informed by a bank's own assessment of its ML/TF risks.

From the perspective of individual financial institutions, the key requirement is to identify and assess the ML/TF threats inherent in their business activities, the ML/TF vulnerabilities in their processes, and the level of AML/CFT controls. Financial institutions should assess the inherent risks of their (a) customer base, (b) products and services, (c) transactions, (d) geographic areas in which they operate or where their customers are located, and (e) delivery or distribution channels for their products, services, and transactions. These risk factors are not exhaustive, and financial institutions can assess additional risk factors depending on, among others, the risk and context of the jurisdiction and sector or the particular business models of individual institutions. In conducting a risk assessment, financial institutions should be free to determine how they do this, as long as the approach is coherent, consistent, and transparent to the supervisor. However, a common approach is to assess the inherent ML/TF risks related to the risk factors and the adequacy of the AML/CFT controls, based on quantitative data and qualitative information. Inherent risks cannot be mitigated entirely, and the risks that remain after AML/CFT controls have been applied are termed residual risks. If an institution's residual risks fall outside its risk appetite, additional controls need to be implemented to ensure that the level of ML/TF risk is acceptable to the institution.

The second key requirement of a risk-based approach is for financial institutions to mitigate the risks that have been identified and assessed. Financial institutions therefore need to have AML/CFT policies, procedures, and controls to mitigate those risks and comply with their legal and regulatory obligations. Such measures should be proportional to and consistent with the level of risks assessed, applying enhanced measures where higher risks have been identified and applying simplified measures where risks are lower. Enhanced measures mean that the scope, intensity, and frequency of controls should be proportionately stronger to mitigate higher risks.

Unless circumstances call for supervisors to set out specific prescriptions, they should not prescribe the specific measures to be applied, except for those cases where enhanced and simplified measures are already prescribed by law or regulation. Financial institutions should have flexibility in determining the most effective way to assess and manage their risks, but decisions should be documented and financial institutions should be able to demonstrate to a supervisor how they came to those risk management decisions. In deciding on the degree of discretion to grant a financial institution, the supervisor should take into account several factors, including the maturity and sophistication of the sector and institution as well as the institution's track record of AML/CFT compliance and its management of other risks. It is also important to take into account the supervisors' experience in conducting risk-based AML/CFT supervision. In jurisdictions where the financial sector and AML/CFT supervisory framework are not well developed, the capacity of financial institutions to assess and mitigate their ML/TF risks may not be fully developed. In such cases, the discretion and flexibility allowed under a risk-based approach should be limited and phased in until such time as the institution's or sector's understanding of risks and experience in mitigating risks improve.

ADVERSE CONSEQUENCES

The risk-based requirements of the FATF and their emphasis on the effectiveness of AML/CFT measures have raised the bar for financial institutions and their supervisors. Jurisdictions that have high ML/TF risk profiles and weak AML/CFT frameworks are vulnerable to abuse by money launderers and terrorism financers, especially if their institutions are weak as well. This situation weakens AML/CFT compliance in the financial sector as a whole. In the end, such financial institutions may lose their correspondent banking relationships, which can have additional effects on international business activities in the jurisdiction. Consequently, having a robust AML/CFT framework is an important prerequisite to mitigating ML/TF risks.

As indicated in the introduction, the adverse consequences of inadequate AML/CFT controls for financial institutions can be grouped into three main interrelated risks:

● Business risk

● Reputational risk

● Legal and compliance risk.

Business Risk

Failure to comply with the AML/CFT legal and regulatory requirements can expose a financial institution to a range of enforcement actions and penalties, including restrictions on business. For more serious offenses, directors and other officials can be subject to civil and criminal liability and be barred from working in the sector. Additionally, a financial institution that is involved, intentionally or unintentionally, in ML or TF activities (or any of the associated predicate crimes) can also be criminally prosecuted. The adverse publicity that can accompany such action can have an especially adverse effect on the business of the institution. Other institutions with which the financial institution has a business relationship may start asking questions and inquiring about remedial actions, as could the supervisory body. Financial institutions listed on an exchange might see an adverse effect on their shares.

In recent years, banks from jurisdictions perceived as having weak AML/CFT frameworks have lost correspondent banking facilities or faced restrictions on their use of such facilities. According to large, international correspondent banks, this so-called de-risking[1] is due, in part, to the imposition of substantial financial fines on banks for AML/CFT violations in their own jurisdictions.

Consequently, to reduce their own risk profile, they have opted to close higher-risk correspondent accounts or cross-border remittances, especially when the cost of compliance was too high to justify maintaining the relationship. For those correspondent accounts that are maintained but considered high risk, the respondent bank may be subject to restrictions and increased costs for maintaining such facilities. The loss of correspondent banking relationships can have negative effects on the international business activities and the ease of doing business in a jurisdiction, and the loss of cross-border remittances can have a negative impact on migrant remittances.

Moreover, where a bank is considered complicit in ML or TF, supervisory authorities can take control of the bank and, in worse-case scenarios, go as far as to close the institution.[2] However, such extreme cases are rare.

Reputational Risk

As Benjamin Franklin said, "It takes many good deeds to build a good reputation, and only one bad one to lose it." This classic saying is still true today for banks and other financial institutions. Unethical business practices, involvement in ML/TF, or enforcement actions by supervisory authorities can affect the reputation of a financial institution. Reputational risk is also difficult to quantify and factor into, for instance, capital adequacy requirements, but it should nonetheless be part of the institution's risk management framework. Reputational damage can attract enhanced supervisory attention, not only in the home jurisdiction but also in other jurisdictions where the financial institution might be active. For developing jurisdictions, the adverse impact of reputational risk on access to correspondent banking should also be factored into the risk management framework of banks and their supervisors.

Legal and Compliance Risk

Banks are exposed to higher legal and compliance costs associated with the risk of enforcement actions and penalties resulting from failure to comply with AML/CFT requirements. Indeed, financial institutions can incur high legal costs if they have to defend themselves from potential enforcement actions. In cases where the supervisory actions include long-term remedial measures, compliance costs can also rise significantly. Additionally, enhanced supervisory monitoring can have material costs on the operations of banks (for example, through more frequent and in-depth on-site inspections and audits). Depending on the financial standing and reputation of the bank, these costs can jeopardize the safety and soundness of the institution.

In some jurisdictions, shareholders (and depositors) can also take legal action against the board of directors and senior management for failure to discharge their fiduciary responsibilities associated with AML/CFT arising from poor governance practices and negligent compliance.

BUSINESS-WIDE ML/TF RISK ASSESSMENT

In order for financial institutions to apply the AML/CFT measures in a risk-based manner, to the extent allowed under domestic law, financial institutions need to understand and manage their ML/TF risks.[3] They should therefore be required to conduct an overall, business-wide risk assessment.[4] To accomplish this assessment, they must identify and assess their inherent risks—that is, the risks to which an institution would be exposed if there were no control measures in place to mitigate them, so that they can apply appropriate and proportionate risk-mitigating controls and systems. The ML/TF risk assessment should be part of, or in addition to, an institution's broader enterprise risk management framework and should be documented and updated periodically. The business-wide ML/TF risk assessment should be available to the supervisor, which can use the additional information to develop the risk profile of the institution.

The first step in conducting a business-wide ML/TF risk assessment is for financial institutions to identify, assess, and understand their inherent ML/TF risks across all business lines with respect to the following risk factors:

- Customers

- Products, services, and transactions

- Delivery channels

- Geographic locations

- Other quantitative and qualitative risk factors, as applicable.

Risks often occur as combinations of these risk factors—because of the interrelationship between a customer and the jurisdictions where the customer originates or is active or because of the connection between a product and the delivery channel. Based on the inherent risk factors, financial institutions can formulate risk scenarios and assess the likelihood that a scenario will occur and the impact should a scenario materialize. The likelihood can be assessed based on the number of times per year that a risk scenario can occur. The impact can be assessed based on the possible financial and reputational risk that can result if a scenario indeed occurs. In this way, the institution can determine the inherent risks.

When assessing its inherent risks, a financial institution should make an inventory of the customers it services and the products and services it offers and define the scope of business areas to assess, including business units, legal entities, divisions, jurisdictions, and regions. To do this, it should use up-to-date information on the type and number of customers (for example, politically exposed persons and casinos); the maturity or stability of its client base; the volume of operations for certain types of customers; the volume of business for products, services, and transactions (for example, trade finance, private banking, and outgoing and oncoming international transactions); and geographic reach (for example, number of customers in high-risk jurisdictions).

Based on the inherent risk assessment, the institution can then set out to determine the nature and intensity of risk controls to apply to the inherent risks. The assessment of inherent ML/TF risks and the level of risk controls will result in the institution's residual risks—that is, the risks that remain when effective control measures have been taken to mitigate risks. It is important for all relevant business lines and staff of the institution to be involved in this process of assessing ML/TF risks. The business-wide risk assessment should not be narrow in scope. In addition to those of the compliance unit and staff, the inputs and views from other relevant units—including risk management, internal control, and human resources—should be taken into account. The results of the assessment need to be communicated to management and relevant staff, including the board of directors.

While financial institutions have discretion to implement their own AML/CFT frameworks, to have some consistency and allow for cross-institution comparisons, supervisors should provide guidance on risk factors and the model or methodology that financial institutions could use to assess their inherent and residual ML/TF risks. Notwithstanding the model used, the adequacy of risk assessment will be influenced largely by the availability, accuracy, and up-to-date nature of information required for the conduct of risk assessments.[5]

The supervisor will review the effectiveness of the AML/CFT risk assessment relative to, among others, the degree and nature of inherent risks. The degree of complexity of a financial institutions' risk assessment model should be commensurate with the nature, complexity, and size of its business. For less complex financial institutions, a simpler risk assessment will suffice, but a large, complex institution will require a more elaborate risk assessment. The customer base, international presence, business products, and other factors contribute to the degree of complexity required.

Risk mitigation is not a zero-sum game, and it cannot be guaranteed that, after applying control measures, there will not be any residual ML/TF risks in an institution's operations. Therefore, when assessing the inherent and residual risks, an institution also needs to assess whether a given risk is within the institution's risk appetite. It is important that this assessment be done in a proportionate manner, with due regard to the specifics of each case, to avoid treating all customers of the same category as presenting equal risk and thus leading to potential de-risking. The level of residual risk may be indicative of the risk-taking culture of the institution's management. It is expected that residual risks will be subject to close monitoring and control by management and that control measures will be enhanced should a residual risk be too high or not within the institution's risk appetite.

The risk assessment should be conducted periodically for all business lines and processes or for one (or more) business line and activity. In particular, the business-wide risk assessment should be conducted when new developments occur, such as the introduction of new products and services. Also, the model and methodology should be subject to periodic review to ensure that their relevance takes into account changes in the assessment of inherent risk factors, including emerging risks and new technologies. In the end, the business-wide risk assessment will form the basis for risk-based AML/CFT policies and procedures.

Proliferation Financing

Financial institutions also need to identify and assess their proliferation financing risks in line with the nature and size of their business. They should have policies, controls, and procedures in place to manage and mitigate effectively the proliferation financing risks that have been identified. This process may be undertaken within the framework of their existing TF supervision or compliance programs.

Group ML/TF Risk Assessment

Financial institutions that are affiliated with other institutions or holding companies often use system-wide AML/CFT risk assessment and compliance systems. In such cases, the financial institution should assess the risks within business lines as well as the consolidated risks across all activities and group members. The lead institution or holding company should frequently reassess and update the ML/TF risks throughout the organization and should communicate any changes to the appropriate business units, functions, and group members. A risk or deficiency that exists in one part of the organization may also occur in other parts of the organization or may raise concerns in other parts of the organization, and management should quickly and diligently address these concerns throughout the organization.

Banks and other financial institutions generally implement group-wide AML/CFT systems across all branches and subsidiaries, domestically and abroad, including group-wide AML/CFT policies and procedures. Banks and other financial institutions should therefore identify and assess ML/TF risks on a consolidated group basis. These risk assessments should be reviewed and updated periodically. Having an assessment of consolidated group risks facilitates the implementation of group-wide AML/CFT compliance measures. Where any cross-border branch or subsidiary cannot implement the group AML/CFT measures (for example, due to differing legal and regulatory requirements), additional risk-mitigating measures for managing the cross-border ML/TF risks need to be applied, and the home supervisor should be informed.

Consideration of a Jurisdiction's National Risk Assessment in Business-Wide Risk Assessments

A jurisdiction's national risk assessment provides essential inputs for business-wide risk assessments. Whenever it becomes available or is updated by the authorities, financial institutions should receive the results. The national risk assessment contains valuable information on ML/TF trends, high-risk products and jurisdictions or regions, and emerging ML/TF typologies and threats. Financial institutions should take this information into account in the assessment and mitigation of their risks.

During the drafting of the national risk assessment, the authorities may request the involvement of or input from the financial sector. If possible, institutions should take part in these activities and provide information as well as their observations and insights about risks. Cooperation and proactive involvement of the institutions contribute to a more accurate understanding of the ML/TF risks in the jurisdiction.

ASSESSING THE INHERENT ML/TF RISK FACTORS

As indicated, there are at least four principal inherent risk factors: customers; products, services, and transactions; geographic locations; and delivery channels. Consequently, any risk assessment model should assess at least the ML/TF risks inherent in these factors.

A key source of information for assessing the adequacy of information used for the business-wide risk assessment is information from national risk assessments, sectoral risk assessments, and ML/TF typologies relating to the specific sector. FATF Recommendation 10 on customer due diligence provides examples of potentially higher-risk situations with respect to customers, geography, products, transactions, services, and delivery channels. These factors are relevant for assessing the risks of an individual customer but also for conducting a business-wide risk assessment.

The following describes the main elements of each of the risk factors that should form the foundation of the business-wide risk assessment.

Customer Risk

It is the institution's responsibility to assess and understand the degree of risk posed by types or categories of customers as well as by individual customers. The assessment of the risk factors used in the business-wide risk assessment is an important input in determining which customers and types of customers pose varying levels of risk (for example, low, medium, and high). When assessing an institution's business-wide risk assessment, supervisors should focus on reviewing whether the information, criteria, parameters, and processes used to assess the level of customer risk are adequate.

The FATF provides the following examples of higher-risk customers:

- Business relationships that are conducted in unusual circumstances

- Nonresident customers

- Legal persons or arrangements that are personal asset-holding vehicles

- Companies that have nominee shareholders or shares in bearer form

- Businesses that are cash-intensive

- Ownership structures that appear unusual or excessively complex given the nature of the company's business.

The following are some examples of lower-risk customers:

- Financial institutions and designated nonfinancial businesses and professions that are subject to requirements to combat ML/TF consistent with the FATF recommendations, have implemented those requirements effectively, and are supervised or monitored effectively in accordance with the FATF recommendations to ensure compliance with those requirements

- Public companies listed on a stock exchange and subject to disclosure requirements (either by stock exchange rules or through law or enforceable means), which impose requirements to ensure adequate transparency of beneficial ownership

- Public administrations or enterprises.

Financial institutions will generally identify certain categories of customers as inherently high risk because they are prescribed by law or regulation (for example, politically exposed persons), customer risks are identified in the national risk assessment or in FIU information and typologies, or their own ML/TF risk assessments identify them as high risk. These customer categories include the following, among others:

- Politically exposed persons

- Casinos

- Nonresident entities, particularly those with connections to high-risk jurisdictions

- Professionals (for example, lawyers, accountants, and trust and company service providers) acting as an introducer or intermediary on behalf of clients or groups of clients (whereby there is no direct contact with the client)

- High-net-worth individuals

- Respondent banks from high-risk jurisdictions

- Private investment or asset protection vehicles.

It is not necessary to categorize all of the persons or entities in one of these groups as automatically high risk, as doing so may not be accurate and may cause financial exclusion. These categories concern the assessment of inherent risks. After mitigating measures have been applied, the risk category might be different. A successful customer risk assessment framework distinguishes between high-, medium-, and low-risk clients.

Product, Service, Transaction, and Delivery Channel Risks

A financial institution should also take stock of the lines of business (products and services) that are more vulnerable to ML/TF abuse. How a customer uses a product or service is what determines the likelihood of abuse. The characteristics of some products make them vulnerable or attractive to abuse (for example, private banking, cash transactions, or virtual assets).

Financial institutions should assess the inherent risks of abuse of products and services by customers, by taking into account factors such as their ease for holding and transferring value or their complexity and transparency. Not all products and services attract the same level of risk, and the model used to assess risk should evaluate their likelihood and impact for being abused for ML or TF. A highly vulnerable product or service may only be used occasionally by a few customers or for small amounts, which could then result in a lower inherent risk of that product or service. To assess the degree of inherent risk, other factors should be taken into account, such as the volume of use, meaning the amount and number of accounts or transactions.

Similarly, financial institutions should also assess the inherent risks associated with their business activities, processes, and transactions with respect to the delivery channels used. Inherently high risks occur in non-face-to-face situations—especially when no safeguards are in place, such as an electronic means of identification—and when professional intermediaries and introducers are used. Financial institutions providing virtual asset services are also likely to have primarily online, non-face-to-face interactions that should be captured by the risk assessment (FATF 2019).

The following are examples of the risk factors related to higher-risk products, services, transactions, or delivery channels as provided by the FATF:

● Private banking

● Anonymous transactions (which may include cash)

● Non-face-to-face business relationships or transactions (without the use of reliable, independent digital identity and other responsible innovative solutions)

● Payments received from unknown or unassociated third parties.

The FATF also provides examples of the risk factors of lower-risk products, services, transactions, or delivery channels:

● Financial products or services that provide appropriately defined and limited services to certain types of customers, so as to increase access for financial inclusion purposes.

Other products and services also have inherent ML/TF vulnerabilities:

● Back-to-back loans

● Financial guarantees (for example, trade finance, stand-by letters of credit)

● Currency exchange

● Trust services

● Wealth management and investment services, including brokerage

- Correspondent banking, including payable-through accounts

- Cash management and custodial services

- Virtual assets.

Geographic Risk

Financial institutions generally have geographic ML/TF risk exposure from both domestic and cross-border sources. These risks arise from (a) the locations where the institution has offices, branches, and subsidiaries; and (b) locations where customers reside or conduct their activities. With regard to geographic risk, financial institutions can obtain information from national risk assessments and the FIU, among other sources, to identify high-risk regions and jurisdictions. For example, branches in border regions, airports, free trade zones, or areas with higher criminality may pose higher ML/TF risks. With regard to cross-border exposures, financial institutions can also draw on the information from sources such as mutual evaluation reports and other reliable reports published by the FATF or the Organisation for Economic Co-operation and Development.

With respect to both the business-wide risk assessment as well as the risk assessment of an individual customer, geographic risk is generally assessed in combination with customer risk or product, service, and transaction risk. For instance, a corporate customer may be active in or have an ultimate beneficial owner from a high-risk jurisdiction, or a customer might send funds to a high-risk jurisdiction.

The FATF provides the following examples of higher-risk jurisdictions or geographic risk factors:

- Jurisdictions identified by credible sources, such as mutual evaluation or detailed assessment reports or published follow-up reports, as not having adequate AML/CFT systems

- Jurisdictions subject to sanctions, embargos, or similar measures issued by, for example, the United Nations

- Jurisdictions identified by credible sources as having significant levels of corruption or other criminal activity

- Jurisdictions or geographic areas identified by credible sources as providing funding or support for terrorist activities or as having designated terrorist organizations operating within their jurisdiction.

The FATF provides the following examples of lower-risk jurisdictions or geographic risk factors:

- Jurisdictions identified by credible sources, such as mutual evaluation or detailed assessment reports, as having effective AML/CFT systems

- Jurisdictions identified by credible sources as having a low level of corruption or other criminal activity.

Other Relevant Factors

A financial institution should also consider factors that may present specific or ancillary risks. These factors can include the following:

- Introduction of new products or services, new technologies, or delivery processes

- Establishment of new branches and subsidiaries locally and abroad

- Unusually high growth or disproportionately large share of profits from a certain branch or subsidiary

- Mergers and acquisitions of businesses

- Significant growth in high-risk products or services

- New typologies on ML/TF

- Changes in AML/CFT laws, regulations, and guidelines

- High staff turnover in high-risk business lines and compliance

- ML/TF investigations or legal and regulatory action affecting the institution.

RISK MITIGATION

A well-thought-out ML/TF risk assessment provides the foundation for financial institutions to develop an effective and proportionate AML/CFT framework. This framework includes AML/CFT policies, procedures, and controls to mitigate inherent risks as well as institution-wide vulnerabilities. Compliance measures need to be enhanced for higher-risk scenarios, while less rigorous controls can be applied to lower-risk scenarios. Standard controls should apply in the areas or scenarios that are identified as medium risk. Additional factors that are relevant to the adequacy of the AML/CFT framework include the size and complexity of operations, regulatory requirements, the economic environment (for example, level of informality and use of cash in the economy), and the experience and capacity of staff. The following are some of the building blocks for an effective AML/CFT framework.

Role of the Board and Senior Management

An effective risk-based approach to AML/CFT implementation requires a board of directors and senior management that are committed to lead and oversee its development and implementation. The AML/CFT framework should be implemented across the financial institution or group. This commitment requires the following actions:

- Fostering a culture of compliance as a core value of the financial institution that focuses on intrinsic motivation to control ML/TF risks

- Implementing robust AML/CFT policies, procedures, and controls adapted to the financial institution's ML/TF risk profile and regulatory environment

- Having transparent and effective governance and management information systems that keep the board and senior management informed of ML/TF risks, emerging threats and trends, and compliance issues—such as statistics on unusual and suspicious transactions, regulatory measures, and sanctions—in a timely manner

- Having effective communication systems to inform staff of ML/TF risks and (changes to) the AML/CFT policy and related matters

- Designating a director or board member to be responsible for AML/CFT compliance and ML/TF risks as well as a chief compliance officer at the senior management level

- Having adequate resources for the main control functions of the institution, especially compliance and internal audits, to enable the board to monitor the effective implementation of the AML/CFT framework

- Having sufficient budget and resources for AML/CFT, including staff training, software, and equipment.

Compliance and Internal Audit Functions

Strong compliance and audit functions are important preconditions for an effective governance, risk management, and compliance framework. As required by the FATF standards, financial institutions should appoint a compliance officer at the management level to signal that AML/CFT compliance is an important function for the institution.[6] The compliance function is intended to ensure effective implementation and compliance with legal and regulatory requirements and with the institution's AML/CFT policies and controls. Compliance should therefore have the necessary independence, authority, resources (including information technology tools), and expertise to carry out these functions effectively, as well as unrestricted access to all relevant internal information, including information from (foreign) branches and subsidiaries. The board and senior management should actively promote the compliance officer's role and responsibility within the organization.

The compliance officer should provide practical advice and ensure that staff receive training on ML/TF risks and the implementation of AML/CFT policies, procedures, and controls and regulatory requirements. The compliance officer should also participate in monitoring and assessing risks across the financial institution and group as well as the effectiveness of compliance measures.

Financial institutions must have an independent audit function to test the institution's AML/CFT system. This function provides a higher level of control for monitoring, among others, the adequacy of and adherence to AML/CFT policies and controls, including the compliance function. The audit function should also review the effectiveness of compliance measures across all business lines, branches, and subsidiaries, both domestically and abroad.

Similar to the compliance function, the audit function should have unrestricted access to all information relevant to its task, including confidential information reported via whistleblowing or other internal mechanisms.

Policies, Procedures, and Controls

In addition to high-level controls on governance, compliance, and internal audits, financial institutions should implement risk-based policies, procedures, and controls to mitigate ML/TF risks that they have identified and assessed with respect to their customers, products, services, transactions, geographic locations, and delivery channels. Customer risk, in combination with these other risk factors, requires a comprehensive set of policies, procedures, and controls. For this reason, the standard on customer due diligence is one of the most comprehensive and important preventive measures in the FATF standards.[7] In addition, the policies, procedures, and controls should extend to monitoring, managing, and mitigating proliferation financing risks.

The BCBS also provides guidance to banks on the management of ML/TF risks, including with respect to a customer acceptance policy, customer and beneficial owner identification, verification and risk profiling, and ongoing monitoring (BCBS 2020).

The following are some of the main risk-based policies, procedures, and controls that a financial institution should implement in order to mitigate inherent ML/TF risks with respect to the above-mentioned risk factors.

Customer Due Diligence

Financial institutions should develop and implement policies, procedures, and controls to mitigate the customer risks they have identified through their business-wide risk assessment. The customer due diligence processes enable financial institutions to obtain and verify information proportionate to the risks that customers represent to the financial institution and in accordance with regulatory requirements.

Financial institutions should assess the level of risk of new customers at the onboarding stage. Based on the customer due diligence information obtained, financial institutions should establish a customer risk profile that will determine whether normal, simplified, or enhanced measures are to be conducted and the level of monitoring of the business relationship that is required. This process can entail an assessment of risk based on the category of customer (for example, resident vs. nonresident), in combination with the type of product and services to be used (for example, retail vs. private banking), expected volume of business and transactions, and place of business.

Thereafter, risk should be monitored through ongoing customer due diligence processes to ensure that the initial risk assessment is still relevant. A customer risk profile can change due to changes in the transaction profile (for example, increase in volume and nature of transactions), products and services used, and business activities or legal form (for example, sole proprietor or partnership), among others. Whatever model is used, an institution should be able to update its risk assessment of customers to ensure that the results are up-to-date and relevant.

Risk profiles can apply at the individual or group customer level, depending on the type of customer and how homogeneous the group is. For instance, certain types of retail customers may be grouped, while corporate and private banking customers may require more tailored customer due diligence and ongoing monitoring. Nevertheless, even with a risk assessment at the group customer level, it is necessary to determine whether certain indicators or red flags require a risk assessment of an individual customer.

Recommendation 10 lists the required due diligence measures that should be applied to customers:

- Identify the customer and verify the customer's identity using reliable and independent source documents, data, or information

- Identify the beneficial owner and take reasonable measures to verify the identity of the beneficial owner, such that the financial institution is satisfied that it knows who the beneficial owner is. For legal persons and arrangements, understand the ownership and control structure of the customer

- Understand and, as appropriate, obtain information on the purpose and intended nature of the business relationship

- Conduct ongoing due diligence on the business relationship and scrutinize transactions under-taken throughout the course of that relationship to ensure that the transactions being conducted are consistent with the institution's knowledge of the customer, its business, and its risk profile, including, where necessary, the source of funds.

Where a financial institution is unable to comply with the customer due diligence measures with respect to a customer, the institution should not open the account, commence a business relationship, or perform transactions. If a business relationship already exists, the institution should terminate it. In both cases, the financial institution should consider whether the circumstances require filing a suspicious transaction report (STR) with the FIU in relation to the (prospective) customer.

Financial Inclusion

Financial institutions should be mindful of the fact that applying an overly cautious approach to customer due diligence can have the unintended consequence of excluding legitimate businesses and consumers from the formal financial system. One of the main obstacles to providing financial services or products to unbanked customers is their lack of reliable documentation of identity and data verification. Low-income individuals or displaced persons such as refugees often do not pos-sess the proper identification documentation and therefore are not able to meet certain customer due diligence requirements. FATF guidance on AML/CFT measures and financial inclusion provides examples of customer due diligence measures adapted to the context of financial inclusion (FATF 2013–17). Those examples illustrate how simplified customer due diligence measures or alternative forms of identity verification—for example, the use of e-identity tools—can support financial inclusion, while appropriately mitigating ML/TF risks. To ensure financial inclusion, financial institutions can apply a certain amount of flexibility to the provision of basic, regulated financial products to a larger proportion of the population.

Ongoing Due Diligence

Depending on the risk profile of the customer, financial institutions should apply ongoing due diligence to determine whether transactions or patterns of transactions are consistent with the institution's knowledge of the customer, its business or activities, and its initial risk profile. Preferably, the risk profile also includes information on the expected transaction behavior of the customer. Such monitoring enables financial institutions to ascertain whether transactions are consistent with the information obtained during the onboarding process or subsequent customer reviews. Transactions and activities of a customer should be monitored continuously, paying special attention to activities or transactions that depart from the known customer profile. Ongoing due diligence also involves updating documentation and data collected through the customer due diligence process.

Ongoing customer due diligence is an important part of a financial institution's overall system for identifying and reporting unusual or suspicious transactions and activities. Depending on the size and complexity of the operations, both manual and automated systems can be used to monitor customer transactions. For customers and business lines with very large volumes of transactions, automated systems may be necessary. In such cases, the automated system should be reviewed periodically and tested for effectiveness to ensure that it is adequate for transaction-monitoring purposes.

Risk-Based Approach to Customer Due Diligence

Financial institutions should apply customer due diligence in all cases, but it should be done in a risk-based manner. The extent of the customer due diligence measures should be consistent with and proportional to the level of assessed ML/TF risks of a customer. In some cases, enhanced or simplified measures will be required or permitted by domestic laws and regulations. In cases where ML/TF risks are higher, enhanced customer due diligence measures should be conducted, which may involve implementing more rigorous information and verification procedures. Alternatively, simplified measures may be permitted where lower risks have been identified and assessed by the financial institution or authorities (for example, in the national risk assessment). Under no circumstances should simplified measures be applied if there is a suspicion of ML/TF.

Record Keeping

Financial institutions should maintain, for at least five years, all of the necessary records on transactions, both domestic and international, to enable them to comply swiftly with information requests from the competent authorities.[8] The records must be sufficient to permit the reconstruction of individual transactions (including the amounts and types of currency involved, if any) to provide, if necessary, evidence for prosecuting criminal activity.

To comply with the AML/CFT statutory and regulatory requirements for recording information, financial institutions should have a record-keeping policy and systems in place with respect to the minimum retention period (not less than five years after the business relationship has ended or after the date of an occasional transaction) and have security protocols and controls in place (for example, storage, backup, and recovery systems) to guard against cybercrime.

The following records should be retained for the legally mandated period:

- All records obtained through customer due diligence measures (for example, copies or records of official identification documents like passports, identity cards, driving licenses, or similar documents)

- Account files and business correspondence, including the results of any analysis undertaken (for example, inquiries to establish the background and purpose of complex, unusually large transactions).

The records should allow for an audit trail and be sufficient for tracing assets and reconstructing accounts for use by competent authorities. The policy should also cover outsourcing arrangements for record keeping.

Ongoing Monitoring and Reporting of Suspicious Transactions and Activities

Financial institutions need to report suspicions of ML/TF promptly, including attempted transactions.[9] Reporting of suspicious transactions and activities to the FIU or any other competent authority is one of the main obligations of financial institutions. Their role in reporting useful financial intelligence to combat ML/TF and related predicate offenses is a critical component of the crime-fighting activities of law enforcement and judicial authorities. Customer due diligence and ongoing monitoring of transactions are important processes that enable the institution to identify unusual and suspicious transactions and activities.

The AML/CFT law should protect not only the financial institution but also its directors, officers, and employees from criminal and civil liability for breach of any restriction on the disclosure of information imposed by contract or by any legislative, regulatory, or administrative provision when disclosing information to the competent authorities. The protection from being criminally prosecuted or held liable under civil law for disclosing information on a customer can only be extended if the institution reported its suspicions in good faith to the FIU, even if it did not know precisely what the underlying criminal activity was and regardless of whether the illegal activity occurred.

Additionally, the AML/CFT law should prohibit the financial institution and its directors, officers, and employees from disclosing the fact that an STR or related information is being filed with the FIU. This so-called "tipping-off" prohibition is intended to prevent prejudice to an investigation, including flight of assets; it is not intended to inhibit information sharing within a financial group, including foreign branches and majority-owned subsidiaries.

In order for financial institutions to report STRs to the FIU, the transaction-monitoring process is an essential element in detecting and investigating possible unusual or suspicious transactions. When setting up a transaction-monitoring process and system, the following conditions apply:

- The transaction-monitoring process should reflect the ML/TF risks identified in the business-wide risk assessment.

- The transaction-monitoring policy should be elaborated in the underlying procedures and processes.

- The transaction-monitoring system should vary depending on the nature and size of the organization and its risk profile. Many institutions will adopt an automated solution for monitoring transactions, especially where the volume of transactions would make manual monitoring impossible.

- Where an automated transaction-monitoring system is used, it should incorporate substantiated and adequate business rules (detection rules with scenarios and thresholds). These business rules should be tested periodically for effectiveness. For manual screening, staff undertaking these tasks should have sufficient expertise to identify suspicious activity in line with the business-wide risk assessment.

- A clearly described process is needed for handling alerts. Investigations of alerts must be documented properly, including the decision to close the alert or to report the transaction to the FIU. Information on alerts should inform the ongoing risk assessment of customers. Even when it does not generate new alerts, transaction monitoring can help to identify patterns that can inform new typologies.

- The governance with respect to monitoring transactions and reporting suspicious transactions should be structured so that duties are allocated clearly and segregated.

- Tailored training programs should allow staff, based on their functions, to identify unusual and suspicious transactions and activities.[10]

The transaction-monitoring systems should be set up so that aggregate customer information can be monitored on a consolidated basis across business lines, branches, and subsidiaries. With respect to operations abroad, the head office should be able to implement the transaction-monitoring system in those jurisdictions and to obtain information on unusual or suspicious transactions and activities detected, subject to local laws and regulations.

ML/TF RISK MITIGATION FOR FINANCIAL GROUPS

Sound ML/TF risk mitigation should extend to each member of a financial group[11] on a consolidated basis, covering all branches and majority-owned subsidiaries of the financial group that operate domestically and in other jurisdictions. Consequently, a financial group should develop group-wide AML/CFT policies, procedures, and controls that are implemented consistently across the group but subject to jurisdiction-specific ML/TF risks and legal requirements. FATF Recommendation 18 states that, where the minimum AML/CFT requirements of the host jurisdiction are less stringent, those of the home jurisdiction should be applied to the extent that local laws and regulations permit. Where doing so is not possible, the financial institution should take additional AML/CFT measures to manage the risks and inform the home-jurisdiction supervisor. When effective implementation of group policies, procedures, and controls abroad is not feasible, the financial group should consider closing its operations in the host jurisdiction.

Under a consolidated AML/CFT compliance framework, the parent bank should implement policies, procedures, and controls on a group-wide basis for all group members, while at the same time complying with local laws and regulations. This framework should include a clear process for sharing information between the head office and all branches and subsidiaries domestically and abroad. Secrecy laws and data protection laws in some jurisdictions may restrict the ability to share customer-related information within the group, which can seriously impede the assessment and mitigation of ML/TF risks. It can also hamper the effective operations of group compliance and group audits.

The financial institution should have a thorough understanding of the inherent ML/TF risks associated with its customers, products, services, transactions, geographic locations, and delivery channels across the group. The institution should ensure that all entities in the group conduct a business-wide risk assessment (as described above) and consolidate these analyses on the level of the group. The risk assessments should be updated periodically. The consolidated risk assessment of the group should determine the type and intensity of AML/CFT compliance measures to be implemented for each member and for the entire group.

The financial institution should also implement, at the group level, key structural controls, particularly risk management, compliance, and internal audits. These functions should evaluate compliance with and the effectiveness of group policies, procedures, and controls, including the ability to share information among group members and respond to information requests from the head office. In this regard, the institution should know the extent to which local AML/CFT legislation allows it to rely on the customer due diligence and other procedures undertaken by other entities within the group, for instance, when a customer has a business relationship with more than one member of the group.

Regardless of the jurisdictions where the group operates, each institution in the group should implement effective compliance monitoring systems with the group's policies, procedures, and controls that are proportionate to the ML/TF risks assessed by the institution in each jurisdiction. A financial institution should monitor significant customer relationships on a consolidated basis, regardless of where the accounts are held. This monitoring should be facilitated by a centralized customer due diligence and transaction-monitoring process to enhance the effectiveness and efficiency of the group's AML/CFT framework. A centralized process should also help the group to monitor and detect suspicious transactions across the group.

An international financial group should also appoint a group AML/CFT compliance officer responsible for compliance with the global AML/CFT framework. This officer should contribute to the development and implementation of group-wide risk assessments and risk mitigation strategies, including compliance with group policies, procedures, and controls.

A financial group should, when required, inform its supervisor(s) about its global framework for identifying, assessing, and managing its ML/TF risks and its consolidated AML/CFT policies, procedures, and controls and group-wide information-sharing arrangements.

Mixed financial groups comprising banks, securities, insurance, and other financial businesses can present additional complexity in the development and consolidation of group processes and systems. Differences in the nature of activities and types of business relationships in each sector may require or justify variations in the AML/CFT requirements imposed on each sector. For instance, simplified customer due diligence measures may be allowed for customers of the group that request term life or non–life insurance products, especially products without a surrender value, while standard customer due diligence will apply to the same customer in other lines of business. At a mimimum, mixed groups should ensure that the required group AML/CFT policies, procedures, and controls are implemented and that information on ML/TF risks and customers is shared across the entire group.

NOTES

1. De-risking is the phenomenon of financial institutions terminating or restricting business relationships with clients or categories of clients to avoid rather than manage risks. See also chapter 6.
2. The 2019 closure of Atlantic International Bank Limited in Belize (an offshore bank) due its alleged involvement in a real estate scam, is instructive in this regard. Also, the so-called 311 Special Measures for Jurisdictions, Financial Institutions, or International Transactions of Primary Money Laundering Concern by FinCEN (the US financial intelligence unit) caused the closure of the Latvian ABLV Bank and of Banca Privada d'Andorra. See https://www.fincen.gov /resources/statutes-and-regulations/311-special-measures.
3. FATF Recommendation 1, interpretive note to Recommendation 1 and Criterion 1.10 of the FATF methodology.
4. The business-wide risk assessment is sometimes referred to as an enterprise-wide risk assessment.
5. For examples of guidance on business-wide risk assessments, see DNB (n.d.-a); IFC (2019); and Wolfsberg Group (2015).
6. FATF Recommendation 18.
7. FATF Recommendation 10 and its interpretive note.
8. FATF Recommendation 11.
9. FATF Recommendation 20.
10. See, for instance, the guidance documents of DNB (n.d.-b) and IFC (2019).
11. The term "group" refers to organizations comprising more than one financial institution, including the branches and majority-owned subsidiaries of the institution wherever they may be located. The term "head office" refers to the parent institution of the group, generally where the group AML/CFT risk management department is located.

REFERENCES

BCBS (Basel Committee on Banking Supervision). 2020. "Guidelines on Sound Management of Risk Related to Money Laundering and Financing of Terrorism; Issued in January 2014 and Revised July 2020." BCBS, Paris. https://www.bis.org/bcbs/publ/d505.pdf.

DNB (De Nederlandsche Bank). n.d.-a. "Integrity Risk Analysis: More Where Necessary, Less Where Possible." DNB, Amsterdam. https://www.dnb.nl/media/1npf44vp/good-practices-integrity-risk-analysis.pdf?msclkid=47a541dbaa1811ec9dc260d298ed5ba7.

DNB (De Nederlandsche Bank). n.d.-b. "Post-Event Transaction Monitoring Process for Banks." DNB, Amsterdam. https://www.dnb.nl/media/glinjegh/guidance-document-transactiemonitoring-banks.pdf?msclkid=03462cd1aa1811ecb5923ff62adab7a5.

FATF (Financial Action Task Force). 2013–17. "Anti-Money Laundering and Terrorist Financing Measures and Financial Inclusion, with a Supplement on Customer Due Diligence." FATF, Paris. https://www.fatf-gafi.org/publications/fatfgeneral/documents/financial-inclusion-cdd-2017.html.

FATF (Financial Action Task Force). 2019. "Guidance for a Risk-Based Approach to Virtual Assets and Virtual Asset Service Providers." FATF, Paris. https://www.fatf-gafi.org/media/fatf/documents/recommendations/RBA-VA-VASPs.pdf.

FATF (Financial Action Task Force). 2020. "Guidelines: Sound Management of Risks Related to Money Laundering and Financing of Terrorism; July 2014; Revised July 2020." FATF, Paris. https://www.bis.org/bcbs/publ/d505.pdf.

IFC (International Finance Corporation). 2019. "Anti-Money-Laundering (AML) & Countering Financing of Terrorism (CFT) Risk Management in Emerging Market Banks." Good Practice Note 2019, IFC, Washington, DC. https://www.ifc.org/wps/wcm/connect/e7e10e94-3cd8-4f4c-b6f8-1e14ea9eff80/45464_IFC_AML_Report.pdf?MOD=AJPERES&CVID=mKKNshy.

Wolfsberg Group. 2015. "Frequently Asked Questions on Risk Assessments for Money Laundering, Sanctions, and Bribery & Corruption." Worlfsberg Group, Ermatingen. https://www.wolfsberg-principles.com/sites/default/files/wb/pdfs/faqs/17.%20Wolfsberg-Risk-Assessment-FAQs-2015.pdf.

www.ingramcontent.com/pod-product-compliance
Lightning Source LLC
Chambersburg PA
CBHW041442210326
41599CB00004B/100